'*Transformational Culture* provides guidance for leaders, managers and HR professionals on the importance of putting purpose, values and people first. David Liddle delivers a blueprint for creating an inclusive, sustainable and high-performing culture.'
Omar Ali, Financial Services Leader, EY

'Clear, straightforward, no grand claims – just simple tools, clear examples of those that have taken the challenge and succeeded, and acknowledgement that while it is hard work, it will bring great value.'
Patricia Grealish, interim Chief People Officer, NHS Blood and Transplant

'The understanding offered by this powerful analysis of organizational culture offers a clear route to transforming work organizations for the future so that those who work in them thrive, the lives of the people they serve are enhanced and the planet they are part of is protected.'
Professor Michael West CBE, Senior Visiting Fellow, The King's Fund, Professor of Organizational Psychology, Lancaster University and Emeritus Professor, Aston University

'A step-by-step guide to creating a business case and framework for a people-centred organization. By utilizing some very honest and thought-provoking case studies, this toolkit is designed to support those with all levels of experience in change management or cultural transformation.'
Juli Oliver-Smith FCIPD, Head of Change, Systems and Integration, P&O Ferries

'David Liddle's deep experience and practical advice is an invaluable tool in helping you to achieve the productive and engaging culture you need in order to achieve your goals and create the organization you want.'

David MacLeod OBE, Co-chair of Engage for Success, co-author of 'the MacLeod Report' on employee engagement and Honorary Professor, Nottingham Business School

'This is the book that all organizations need. With the development of a Resolution Framework based on the 7Cs model, organizations can begin to put employee wellbeing and inclusion at the heart of their activities. Only with a comprehensive and integrated approach to culture change can we begin to effectively address the challenges and opportunities that a diverse workforce offers – and create the types of organizations employees want and need to flourish and thrive. Although this is not easy, anyone using this book as a guide should see a genuine transformation and a way to navigate their aspiration to maximize the potential of all their employees. Highly recommended'.

Jill Scott, CEO, Inclusion Solutions

'This comprehensive book uses accessible and understandable tools and case studies to challenge our thinking and provoke us to action. It is as professionally challenging as it is enjoyable. This book has captured the current passion and enthusiasm of many leaders and HR professionals to use the past year as a catalyst for real, sustainable change.'

Dean Royles, President of HPMA and strategic HR consultant

'Written with leaders and HR professionals in mind, this book provides a solid framework and practical playbook for helping organizations to shift their culture into one that is not only transformational in nature but fair, just, inclusive, high-performing and sustainable.'

Victoria Leach, Head of People and Culture, North East Lincolnshire Council

'*Transformational Culture* strikes a great balance between providing theory that underpins its key messages and practical examples that

will help to make changes to how an organization works. In providing an alternative to retributive justice it helps to overcome the biggest barrier to change: the current systems and processes that we use to deal with conflict in the workplace. For me, the added value of what David Liddle says is that it makes for better-run and more successful organizations, and he absolutely demonstrates why.'
Graham Boyack, Director, Scottish Mediation

'David Liddle sets the tone straight away: 'Develop a people-centred organization for improved performance'. Why? Because people are any organization's most valuable asset! Without them you don't have an organization. A truly educational and inspiring book, which I would recommend to any leader or HR practitioner to read cover to cover!'
Lisa Seagroatt, Associate CIPD and Founder and Managing Director, HR Fit for Purpose

'*Transformational Culture* provides a blueprint for leaders and organizations to journey towards something better. David Liddle expertly outlines a different, more balanced way of working and offers a pragmatic and considered framework for making progress. Complex and nuanced subjects such as justice within organizations are examined and the limitations of conventional approaches are methodically laid bare. This is an essential read for anyone who believes workplaces can build performance while nurturing enhanced fairness, justice and learning.'
David D'Souza, Membership Director, CIPD

'This book is nothing short of amazing. I have found it truly relevant for the current time and particularly useful for the work I undertake as an HR professional. David Liddle, I salute you for a job well done.'
Akua Richardson, Director, People First Initiatives

'In this interesting and highly relevant book, David Liddle clearly illustrates what good and bad culture looks like, describes the different factors that influence culture and explains the problems we face in trying to solve modern problems with traditional ways of thinking. More than that, though, he has pointed the way and helped us establish a route to a more just, more human and more productive way of doing things.'

Jonathan Goodger, Employee Relations Manager, global pharmaceutical company

'David Liddle has produced another gem of a book which should be compulsory reading for all leaders, managers and HR professionals alike. He makes a compelling case for the power of transforming cultures to be kinder, more compassionate and to achieve a win/win approach for everyone. This book is full of case studies showing transformational cultures in action, sound models and a comprehensive, practical toolkit to help transform organizational culture. This is a book I will return to time and again.'

Pam Williams, HR director and leadership coach

'The next time I encounter yet another excuse for not addressing racism, injustice or fairness by an employer, I will whip out David Liddle's *Transformational Culture*. I DARE every leader, manager, lawyer and HR person to read this book. He stops us getting too cosy as he challenges our conventional organizational thinking and reminds us why transformational cultures are needed at work, now! He transforms outdated, rigid and harmful disciplinary processes based on retributive justice towards what this weary world needs: restorative justice, focused on learning and collective organizational safety.'

Animah Kosai, Founder, Speak Up Collective and Counsel

'*Transformational Culture* is the brainchild of David Liddle whose phenomenal, diverse career leaves you with that comfortable feeling you can trust what you read. All the blood, sweat and tears articulating how a leader can get organizational culture on point has been absorbed by the author and he is handing over all this wisdom on a plate in the guise of this shiny book ready to dip into time and time again.'

Mandy Wardrop, senior lecturer and HR programme leader

Transformational Culture

Develop a people-centred organization for improved performance

David Liddle

KoganPage

First published in Great Britain and the United States in 2021 by Kogan Page Limited

2nd Floor, 45 Gee Street	122 W 27th St, 10th Floor	4737/23 Ansari Road
London	New York, NY 10001	Daryaganj
EC1V 3RS	USA	New Delhi 110002
United Kingdom		India

www.koganpage.com

Kogan Page books are printed on paper from sustainable forests.

ISBNs

Hardback	978 1 78966 110 1
Paperback	978 1 78966 108 8
Ebook	978 1 78966 109 5

British Library Cataloguing-in-Publication Data

A CIP record for this book is available from the British Library.

Library of Congress Control Number

2021941637

Typeset by Integra Software Services, Pondicherry
Print production managed by Jellyfish
Printed and bound by CPI Group (UK) Ltd, Croydon, CR0 4YY

For Jayne, Daniel, Ethan and Imogen.
Thank you for transforming my life xxx

CONTENTS

FOREWORD

Everyone reading this book will have heard 'culture eats strategy for breakfast' attributed to Peter Drucker. While he may never have said these actual words (hint: if you have a great quote you want repeated, attribute it to Peter Drucker), he and almost all those who study or practice management believe it. 'Culture' matters.

We experience an organization's culture whenever we participate in an organization where we work (my job), where we shop (retail stores), when we eat out (restaurants), when we travel (airlines, hotels), where we play (teams or groups we follow or play on) and how we worship (church, mosque, or temple). Organizations pervade our lives and an organization is known by its culture.

As David Liddle points out, millions of ideas have been shared about culture. In their book *Culture: A critical review of concepts and definitions*, authors Alfred Kroeber and Clyde Kluckholn identified 164 different definitions of culture, in 1952! In our efforts to synthesize the vast 'culture' literature applied to the organization setting, we have identified four phases of understanding an organization's culture (see Figure 0.1) that have evolved over time:

FIGURE 0.1   Ways of understanding culture

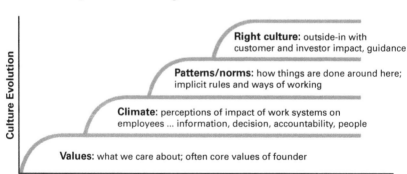

What is remarkable about David's book *Transformational Culture* is that he addresses all four phases of culture and adds to each:

Culture as values: This work recognizes the importance of an organization's core values and how they shape individual behaviour. To have a truly transformational culture, he identifies the key values of being just, fair, inclusive, sustainable and high performing. When employees act on these values, not only do employees experience higher personal wellbeing and productivity, but the organization also thrives.

Culture as climate and work systems: This work recognizes that culture shows up as an organizational climate and is embedded in work systems. HR practices around people (staffing, training, careers), performance (appraisal, rewards), communication (sharing information, engaging employees) and work (where and how work is done) reflect and sustain a culture. Leaders who use these HR practices and who model the values become the carriers of the culture.

Culture as patterns/norms: This work highlights that transformational culture creates positive patterns and norms inside the organization. Patterns become governance mechanisms that shape employee behaviour more than rules and incentives. It does not take long to feel the difference between an abundant vs toxic organization culture. The transformational culture laid out in this book enables employees to fulfill their full potential.

Culture as identity: This work goes beyond culture within the boundaries of the organization and relates it to the identity of the firm in the minds of external stakeholders. It is not enough to have a culture; it is critical to have the right culture that creates an identity in the marketplace that impacts the workplace. Customer experience comes from employee experience. Investor confidence comes from the intangibles embedded in a culture. Community reputation evolves from creating the right internal culture.

By addressing culture at all four levels, this book defines the outcomes of culture for all stakeholders. Employees can select and work for companies that match their personal values. Leaders can proactively create the right culture that delivers strategic and marketplace success. Customers can do business with organizations who have made a firm brand into organizational practices. Investors can invest in companies who have successful patterns of behaviours. Communities can support companies whose reputations sustain contribution to societal progress.

To reach these outcomes, the Transformation Cultural Model David proposes offers a blueprint for thinking and roadmap for action to create culture at all four levels. The transformational hub becomes a forum for sharing ideas that create the blueprint for culture. The eight transformational enablers became the roadmap for making culture happen with discipline and rigor. The 7 Cs of transformational culture become the fuel that drive the culture transformation journey.

Many today recognize organizational culture as a reality. This book turns that reality into ideas with impact. The ideas are insightful and the tools practical and useable. Combined, *Transformational Culture* will be a useful guide for anyone wanting to move beyond advocacy that 'culture matters' to application to make 'culture happen'.

Bravo!

Dave Ulrich
Rensis Likert Professor, Ross School of Business,
University of Michigan
Partner, The RBL Group
dou@umich.edu

PREFACE

'Why can't people just be kinder to each other?'

DANIEL LIDDLE, AGED 12¾

Imagine working in an organization with a clearly defined purpose and a set of core values which connect us with our organization, with one another, and with our customers. Where our leaders are committed to unlocking our inner brilliance and engaging with each of us as human beings – during the good times and the bad. Where each voice is heard, each contribution is valued, and our differences are a source of celebration.

Imagine a workplace where disputes and disagreements are resolved constructively, equitably and with empathy. Where managers feel confident and courageous to have the right conversations, with the right people at the right time. Where compassion is a sign of strength, dialogue is a foundation of justice, and collaboration is at the core of every team.

Imagine a workplace where the policies of the organization shield us from harm and hold us to account but are equally concerned about protecting relationships and building an inclusive, collaborative, and humanizing workplace.

Imagine working in an organization where our managers value and nurture our happiness, our health, and our harmony. Where mistakes become opportunities to learn and grow, and where failure becomes a catalyst for insight and innovation.

Imagine our organizations thriving and growing, where boardroom executives listen and respond to the needs of our diverse stakeholders. Where investments can be made safe in the knowledge that our organizations will act responsibly and justly. Where profit and integrity go hand in hand, and where corruption, exploitation and abuse of power is challenged and resolved through fair, transparent and robust systems of governance and accountability.

Imagine all of this in a workplace which recognizes it has a responsibility to our planet, and which works hard to protect the rich and diverse ecosystems within which we all live, play and work.

This is not a childhood fantasy. This is a transformational culture.

Welcome to Transformational Culture

This book offers leaders, HR professionals, line managers, unions, lawyers, employees, and many others a blueprint for a new form of organizational culture – a transformational culture. A transformational culture is fair, just, inclusive, sustainable and high performing.

To assist an organization to succeed, a transformational culture is one which embraces diversity, promotes learning, encourages accountability and drives engagement. It does so in ways that matter not only to employees, but to customers, investors and other stakeholders. This is not a soft option. When the internal culture matches customer and stakeholder expectations, organizations achieve hard business outcomes, drive up productivity, act responsibly, and create a high performing workplace where individual, team and organizational objectives can be met, and exceeded.

> 'A strong organizational culture can clearly differentiate a business from its competitors. Companies that align culture with business have 58 per cent more growth and 72 per cent more profitability.' (Cappellanti-Wolf, 2019)

Transformational culture draws from a variety of models and theories including, but not limited to, positive psychology, emotional intelligence (EQ), systems thinking, nudge theory, principled negotiation, restorative justice (RJ), transactional analysis (TA), and non-violent communication (NVC). I have provided an overview of these models and framework throughout the book and on pages 282–285.

Why have I written this book?

In my first book, *Managing Conflict* (Liddle, 2017), I set out a simple challenge for business leaders, HR professionals, unions and others. I challenged them to make the management of conflict a strategic priority, and to integrate a people-centred and values-based approach for resolving issues in the workplace. I offered a variety of tried and tested toolkits to help them to prevent, resolve and transform conflict.

My work in the fields of conflict and change management has given me the unique opportunity to work with organizations and teams at times of distress and dysfunction. I have learned so much about corporate culture and the climate within teams and divisions. I now appreciate that culture is the greatest asset, or the greatest liability, an organization has. Yet, for so many, culture is barely talked about and it is the only asset, or liability, that no-one has direct ownership of. In some respects, corporate culture reminds me a great deal of workplace conflict: widely misunderstood, routinely ignored; yet a potential source of riches when it is managed well.

As an asset, good company culture can drive employee experience, it engenders trust and respect, it can create safe and healthy workplaces and it can ensure customers, investors and stakeholders receive the very best that the company has to offer. In a good culture, customers and employees are naturally inclined to spread the good word and become an advocate and supporter for what you do (Klinger, 2021). Conversely, when cultures go wrong, they can become a liability. They can be stifling, toxic, dysfunctional, destructive, corrosive, divisive, confusing, fear-inducing and unsafe places to work within, or to do business with.

> 'A bad workplace culture can derail an organization, creating a toxic atmosphere that leaves employees frustrated and produces a very real bottom-line impact. A strong workplace culture, however, ensures employees act in the best interest of their organization and feel fulfilled within it. Organizations that build a great workplace culture will ultimately win the war for talent, innovating and growing for years to come.' (Taylor, 2019)

We need a new cultural paradigm

Following the global coronavirus pandemic, and the socio-economic and health inequalities that have been laid bare, it is right that the question of company culture is being hotly debated. Research has found that 94 per cent of executives and 88 per cent of employees believe a distinct workplace culture is essential to business success (Deloitte, 2012). Set in the context of a rise in social justice movements such as Black Lives Matter (BLM) and #MeToo, increasing levels of employee activism, rising demands for flexible workplaces, worsening divisions within and between our communities, and an unfolding economic and climate emergency, if there was ever a time to seek out a definition of good company culture, it is right now.

In writing *Transformational Culture*, I set out to define what good looks like. I did so by building a cultural model around five terms which I believe are central to good organizational culture:

- **Just.** Where organizations blend the need for accountability with the need to protect relationships and to engender dialogue, learning and growth.
- **Fair.** Where organizations' systems and structures deliver equity, where employees' voices are heard, and where concerns, conduct, complaints and conflicts are resolved constructively.
- **Inclusive.** Where leaders and managers recognize and amplify the inner brilliance of all their employees.
- **Sustainable.** Where organizations minimize harm to our planet whilst meeting the needs and aspirations of their organization.
- **High-performing.** Where we work together with a common purpose to achieve the best possible outcomes: for ourselves, for each other, for our communities and for our organization.

I have been motivated by a growing body of evidence which suggests that there is a negative outcome for employees from traditional systems and cultures such as the dominant hierarchical structure – typified by a preoccupation with target setting, rules and regulation (Armit, 2015).

In *Transformational Culture*, I wanted to create a cultural blueprint which would be applicable to any organization – irrespective of size, location, sector or maturity. I hope that what I offer here will instigate a dialogue regarding the interaction between purpose, values, culture, team climate, corporate strategy, rules, behaviours, policies, justice, leadership, HR, unions, employee experience, customer experience and the environment. The various models and frameworks that I have developed are designed to be used and adapted. They will only work if they are lifted off the pages off this book, and brought to life in real organizations, consisting of real people, experiencing real challenges.

Time's up for retributive justice

A core message in this book is the need for organizations to shift from a reliance on retributive justice (fault, blame and punish) to transformational justice (just, learning and restorative). I speak to employees, HR professionals, unions, managers and leaders every day and there is a palpable desire to change the way that they deliver and access justice. However, retributive justice is deeply ingrained in our organization's systems, structures and psyches. It is punitive, draconian and malignant. Like other malignant ailments, it is poisoning the whole system and its influence is far reaching and corrosive. Retributive justice, and the desire for blame and punishment, has bound itself to so many of our HR systems and management processes. It has become the elephant in the room, that everyone can see, but no one dares to discuss.

Retributive justice – as so clearly viewed through the prism of our traditional discipline, performance and grievance policy frameworks – is binary, polarizing, adversarial and reductive. It focuses on winning or losing; on right or wrong; on black or white; on attack or defend. This model of justice disregards the deeper needs and interests of the parties and needs and interests of the organization. It is a model of justice which is often poorly administered, is open to abuse, which supresses innovation, impedes creativity, and engenders a climate of fear and division. In other words, retributive justice offers a mirage of justice and it creates an illusion of fairness. Within *Transformational Culture*, I describe a new model of justice which is becoming embedded into the rule books and employee handbooks of a great many organizations.

Procedural justice (which ensures that an organization delivers due process and is able to meet its statutory and regulatory obligations) has been blended with restorative justice (which is concerned about reducing harm, promoting dialogue, acting fairly, learning lessons, taking responsibility, engendering compassion and driving behavioural change). I have coined the phrase transformational justice to describe this new and progressive model of justice.

The future of culture is transformational

The Transformational Culture Model set out in this book is designed to support you and your colleagues as you create a fair, just, inclusive, sustainable and high-performing organization. Integrating a transformational culture requires commitment and tenacity. It will challenge much of the conventional wisdom about the prevailing systems, structures, processes and rules which we have come to rely on for many years.

Maria Arpa MBE, a global leader in the fields of restorative justice and non-violent communication (NVC) believes that the time has come for a radical overhaul of the existing cultural and justice paradigms. Maria explains:

'Now, more than ever, we need a new set of lenses through which to view our world. Moreover, we require the presence and enlightenment to question and challenge the systems of society that we have accepted for so long as the "way it is", even when they continue to create so much unnecessary human suffering.'

Drawing on her extensive experience of working with people and organizations, helping them to make the shift towards a progressive model of justice, Maria goes on to suggest that:

'The time for robust dialogue, human compassion and liberation from domination culture is upon us, both at grass roots and leadership level. Within our organizations, the shift towards a just, fair, inclusive and sustainable model of management, leadership and human resources will reduce the unnecessary human suffering that is so often the hallmark of top-down, punitive systems. In a world where people are justly demanding inclusion and equality, the consequences of being late to the party will further harm society. The development of a transformational culture offers a pioneering model for this new kind of organizing so I urge leaders to look to these models of change and find the humility to shift from "power over" to "power with".'

Within this text, I propose that the current cultural orthodoxies are not working and are no longer fit for purpose. They are being dismantled in front of our eyes. We can either leave the development of our organizational culture to chance, or we can actively develop the culture in a way which ensures that our organizations will be competitive and sustainable long into the future. I predict that the smart investors, the smart candidates, and the smart customers will choose the latter.

References and resources

Armit, K (2015) Evidence, culture and clinical outcome, *Royal College of Physicians Future Healthcare Journal*, https://www.ncbi.nlm.nih.gov/pmc/articles/PMC6460145/ (archived at https://perma.cc/PD6Z-4B4C)

Cappellanti-Wolf, A (2019) Developing a high-performance culture that enables your company to grow and thrive, www.shrm.org/about-shrm/press-room/press-releases/pages/shrm19-annual-conference-and-exposition-monday-speaker-quotes,-june-24,-2019.aspx (archived at https://perma.cc/6JRP-9358)

Deloitte (2012) Core Beliefs and Culture: Chairman's survey findings, https://www2.deloitte.com/content/dam/Deloitte/global/Documents/About-Deloitte/gx-core-beliefs-and-culture.pdf (archived at https://perma.cc/VEW2-3DSZ)

Klingler, S (2021) Why your employees are your best brand ambassadors, *Forbes*, www.forbes.com/sites/forbeshumanresourcescouncil/2021/05/06/why-your-employees-are-your-best-brand-ambassadors/?sh=286c96c951e0 (archived at https://perma.cc/5H8E-N9GE)

Liddle, D (2017) *Managing Conflict: A practical guide to resolution in the workplace*, Kogan Page, London

Taylor, J (2019) *The High Cost of A Toxic Workplace Culture*, SHRM

ACKNOWLEDGEMENTS

Writing this book has been a collaborative effort and I would like to thank the following people for their generosity, their support and their guidance.

Thank you to my wonderful wife and three children for your love, patience and words of encouragement. I wrote much of this book in a converted shed, during the third lockdown and a very cold winter. Your delicious cakes, cups of tea and big hugs kept me going. Thank you also to my parents, Sue and Bruce, for your love and support.

I would like to thank everyone who contributed to *Transformational Culture* by way of sharing your insights, your wisdom and your stories. Each case study has highlighted best practice in people-centred and values-based approaches. You have helped me to paint a picture of what a transformational culture might look like and the benefits it can deliver. The world of work is changing, and you are at the vanguard of that change.

Thank you to everyone involved with The TCM Group. You have given me the confidence and the courage to write this book. You inspire me and you demonstrate the transformational principles every day, in all that you do. I would like to say a special thank you to Lisajay, who has been a rock, and to Erika, who provided much-needed coaching and support as I wrote the book.

Thank you to everyone at the Institute of Organizational Dynamics (IOD) for your support and your guidance. There is more work to be done to understand the impact of a transformational culture. I look forward to working with you, and a growing number of like-minded academics and researchers, to achieve that objective.

A huge thank you to everyone at Kogan Page for having the confidence in me and asking me to publish my second book with you. Thank you also for all your support for my first book, *Managing Conflict*.

My final thank you is to all the mediators and the peacemakers out there. You are the unsung heroes of our communities, our workplaces and our society. You work quietly, every day, to transform relationships, to resolve disagreements, to establish harmony and to make people's lives better. The root causes of intolerance, violence, prejudice and division can only be resolved through insight and understanding – born out of dialogue. You give dialogue primacy. You build bridges where others build walls, and I am humbled by your tenacity and the immense impact that you have on all our lives.

PART ONE

The Case for Change

01

The transformational culture and why it matters

TRANSFORMATIONAL LEARNING

Within this chapter, you will discover answers to the following questions:

- What is a transformational culture and why does it matter?
- Why is the need for a new cultural paradigm pressing and urgent?
- What is the transformational culture triangle?
- How does transformational justice balance procedural justice with restorative justice?
- How can a transformational culture support our organizations to 'build back better' following Covid-19, socio-economic uncertainty and ongoing geo-political turbulence?
- Why are power, profit and process no longer the symbols of a successful organization?

What is a transformational culture?

A transformational culture is an organizational culture which is fair, just, inclusive, sustainable and high performing. It offers a new cultural paradigm and a practical framework for organizations which are committed to putting their purpose, their people and their values first. A transformational culture is suitable for organizations of any size and in any sector, bound by a common purpose to develop a workplace where the success of the organization and the success of its employees, customers and stakeholders are inextricably aligned.

The overarching purpose of a transformational culture is for leaders, managers, human resources (HR), trade union officials and others to create the conditions for their employees to reveal the most brilliant versions of themselves. This brilliance can be displayed in an extraordinary and infinite number of ways, each of which is unique to them and which creates a sense of humanity, harmony, interconnectedness and common purpose. This ability to be brilliant and to have the brilliance recognized, nurtured and celebrated by our leaders and our managers is the key to unlocking great employee experience (EX) and world-beating customer experience (CX).

In a transformational culture, the HR systems and management processes which promulgate mistrust, fear, injustice, exclusion, blame and retribution are supplanted with new systems and new processes which institutionalize trust, fairness, learning, growth, dialogue, inclusion, insight and collaboration. This new form of organizational culture requires a significant shift in focus and emphasis. The rewards will be great, measured in terms of enhanced competitive advantage, attracting investment, enhanced brand values and the ability to attract and retain the top talent.

> 'People who are influenced so that they feel more in control of their role, more engaged with the organization and who feel they are contributing to the wellbeing of others are more likely to be self-motivated, loyal, productive, creative and healthy.' (Swart *et al*, 2015)

To realize these rewards, we will all need to embrace radical change in the way that we lead, manage and administer our organizations. For instance, a transformational culture requires leaders, managers and HR to eliminate their reliance on traditional retributive justice orthodoxies (blame, shame and punish) and embrace a new and exciting form of justice: transformational justice. This new form of organizational justice brings together procedural justice (concerned with due process and protecting rights) and restorative justice (concerned with reducing harm, promoting dialogue and encouraging learning). In so doing, leaders, managers and HR will be demonstrating the very best of transformationalism: putting people before process, resolution before retribution, dialogue before dogma and action before entropy.

The axis of organizational culture is tilting

In recent times, we have witnessed a widespread reorientation of the employee's relationship with the employer, and this is profoundly changing company culture. New rules are being drawn up around a modern form of social contract between the company and its employees. New lines of acceptable behaviour, tolerance and inclusivity are being defined through behavioural frameworks which align corporate values with the desirable and undesirable behaviours.

In this precipitous, fast-paced and fluctuating world there can be no doubt that concepts of organizational culture and workplace climate have become confused and muddled:

- Home has become work.
- A response to a social justice issue has become a yardstick of an organization's brand.
- Individualism has become activism.
- Leaders have become servants.
- Investors have become the guardians of our climate.
- Employees have become customers.
- Shareholder value has become stakeholder value.

Add to this mix the fact that organizational culture, workplace climate and leadership behaviours play out in the glare of a relentless social and mainstream media, which can destroy reputations – individual and organizational – in the blink of an algorithm.

To fail to perceive this shift, and to fail to embrace the necessary changes to maintain pace with and keep ahead of the culture curve, could prove catastrophic. But for the organizations which get this right, this could be their greatest moment. The stakes are high and organizational culture seems to be the trump card.

Within this book I do not flinch from asking some of the big questions about culture. I am also privileged to be able to include various interviews and testimonies from organizations which are committed to putting their people and their values first. People such as Jon Slade, chief commercial officer (CCO) at the *Financial Times* (the *FT*), whose full interview appears on page 216. I asked Jon why he believes the need for a transformational culture is so pressing:

> 'We often talk about "company culture", but what we really mean is a collection of individual departmental "micro-cultures" that in sum add up to something bigger. The idiosyncrasies of departmental climate run deep with prevailing identities, personality, attitudes and ways of working. They are derived from the personalities who have dominated in the past, the victories, and losses the department has enjoyed or endured over the years, the traditions that have become mainstays of life. But now we encourage our staff, particularly younger staff, to "bring their whole selves to work" – and they are. They are bringing their outrage, their distress and their hopes around social questions such as ethnicity, gender, sexual orientation into the workplace. How they define themselves "out of the office" has become how employees choose to define themselves "in the office". It is just that there is no longer an office. All this means that we are moved from departmentally-defined culture to demographically-defined culture.'

Clearly, our leaders and managers must learn to engage with and listen actively to their people and do so with a constructive, empathetic and compassionate mindset. Failure to listen, and a failure to engage with their people, will fuel a perception that these leaders are out of touch with the reality of their lives and that they cannot be trusted. These are significant but often overlooked antecedents of organizational decline.

Why is the need for a new cultural paradigm so urgent and pressing?

Organizations are straining every sinew to build back better following some of the most challenging and turbulent times in the past 20 years:

- the 2008 financial crisis with all the serious (and continued) repercussions that the crisis had on organizations, communities, families and individuals around the globe;
- Covid-19 and the tragic toll it has taken, the growing health and social inequalities that it has exposed, the economic and social impact of continued lockdowns, and the rocky and uncertain road to recovery;
- the unfolding climate emergency and the urgent need for organizations to reduce waste, to cut emissions and to achieve net zero in record time;
- continuing division and inequality in our society which has led to a rise in social justice movements such as the Black Lives Matter (BLM) and #MeToo movements.

Some of this is being defined as a growth of 'employee activism'. I fear this term relegates the shift to the category of 'unwanted noise'. It is not. Leaders should pay heed and welcome the opportunity to engage with their people on issues that matter to them and establish those new parameters. To do so will engender trust and it will create and sustain a new social contract within our organizations.

Nonetheless, let us not kid ourselves here; these are huge and daunting topics. Very few, if any, of us have had to deal with anything like this before. This is VUCA (Volatile, Uncertain, Complex and Ambiguous) on steroids.

'I cannot recall a time where it has been more important for companies to respond to the needs of their stakeholders. We are at a moment of tremendous economic pain. We are also at a historic crossroads on the path to racial justice – one that cannot be solved without leadership from companies. A company that does not seek to benefit from the full spectrum of human talent is weaker for it – less likely to hire the best talent, less likely to reflect the needs of its customers and the communities where it operates, and less likely to outperform.' Larry Fink, Chairman and CEO of BlackRock (2021)

The challenges and the opportunities of a transformational culture

As this book demonstrates, a transformational culture is not for the faint of heart. However, the existing cultural paradigms are not working and something needs to change, urgently. As seen earlier, the list of factors affecting our organizations is getting longer each day and my guess is that I have merely exposed the tip of the iceberg. These are not issues that can be resolved by simply heading off on a 'board away day'.

Under this unsurmountable pressure, our workplace cultures are likely to slowly unravel and expose the fragility of our organizations and the inadequacies of the underpinning systems such as leadership, management, HR policies, inclusion, wellbeing, engagement and overall employee experience.

In the following section, I set out some of the specific challenges for leaders, managers and HR, as I see them.

Some of the big questions about culture

If you feel overwhelmed or daunted by the amount of content there is flying around about organizational culture, you are not alone. The area of culture is probably one of the most popular topics of conversations, blogs, webinars, articles, books and podcasts right now. Pretty much everyone seems to have their own ideas of what culture is and what it is not, what a good culture looks like and the impact of a bad culture. It is good news, of course. For those of us who are passionate about this topic, the debates are deeply exciting and energizing. This topic needs a proper discourse and a lively debate. However, my fear is that, as with so much in our lives, the topic of organizational culture becomes overly complicated and too contentious. All fine if we have hours to spend in seminars and workshops studying and debating the topic; however, in our seemingly busier and busier lives, this is a luxury many of us simply cannot afford.

To try to resolve this issue, in terms as straightforward and useful as possible, this text explores the meaning and benefits of a transformational culture in a practical and jargon-free way. It offers tested toolkits and practical checklists to support you as you go about developing your own version of a transformational culture.

So, before we get immersed in the detail, let me start by asking you to reflect on some of the big questions of the day.

TRANSFORMATIONAL THINKING

- What does the term 'culture' mean to you?
- Who owns your organization's culture?
- What impact do your leaders and managers have on your organizational culture?
- Does everyone experience culture in the same way and what are the issues which influence people's experience of culture?
- What changes would you make to your organizational culture if you could?

These are complex questions. Maybe it is because they are so tough, and so hard to answer, that they have regularly been overlooked and put in the 'too difficult to deal with today tray'. But we know these questions will not go away.

The question concerning 'what culture means' is an interesting one. It is a question which has perplexed us for years, and still eludes so many of us. I have spent a great many years examining organizational culture and working with senior leaders and other stakeholders who know what culture feels like – they know what it looks like, they know that it is important and they know the effect it can have when it goes wrong. However, achieving a common definition of the term 'culture', even in just one organization, let alone universally, can best be described as challenging. One only needs to run a quick search on Google to see that the term 'organizational culture' will generate millions of search results (I received 44 million results when I last ran a web search). Of course, now that this book is published, that has become 44 million and one.

The definitions of organizational culture are as wide as they are broad. I have set out below some of my favourite quotes and anecdotes about organizational culture:

'While successful culture can look and feel like magic, the truth is that it's not. Culture is a set of living relationships working towards a shared goal. It's not something you are. It's something you do.' (Coyle, 2018)

'An organization's culture defines the proper way to behave within the organization. This culture consists of shared beliefs and values established by leaders and then communicated and reinforced through various methods, ultimately shaping employee perceptions, behaviours and understanding. Organizational culture sets the context for everything an enterprise does. Because industries and situations vary significantly, there is not a one-size-fits-all culture template that meets the needs of all organizations.' (SHRM, 2021)

'Corporate culture is the only sustainable competitive advantage that is completely within the control of the entrepreneur.' (Cummings, 2011)

'If you get the culture right, most of the other stuff – like great customer service, or building a great long term brand, or passionate employees and customers – will happen naturally on its own.' (Hsieh, 2010)

'The culture of any organization is shaped by the worst behaviour the leader is willing to tolerate.' (Gruenert and Whitaker, 2015)

There is certainly a lot to think about here. The concept of organizational culture remains something of a paradox – powerful yet elusive. Perhaps, in the complex and volatile worlds that we inhabit, culture is more elusive now than it has ever been, yet it has never wielded such power. The need to resolve the culture paradox is a nettle which organizations must grasp if they are going to succeed. Some organizations are indeed grasping the nettle and the results are amazing. One such organization, where a purpose-driven and people-focused culture is viewed as being central to its long-term commercial success, is TSB Bank. TSB Bank plc is a retail and commercial bank in the United Kingdom and a subsidiary of Sabadell Group. It operates a network of 536 branches across England, Scotland and Wales. TSB in its present form launched on 9 September 2013 when it separated from Lloyds Banking Group.

CASE STUDY
TSB embraces a transformational culture

A purpose-driven and people-focused culture is helping TSB change the face of retail banking in the UK. 'Consciously transforming the culture to one where people could be themselves, perform at their best and do the right thing for customers was central as TSB planned to launch its new strategy in 2019,' explains Liz Ashford, the bank's HR Director. 'After an intensive period of research and feedback from customers and colleagues, the business agreed on its core purpose (Money confidence. For everyone. Every day) and launched an ambitious three-year strategy for future growth.'

This purpose is supported by three strategic drivers and a set of core behaviours. These core behaviours act as a guide for colleagues when they are taking actions, interacting with customers and each other, and making decisions. 'Feel what customers feel', for example, encourages colleagues to step into customers' shoes, while 'look for better' highlights TSB's belief that there is always room for improvement. Colleagues are also encouraged to 'do what matters' as they go about their day-to-day jobs, and to 'say it straight', taking pride in being open and honest.

The challenge in achieving a purpose-driven and people-focused culture is bringing these statements to life and making them genuine organizational habits, not just intention. TSB recognized that to achieve money confidence, for everyone, every day it needed to deliver more than just commercial performance. Liz explains how the organization used its core behaviours to build a tangible plan 'Working closely with our 6K colleagues, we developed a responsible business plan, putting "Do What Matters" into action and integrating it to set high standards for the way the bank operates, engages with employees and focuses its social and environmental contribution.'

The TSB Do What Matters plan has five key pillars:

- Doing what matters for customers (focusing on helping people to be more money confident).

- Doing what matters for businesses (treating businesses fairly and helping them grow).

- Doing what matters for colleagues (ensuring TSB is a truly inclusive organization).

- Doing what matters for communities (donating time and money to vital local projects).

- Doing what matters for the environment (a commitment to reduce the environmental impact of operations to net zero by no later than 2030).

The Do What Matters plan was launched in July 2020 and by early 2021 had been embedded into every part of the business. Colleagues have fully embraced the initiative, with four out of five saying they understood their role in achieving it just six months after launch. Half of the initial goals set had already been achieved during the first six months and were updated for 2021. 'Every aspect of our plan is geared around our purpose and behaviours. People very much understand it and are enthusiastic about it, and it shows up all the time in everyday life,' says Liz.

Do what matters for colleagues

Progress under the 'Do what matters for colleagues' pillar has been particularly strong. TSB already had inclusion affinity groups for Ability, BAME, Gender Balance and LGBTQ+, and during 2020 it took proactive steps to work more closely together to achieve a truly inclusive culture. Gender balance has improved, with 40 per cent of senior roles now held by women, and in January 2021 TSB established a new set of holistic goals to increase the diversity of the overall workforce and senior teams. By the end of 2020, around half of line managers had completed training in mental health awareness and inclusive behaviours, and the bank was on track to meet its goal of all line managers completing the full programme by the end of 2021. One in three colleagues were engaging with proactive mental health support to take care of their mental wellbeing.

'What's really exciting is the intersectionality of the agendas,' explained Sarah McPake, Head of Talent, Insights and Inclusion at TSB. 'The networks are working together as a force for good on topics that affect the broadest number of colleagues, and that's having a really positive impact.'

TSB has also made a significant change in the way it manages conduct, conflict, complaints and concerns. They have implemented a resolution framework, where the emphasis is on resolving issues quickly through effective conversations and mediation, thereby developing enduring, productive and respectful workplace relationships. The launch of this resolution-focused approach coincided with the emergence of Covid-19, but the business felt it was such an important initiative that it should not be put on hold. Following official endorsement by the executive committee, the first mediation case was taking place virtually within weeks.

'We wanted to create a culture where people could challenge the status quo and feel that they were operating in an environment where you could have different perspectives and points of view and still feel safe speaking up,' said Sarah.

Evaluating progress

Tools were put in place to track and measure the evolution of the culture from the beginning, with insights drawn from colleague feedback as well as a range of people- and customer-related metrics.

Data has already shown the majority of colleagues agree the business treats its people fairly and with respect, together with an increase in the number of colleagues who feel they can speak up freely and positive feedback about levels of wellbeing – remarkable results given the backdrop of Covid-19. 'The power of listening really kicked in. Our leaders were out and about listening to people all the time. All of this listening gives us a brilliant opportunity to reframe and rethink and ensure what we are doing remains relevant across the whole of the organization,' says Liz.

Lessons learned

As the culture continues to transform, HR practitioners at TSB have had the opportunity to reflect on what they have learned from the process.

'Simplicity and taking it in bite-sized chunks has been key,' says Liz. 'We didn't set out to do everything at once, it has been a gradual build and there's always more to do. Culture can be difficult to define, and it means different things to different people, but if you can keep the concept and principles as simple as you can, it will serve you well and keep you grounded.'

The transformational triangle

The transformational triangle model represents the three elements of transformationalism: transformational HR, transformational leadership and transformational justice (see Figure 1.1). These three elements work in harmony to influence the development of a transformational culture.

FIGURE 1.1   The transformational triangle

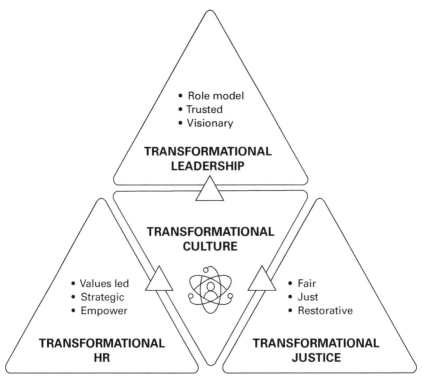

Transformational leadership

The transformational leader demonstrates an alignment of their behaviour with the purpose and the values of the organization. They know that it is important to walk the talk because they understand that they are a role model – that the way they behave sets the tone for the culture of their organization. Moreover, it defines the climate and the terms of engagement (the micro-culture) within their teams, divisions and departments.

In his 1985 book, *Leadership and Performance Beyond Expectations*, Bernard Bass defined what we have come to understand as transformational leadership. He described such leaders as having the capacity to influence followers, to transcend self-interests for the greater good of their organization and inspire focus, energy and effort in people to achieve results beyond expectable limits (Bass, 1985). In their book, *Multipliers*, Liz Wiseman and Greg McKeown catchily described such a leader as a multiplier (as opposed to a diminisher - those who uses the opposite, more transactional, leadership style). 'A multiplier is someone who uses his or her intelligence to amplify and bring out the smarts and capability of those around them... Multipliers are leaders who look beyond their own genius and focus their energy on extracting and extending the genius of others' (Wiseman and McKeown, 2010).

Transformational leaders and managers act with courage and kindness. They listen actively, they respond constructively and they lead with integrity. They do this because they know that these behaviours underpin the development of high-performing and highly resilient teams and organizations. In addition, they know how to handle conflict, change and crises effectively, by:

- being courageous and having difficult conversations;
- creating psychologically safe spaces for dialogue;
- acting with objectivity;
- being comfortable with their own and others' emotions;
- demonstrating self-awareness and empathy;
- seeking constructive win/win remedies to problems;
- empowering others.

Within a transformational culture, leaders and managers possess the courage, the confidence and the competence to spot and resolve concerns, conflicts and complaints constructively. Leaders and managers must also be empowered to take action to resolve issues at work rather than subcontracting problems to the HR function or relying on two of the popular management norms that I observe: extensive inaction or expensive overreaction.

Developing a transformational culture requires our executives, leaders and senior managers to shift the way they think about leadership. They need to lead with values, and they need to recognize that compassion for others, and compassion for our planet, is a sign of strength, not a sign of weakness.

Our leaders must integrate the purpose and the values of their organization into their corporate objectives and strategy (as so vividly demonstrated by the BRC on page 149). Our leaders and managers should create and sustain an overarching strategic narrative which supports the deployment of a fair, just, inclusive, sustainable and high-performing culture (like Imperial College Healthcare NHS trust did on page 140).

Our leaders should be able to create an inspiring vision of the future by motivating people to buy into, and deliver, the vision. They are exceptional listeners, and they go to where their people are before they ask their people to follow them. They are proactive at spotting and preventing issues from escalating and they are confident and courageous when it comes to engaging in and facilitating dialogue.

In summary, within a transformational culture, leaders and managers know how to build and sustain working and business relationships forged with trust, respect, tolerance and a commitment to fairness and inclusion.

Transformational justice

A transformational culture is not simply about giving a label to a 'good culture'. It goes far deeper than that. A transformational culture is about enabling a radical shift in the way that our organizations think about justice. After all, justice is at the heart of a civilized society – it is the reason so many of our rules and procedures exist, it is the basis for so many of our institutions and people spend their lives going in search of it. But the question begs to be asked: do our organizations' rules, procedures and policies deliver justice? I would – and this is with the greatest respect to everyone involved in designing and administering these rules and processes – suggest not.

Transformational justice, as I explain in detail in Chapter 2, is a modern and progressive amalgam of procedural justice and restorative justice. This new model of justice balances the rules of the organization, the rights of the employee, and the need to generate fair, just and inclusive outcomes when things go wrong. Transformational justice, at its core, is about reducing harm, building trust, protecting relationships, promoting psychological safety and creating opportunities for insight, reflection and learning.

Transformational justice replaces the retributive models of justice which are deeply ingrained through organizational processes such as the traditional performance management, discipline and grievance procedures. These retributive justice processes are concerned about risk mitigation, blame and punishment. They disregard learning, compassion and the emotional and psychological needs of the parties involved. These procedures, and the entire retributive justice paradigm, are being shown to be harmful, damaging and divisive, with the potential to be discriminatory. Worse still, their sheer existence invokes an adversarial and confrontational mindset and dynamic in teams, departments, divisions and across entire organizations. They sow the seeds of toxicity which are watered, often ably, by poor management behaviour and team discord. While trust and equity are core features of any justice model, trust in the retributive justice model has broken down irrevocably. It is time for it to go.

In Chapter 5, I set out a radical new Resolution Framework to assist organizations that wish to make transformational justice a reality. I set out the benefits of using the Resolution Framework and its associated transformational principles for handling concerns, conduct, complaints and conflicts at work. I also share examples of organizations which have adopted this new approach, including Center Parcs, TSB Bank, London Ambulance Service and Aviva. Thankfully, these and many other organizations are waking up to the harm that these retributive systems are causing and they are beginning to embrace transformational justice.

Transformational HR

If organizations are going to adopt a transformational culture, the human resources function must take urgent action to become purpose, people and values led. HR must transform itself into an overarching people and culture function and it should act now to release itself from the burden of its perceived proximity to management. The term 'business partner', so casually used, is a divisive and loaded term which results in HR being perceived by many as the 'long arm of management'. This perception of systemic bias impedes the effectiveness of HR and it erodes trust in its role and its systems. Ironically, it also impedes HR's ability to support managers effectively.

For HR to remain a trusted and effective function in our organizations, it must rise above the paradigms of power, hierarchy and control. It must become obsessed with delivering great employee experience (EX) and becoming a catalyst for world-class customer experience (CX). HR should be the function within our organizations that connects EX with CX. To assist with this transformation, I have created a powerful organizational culture model, which I set out in Chapters 2 and 3.

Released from the burden of HR being perceived as the 'long arm of management' or the perception that HR has had to sell its soul to 'secure a seat at the board table', HR will experience some exciting and new strategic and operational challenges:

- No longer using the divisive term 'business partner' to describe the role of HR practitioners. People and culture partners will partner with all stakeholders to build trust, deliver accountability and drive growth.
- Creating and sustaining a transformational culture hub (see page 233) and its associated subgroups.
- Integrating a suite of new processes for driving organizational development (OD), learning and development (L&D) and employee relations (ER), including positive psychology, systems thinking, principled negotiation, appreciative inquiry, restorative justice and non-violent communication.
- Partnership working with unions and management to develop and deploy a new model social contract.

- Administration of a justice model which is fair, just and restorative – transformational justice.
- Systematizing coaching, mentoring, facilitation and mediation.

Chapters 2 and 3 provide the blueprint to assist HR to make this transition. In Chapter 5, I explain how the new people and culture function can develop and deploy an overarching Resolution Framework for addressing concerns, conduct, complaints and conflicts in the workplace. This includes integrating collaborative, inclusive and constructive remedies to people issues. As a result, organizations, and the people and culture profession, will reap the rewards from a culture which is values based and people centred.

As I was researching this book, I had the privilege to speak with renowned author and transformational HR activist Perry Timms about the concept of transformational culture. He explained to me: 'Culture is undeniably powerful and complex in equal measure. My view is clear: people are the transformative force in work. The systems we build, and the technology we deploy that aims to be transformational, is nothing without people bringing it to life and making it deliver the value it is intended to create. HR has willingly and somewhat coercively "owned" this area of the organizational system as it directly relates to people. I would suggest that HR's role in stimulating, promoting and leveraging a transformational culture comes in creating safety, measured experimentation, commitment to improve and diversify, and being bolder, braver and more edgy in how work gets done. In essence, an act of defiance against operational mediocrity.'

A transformational culture requires a shift in mindset by employees also. Employees should align their behaviours to the purpose, values and culture of the organization. In a transformational culture, employees and their representatives should be encouraged to raise issues as early as possible so that they do not fester and do not escalate into more significant problems and disputes. Employees should know that dialogue has primacy in a transformational culture. It is not possible to secure a fair, just, learning or restorative outcome without sitting down together, talking, listening and finding a mutually acceptable way forward.

In addition, union partners and employee representatives should be viewed as equal partners. As such, their voice should be heard, and they should be given the opportunity to engage in predictive and proactive problem solving with leaders, managers and people and culture (HR) colleagues. A transformational culture provides an opportunity to forge a new social contract – an exciting new partnership between the management of the organization and its workforce. The principles of transformationalism (fair, just, inclusive) and this new model of social contract can be used to build a culture of mutual trust, respect and accountability between management, HR, employees and employee representatives.

TRANSFORMATIONAL THINKING

- How could you deploy the transformational triangle within your organization?

- Are your leaders transformational?

- How can your HR function become more transformational?

- Is your organization ready to deliver transformational justice?

- What potential benefits does the transformational triangle offer to your organization?

Power, profit and process are no longer the symbols of a successful organization

You cannot build back better when your workforce is unhappy, unhealthy and disengaged; when your rules and procedures fuel discord, dogma and division; when your managers lack the basic skills to handle even the simplest quarrels and disagreements; where diversity creates adversity; where your response to failure is to blame others and to create a culture of fear and retribution; and where inequity and unfairness are systemic.

Creating a sustainable and high-performing organizational culture means that we must take urgent action to tackle the thorny issues of mistrust, fairness, inequity, climate change, stakeholder value, employee engagement, digitalization, agile and flexible working, diversity, inclusion, the productivity gap, and our employees' mental and physical wellbeing. To achieve a transformational culture, leaders, managers, HR, employees and unions must work together to address these urgent issues.

Measuring culture

The debate that perplexes a great many is the question of whether culture can be codified, measured and evaluated or whether it is even desirable to evaluate the return on investment (ROI) from a culture. Following a series of seminars run in collaboration between ACCA (Association of Chartered Certified Accountants) and the ESRC (Economic and Social Research Council), a final report concluded that senior leadership teams should be proactive in considering the shape and tone of the company culture and that cultural change should begin at the top of the organization. 'The board should consider what sort of culture the company wants before it assesses its existing culture' (Moxey and Schu, 2014).

The report suggests that recent corporate failures have highlighted that the following considerations are basic to good corporate governance and before proceeding to any assessment of their culture, the board should ask themselves the following questions:

- What are the goals and purposes of the organization?
- What sort of behaviours does it wish to encourage and discourage?
- How is the tone at the top set out and conveyed through the organization?

The report goes on to say: 'An organization's culture should be one of its most important assets as it is heavily linked to decision making, productivity, capacity and its brand/image (and therefore reputational risk)' (Moxey and Schu, 2014).

I believe it is both possible and desirable to codify, classify, measure and evaluate a transformational culture. Where there is a will, there is a way. Increasing access to digital technologies coupled with a desire by leaders, managers, HR and others to measure and evaluate areas such as wellbeing, engagement, inclusion and employee experience means that meaningful cultural analysis is now entirely plausible. In Part Two of this book, 'The Transformational Culture Playbook', I provide checklists and guidance notes to assist you to integrate and evaluate a transformational culture. For instance, on page 219 I explain the business case for a transformational culture, and I offer guidance to help organizations to codify, measure and evaluate their current cultures and micro-cultures.

Conclusion and calls to action

It is clear to me that it will not be possible to emerge from this current set of crises with the old cultural paradigms still in play. Developing and sustaining a transformational culture must feature at the top of the inbox of every executive, HR professional, manager and union official. Culture must become the number one strategic priority for our organizational leaders. One thing is for certain: organizations that get this wrong will be the ones that fail, some slowly and inexorably, others in a blaze of media headlines and a social media storm. The ones that get it right will be the successful enterprises in the future. That is where the smart money and the top talent will head.

A transformational culture by its very nature encourages and enables disparate and sometimes competing beliefs, needs, priorities and agendas to be aired, to be understood and to be resolved. As this text will demonstrate, a transformational culture delivers a happier, healthier, more harmonious and high-performance workplace – four outcomes which underpin the most strategically important objectives of enhanced EX and great CX.

We no longer need systems in our organizations which seek to suppress or control debate and diverse thinking, or which blame, shame or punish people when mistakes are made. They have failed – they have no place in a modern workplace. We need to create systems and processes which promote and value dialogue, which engender compassion, which reduce harm, which promote learning, which bring people together, which protect relationships, and which create a humanizing space for every one of us to be the very best versions of ourselves – individually and collectively.

A transformational culture, as this book will reveal, is the key to unlocking individual, team and organizational success. It is time to get to work.

References

Bass, B M (1985) *Leadership and Performance Beyond Expectations*, Free Press, New York

Coyle, D (2018) *The Culture Code: The secrets of highly successful groups*, Random House, London

Cummings, D (2011) David Cummings on startups: The top 3 things every entrepreneur needs to know [Blog] 7 December, https://davidcummings. org/2011/12/07/the-top-3-things-every-entrepreneur-needs-to-know/ (archived at https://perma.cc/9FUR-CQUX)

Fink, L (2021) Larry Fink's 2021 letter to CEOs, www.blackrock.com/corporate/ investor-relations/larry-fink-ceo-letter (archived at https://perma.cc/FJ9G-YDDP)

Gruenert, S and Whitaker, T (2015) *School Culture Rewired: How to define, assess, and transform it*, ASCD, Alexandria, VA

Hsieh, T (2010) *Delivering Happiness: A path to profits, passion, and purpose*, Grand Central Publishing, New York

Moxey, P and Schu, P (2014) Culture and channelling corporate behaviour: Summary of findings. Joint report produced by ACCA and ESRC

SHRM (2021) Understanding and developing organizational culture, www.shrm.org/resourcesandtools/tools-and-samples/toolkits/pages/ understandinganddevelopingorganizationalculture.aspx (archived at https://perma.cc/BSV2-Z23V)

Swart, T, Chisholm, K and Brown, P (2015) *Neuroscience for Leadership: Harnessing the brain gain advantage*, Palgrave Macmillan, Basingstoke

Wiseman, L and McKeown, G (2010) *Multipliers: How the Best Leaders Make Everyone Smarter*, Harper Business, New York

02

Shift happens: from retribution to transformation

How to harness the power of restorative justice

TRANSFORMATIONAL LEARNING

Within this chapter, you will discover answers to the following questions:

- Why do the favoured retributive justice models fail to deliver fairness, accountability, consistency or justice?

- Why has the time come for a review of the prevailing retributive justice systems in use in our organizations?

- What is transformational justice and how does it work in practice?

- What is the power of restorative justice (RJ) and where can RJ be applied in the workplace?

- How does transformational justice promote dialogue, deliver accountability and build trust?

- What role does transformational justice play in modern employee relations?

Amul and Joanna have been working together for the past six years in the finance department of a large multinational company. About a year ago, Joanna was promoted to the role of finance manager. Amul had also applied for the position but was unsuccessful. He was unhappy about the recruitment decision as he believed he was better qualified and more experienced than Joanna. He suspected it was a decision made based on his ethnicity. He has since spoken to other minority ethnic colleagues who experienced similar adverse outcomes from internal recruitment processes.

Amul chose not to appeal the recruitment decision, however. For the past 12 months, he has been feeling increasing levels of resentment towards Simon, the Director of Finance, who chaired the recruitment process. However, Simon has not spoken to Amul since the interview process. Amul has been channelling his feelings of resentment and frustration towards Joanna.

At a recent meeting, Amul and Joanna were having a robust discussion about a funding application for a new project. Amul became cross with Joanna; he began to make comments under his breath (which Joanna could not hear, but which she perceived to be derogatory). During the conversation Joanna said she felt that Amul had put a 'black mark' against her name ever since she had been promoted to the finance manager role. In the commotion, Amul misheard this comment. He thought that Joanna had made a racist comment, he heard 'black something'. Already feeling stressed and frustrated, he lost his temper with Joanna and called her 'a bully and a racist'. He added that 'she did not deserve the new role'. Feeling attacked and undermined, and shaking with anger, Joanna told Amul to go home and cool off for the rest of the day. In a state of shock, distress and confusion, Amul went home.

That evening, Amul raised a formal complaint against Joanna. He sent his complaint to the VP for finance, the HR director and the head of audit and compliance. The next day, Joanna was suspended pending an investigation into gross misconduct under the company's fair treatment and disciplinary procedures. The day after that, Amul went to see his GP and was signed off work for stress. He has not been back to work since.

Following Amul's allegations, the company policies were followed correctly at every stage. The investigation was impartial and thorough; indeed, the entire process of managing the case was meticulous and robust. It was an exemplar of best practice in procedural fairness.

Fast forward three months from the incident. Joanna has just heard that she has had her appeal overturned. She has been dismissed, without notice, for gross misconduct, a sanction which the company's counsel believed fell within the range of reasonable responses. She was unable to prove that she did not make a racist comment and the disciplinary panel felt that Amul was a credible complainant and that his allegations of bullying, harassment and discrimination were proven, on the balance of probability. The company was proud to have delivered on its zero-tolerance policy on racism and bullying. The senior management and HR felt that this case would send out a clear message to all employees that bullying and harassment are not acceptable in any form.

Joanna's partner and her three children are extremely worried about her mental health. Joanna has not slept properly since the incident and has been having troubling and suicidal thoughts. She has been referred to counselling and psychotherapy, which begin to help, and over time she does, thankfully, begin to recover. She will never work in finance again and she will never again hold a management position.

Amul has now left the company. He felt traumatized by the entire process. He quickly realized that the situation had escalated out of control and his substantive complaint, in relation to the adverse recruitment decision, had been brushed under the carpet. When he raised this with the investigator, and during the hearing, which was chaired by Simon, he was told that his 'conjecture' of an unfair recruitment process was not relevant in the disciplinary case against Joanna. Amul is carrying a huge amount of guilt about what happened. He knows that he should not feel guilty, as he has done nothing wrong. However, the entire process has made him feel this way. When he heard that Joanna had been dismissed, he wept, the first time he had wept since his mother died 10 years ago. Amul has now set up a small website development consultancy and he does occasional freelance work for firms in his local area.

Simon has just been promoted to VP of finance. His career at the company looks brighter now than it has ever done.

Author's note: this case is fictional. Any resemblance to any person(s) is entirely coincidental.

TRANSFORMATIONAL TAKEAWAY

- How did this case make you feel?
- Could this situation happen in your own organization?
   - If yes, why?
   - If no, why not?
- Did this case deliver justice? If so, for whom?
- How could the case have been handled differently?
- Have the parties in this case learned any lessons?
- Has the organization learned any lessons?
- Has this situation made Simon a better leader?

What is transformational justice?

The story of Amul, Joanna and Simon may be a work of fiction, but it is a story that I have heard a great many times over the years. I have seen, first hand, the terrible human and entirely disproportionate damage caused by our reductive, divisive and destructive HR processes and management systems. In Chapter 5, and supported by numerous sources and case studies, I highlight how more and more organizations are rejecting the retributive orthodoxies of blame, shame and punish and introducing the transformational principles through systems such as an overarching Resolution Framework. I work closely with a great many senior leaders and HR professionals who share my view that the time is up for retributive justice. One of them, Roujin Ghamsari, is a strategic lead on the development of HR and leadership practices in the National Health Service (NHS). Roujin has been one of the leading advocates for a new model of transformational justice. She explained to me: 'Blame and retribution are no longer viable outcomes in the modern workplace. If organizations are serious about putting people and values first, and embracing a culture that encourages learning, not punishment, they need to consider deploying a model of justice which is fair, just and restorative.'

It is evident to me that organizations are tired of the old justice paradigms and are frustrated at the damage they do. In this chapter I will describe how the traditional systems for managing performance, discipline and grievances create untold stress, they damage relationships and they rarely, if ever, yield a positive outcome for anyone unfortunate enough to encounter them. We have built an entire industry around them and, on an industrial scale, they are destroying lives and they are eroding any ability to deliver meaningful employee or customer experience. These traditional HR policies and management systems will, in my view, block any attempts made to adopt a transformational culture, and they will severely impede efforts to develop people-centred and values-based leadership and management systems and behaviours.

Retributive justice is a flawed model of justice

The one factor that is common in each of these policy frameworks is that they are built around a flawed model of justice – a model of justice where the primary focus is on blame and punishment. In his book *Just Culture*, Sidney Dekker explains that the retributive justice model is concerned with three key factors: 1) which rule has been broken, 2) who did it, and 3) what punishment the wrongdoer deserves to receive (Dekker, 2017).

I am often told that our traditional HR processes and management systems deliver procedural fairness and due process. They may do so, but at what cost? According to latest research, workplace conflicts cost the UK economy £28 billion a year and the formal processes used to manage conflict, such as disciplinary and grievance procedures, cost more than £15 billion per annum (Saundry and Urwin, 2021).

These costs are staggering and are entirely unnecessary. It is possible to deliver procedural fairness and due process without incurring such excessive costs, destroying people's lives and undermining their relationships. As this chapter will illustrate, when organizations align procedural fairness with the restorative principles, the outcomes are so much better. And please do not worry, there is no greater risk of an adverse outcome at tribunal if we are kind to people.

Procedural justice and retributive justice are not one and the same, even though they appear to be so when one reads through any standard employee handbook. One could easily be mistaken to believe that they have been coupled together by people who either a) do not understand the nature of people or organizations, or b) have a vested interest in the worsening of workplace relationships. Either way, these retributive processes and systems do not have a place in a transformational culture.

In our retributive justice systems, our humanity is overlooked and our perceptions, feelings, needs, goals, hopes, fears and aspirations are treated with disdain and as an irrelevance. Our retributive justice systems are built around a culture of risk mitigation – they do not take account of the harm that they do to people or to relationships, and they fail to instil any sense of good people management. The needs of human beings are conveniently pushed aside in favour of reducing the risk of an adverse outcome in any future litigation.

Retributive justice creeps, like a thief in the night, into the culture of our organizations and the climate of our teams. It steals the goodwill that has built up, it makes off with the trust that has been earned and it appropriates the camaraderie which has been the glue that has held our teams together. These retributive systems render our organizations, divisions, departments and teams increasingly adversarial, hostile and confrontational, destroying relationships and sowing the seeds of division. I would go as far as to say that our current penchant for retributive justice erodes and undermines the very fabric of our organizations: trust, fairness, mutual respect, inclusion and open dialogue. In other words, retributive justice breaks the fragile social contract in place in our organizations.

There is an imperative for a new model of justice

So many case studies and stories in this text demonstrate that there is an imperative for change. Within this chapter, I propose the development of a new model of organizational justice which I call transformational justice. This model of justice blends procedural justice (which is concerned with employee rights and the need for due process) with restorative justice (which is concerned with reducing harm, promoting dialogue and restoring relationships). Transformational justice delivers a system of rules, behaviours and processes which keep people safe, which build trust, which promote accountability, which protect relationships and which generate constructive outcomes through meaningful dialogue.

Transformational justice is fair, empowering, inclusive and tough. It holds people to account in a direct and powerful way. Drawing heavily on the restorative principles mentioned above, it holds up a mirror to us and requires us to ask ourselves some tough questions about the choices that we make and the impact of our actions, interactions and reactions.

Through a process of direct engagement with the person(s) affected by our behaviour or impacted by a mistake, transformational justice delivers behavioural changes which are as profound as they are sustainable, and ultimately it delivers organizational learning which has a legacy.

The principles of transformational justice (aka the transformational principles) are as follows:

- It delivers procedural justice and offers a due process for addressing issues in the workplace.
- It places greater emphasis on the harm caused and the sources and the impact of the harm on people and relationships.
- It allows those directly involved to explore and discover:
  - the meaning of what the other is saying (or has been trying to say);
  - the perceptions and opinions the other has formed;
  - the impact of each party's actions, interactions and reactions;

○ the intention behind the actions, interactions and reactions;

○ the needs that the parties have (including the organization) to restore the relationship or to take remedial action to resolve the issue or mistake.

- It applies a powerful narrative form. By encouraging the parties to reflect on the past, the present and the future, it focuses on repairing the harm caused and it empowers the parties to resolve issues in a direct and constructive way. It allows the parties in a complaint, with a concern or in conflict to tell their own story and for those stories to be shared. Stories can be congruent in a metaphorical way, even if the facts seem diametrically opposed. With story you can address both sides of unresolvable paradoxes (Simmons, 2000).

- It promotes deep learning which helps the parties to make new choices and to develop new strategies. These strategies will assist them to modify how they act, interact and react in the future. In other words, transformational justice nudges people to move towards behavioural change rather than threatening them with a sanction or a punishment.

- It delivers a clear commitment to the safety, healing and constructive support for all employees.

- The focus shifts from punishment to enlightenment. It focuses on delivering accountability/acceptance of responsibility and a positive transformation for people who harm others. For instance, as disciplinary warnings become reminders and performance improvement plans (PIPs) become resolution action plans, the fear of the performance conversation is removed.

- It delivers a highly empowering model of justice, where the outcomes are crafted and agreed by the parties themselves wherever possible. There are various options for assisted dialogue, such as mediation and facilitation, where the parties are unable to resolve a situation directly. In this way, the parties are actively engaged in securing a just and learning outcome rather than being passive participants in an abstract process.

- Transformational justice is concerned about the past and righting the wrongs. But that is balanced by being future focused and outcome oriented. The outcomes from transformational justice address the harm caused and reduce the risk of future harm.

- Procedural justice and due process remain core elements of transformational justice. There is a mechanism for escalation and serious and complex cases can still be investigated and a sanction applied where required, such as serious negligence, repeated violations or a serious breach of the agreed organizational behaviours.

The power of restorative justice

One of the fundamental tenets of transformational justice and, by default, a transformational culture is restorative justice. I first encountered RJ and the restorative principles in the mid-1990s when I was trained as a restorative practitioner by the wonderful Barbara Tudor, award-winning advocate of restorative approaches and co-author of *The Pocket Guide to Restorative Justice* (Wallis and Tudor, 2008).

Having gained my first degree in race and community relations and having worked in the areas of social regeneration and inclusion, I had set up and was running a large charity which specialized in delivering mediation and non-violence in a wide variety of settings: communities, neighbourhoods and schools. At that time, RJ operated predominantly in the criminal justice system and was used to divert young offenders away from a custodial sentence. It involved offenders and their victims meeting each other in carefully facilitated sessions or communicating via letter exchange.

I worked with various crime reduction and law enforcement agencies to develop and integrate restorative justice approaches which included:

- letter exchanges between the victim and the offender(s);
- indirect dialogue between the victim and the offender(s) through a process called 'shuttle mediation';

- direct dialogue between a victim and the offender(s) at a restorative meeting;
- restorative conferencing which was used to bring together multiple stakeholders (police, council, neighbours, young people, youth workers, etc) to address issues such as anti-social behaviour, nuisance and low-level criminal activity.

I learned that RJ gave victims a much greater stake in the justice process. It gave them a voice, when so often they were excluded from the formal systems of justice. I learned also that RJ provides a safe space for offenders (many of whom are very young and often disadvantaged) to learn about the impact of their offending behaviour on a real person and the harm that they create due to the choices they make. It also allowed the offender to apologize for the harm they had caused, and in many cases (not all, but in a great many) for the victim to forgive the offender. I will come back to the power of apology and forgiveness several times in this book.

A lack of empathy led many of the young people I worked with to make desperately bad decisions and choices. During an RJ process, developing empathy has a significant impact on the offender and indeed on the victim. Of course, it is impossible to go back in time to undo the wrongs of the past; however, empathy, and the self-awareness that is built around it, gives them a basis by which they can make better decisions in the future.

I call it the three second rule. In the three seconds after they spot a window ajar, or a car door unlocked, can they walk past and not commit an offence? All RJ must do (and this is a big ask, given that very few others had managed to do it up to that point), in those three seconds, is to persuade them to put the victim first and to choose not to commit an offence. It worked – the power of empathy and the ability to put another human's need ahead of our own really could reduce the risk of reoffending. In the criminal justice system, reoffending is known as recidivism; RJ is proven to deliver quite staggering results in terms of user satisfaction and a reduction in recidivism. Following a seven-year evaluation by the Ministry of Justice of three restorative justice schemes, a final evaluation report was published in 2008 (Shapland *et al*, 2008) which suggested that:

- restorative justice led to a 14 per cent reduction in the rate of reoffending;
- 85 per cent of victims were satisfied with the process of meeting their offender face to face, and 78 per cent would recommend it to other people in their situation;
- 62 per cent of victims felt that restorative justice had made them feel better after an incident of crime while just 2 per cent felt it had made them feel worse;
- for every £1 spent on delivering a face-to-face meeting, £8 was saved through reductions in reoffending.

I have been swept up by the transformational power of RJ and the shift in emphasis from blame and judgement to insight and understanding. Thankfully, RJ is now predominant across most of the UK's justice systems, except, and I sincerely hope this will change soon, in the areas of human resources management and workplace and employee relations.

Where can RJ be applied in the workplace?

Accountability, remorse, understanding, apology and forgiveness are the currency of RJ. Parties who had so little in common, other than that one had chosen to commit an offence against the other and one had been harmed by the choices that the other had made, find a shared narrative, a powerful connection and a deep understanding. In the workplace, RJ takes the form of local resolution, team facilitation, mediation, coaching and team conferencing. I will explain these processes more in Chapter 5.

Within the workplace, RJ can be applied effectively in the following settings:

- By ensuring an open and honest dialogue between a manager and an employee to resolve a performance or a conduct issue.

- By facilitating a conversation between two disputing colleagues in a work or a project team.

- By mediating between an employee and a manager, where an employee has a complaint about the behaviour or conduct of their manager.

- By mediating between a member of a team and their employer or their manager where the employee has alleged bullying, harassment or discrimination.

- When a manager is coaching members of their team to improve performance or to build resilience.

- When a team is in distress because of an unresolved conflict or it is experiencing a change, such as a merger or an acquisition (M&A).

What is retributive justice?

In comparison with the transformational approaches, the models of retributive justice are predicated on the principle that an offender should be punished when the rule of law is broken.

Retributive justice can be summarized as follows:

- It is an adversarial process where each of the parties may be represented by an advocate. In the UK workplace this is not possible. Rather, the accused party is given the right to be accompanied to hearings rather than having the right to be represented (Employment Relations Act, 1999). This does not have the effect of rendering workplace processes less adversarial. On the contrary, it means that the parties become more traumatized and increasingly anxious, which often manifests as hostility and defensiveness.

- A senior manager will hear the case to determine the truth. They are concerned with which rules have been broken, how badly, with what impact and what sanction should be applied. Interestingly, in many workplaces, HR administers this damaging process and HR personnel support the chair during the hearing. This has the net effect of undermining trust in the HR function, which many regard as the 'long arm of management'. For the past 20 years, I have seen this dynamic play out time and again and it genuinely baffles me why this is not a bigger concern to HR personnel, most of whom are fair-minded and reasonable people.

- It considers who is right and who is wrong. In other words, it is concerned with who is to blame. The entire process looks backwards rather than forwards. It is consequence based and a sanction (punishment) is applied to the wrongdoer. The punishment should be proportionate to the offence. However, the only real sanction available in workplaces is dismissal. All other sanctions are in fact warnings rather than sanctions. Therefore, for so many, a warning feels like the first step towards dismissal as that is, in fact, precisely what it is.

- The process of retribution should act as a deterrent to others. It does not.

In the workplace, retributive justice can be viewed most clearly through the prism of the traditional performance, discipline, conduct, absence and GBH (grievance, bullying and harassment) procedures. It is these procedures which cause the greatest harm and yield the least valuable outcomes.

Why do retributive justice models fail to deliver fairness, accountability or consistency?

The argument that I frequently hear in favour of the retributive justice system is that it delivers accountability and consistency and is procedurally fair. Maybe, but who is going to tell that to Joanna and Amul?

I hear, every day, harrowing first-hand accounts that tell me that these traditional procedures are broken. They are the antithesis of a transformational culture. At best, they are poorly designed and poorly administered. At worst, they are destructive, harmful and discriminatory. One of the key functions of workplace policies is to protect the vulnerable. They fail in that basic requirement. They do not protect the vulnerable – they undermine the human rights and the human needs of the most vulnerable within our organizations.

TRANSFORMATIONAL THINKING

Please undertake an evaluation of your own disciplinary, conduct, grievance and bullying and harassment cases over the past 12–24 months:

1 How many allegations of bullying and harassment has your organization dealt with? Of these, how many allegations were upheld?

2 How many bullying, harassment or discrimination cases were raised by black, Asian or minority ethnic (BAME) employees against a co-worker or a manager? Of those, how many cases were upheld?

3 What impact do your processes have on your attrition rates?

4 How many disciplinary cases have been held and what sanctions were applied? What is the breakdown of white to BAME employees in those cases? Does that ratio align to your working population?

NB: you could also apply the analysis to issues raised by women, LGBTQ+ employees and disabled employees, etc.

Analysis undertaken by my own organization, the TCM Group, suggests that less than 10 per cent of complaints of bullying, harassment or discrimination result in a sanction against the wrongdoer. That leaves 90 per cent of allegations resulting in no further action being taken and the complainant left with no answers, no insights about what went wrong and why, no reassurance that the situation will not reoccur. It leaves a bad taste in the mouth, accompanied by a deep sense of injustice. The experience of black and ethnic minority employees is only just starting to be considered, but the evidence from some sectors of our economy is showing that they have a worse time of it than their white colleagues. 'There is a disproportionate ethnicity gap in entry into the formal disciplinary processes' (NHS England and NHS Improvement, 2019).

While this research comes from the NHS, and thankfully the NHS is taking this seriously, I am going to go out on a limb here and suggest that systemic bias in the application of these processes is not just a healthcare issue. No wonder so many employees remain disengaged, excluded, unhappy, unhealthy and unmotivated.

Anthony Robinson, Assistant Director, Professional Regulation at the Nursing and Midwifery Council and co-editor of *Blackstone's Guide to the Equality Act 2010, Fourth Edition* (Robinson, 2021), spoke to me recently about his frustrations with the status quo. 'The traditional systems for resolving allegations of bullying, harassment and discrimination fail to address these issues adequately. In all but a few cases, they fail to provide justice for the victims, or to drive the necessary systemic changes for the future. Ironically, the policies and processes which are in place to reduce the risk of victimization and discrimination maintain a culture of inequity and injustice – where the needs of the victim are disregarded. It is not just employers who fail. The whole system fails to support those who have been discriminated against.'

A flawed model of justice borrowed from the civil justice system

The effect that the traditional performance, discipline and grievance procedures have on our people and our organizations is chilling. Issues are suppressed, problems are avoided, power is abused, rational thought is hindered, communication is broken, trust is destroyed, relationships are torn asunder.

Because the workplace justice model is derived primarily from the civil justice system, it is perhaps little surprise that our traditional HR processes have adopted a quasi-litigation and adversarial structure and tone. However, the 1996 Woolf reforms of the Civil Procedure Rules set into play a steady adoption of alternative dispute resolution (ADR) across the various civil justice processes.

Organizational justice has failed to keep up. It has shown little, if any, creativity and innovation in how we handle disputes and disagreements. The 2007 review of the then statutory dispute resolution regulations (DRR) by Michael Gibbons had the potential of being a turning point for dispute resolution in the UK. While calls had been made for common sense to prevail and for the enhanced role of ADR (Gibbons, 2007), what happened was the briefest mention of mediation in the new Acas code on discipline and grievance. A very late model of 'early conciliation' (George Orwell, who coined the phrase 'doublespeak' in his classic book *1984* (Orwell, 2004), would be proud) was introduced and a series of employment tribunal (ET) reforms were made which were subsequently found by the Supreme Court in 2017 to be a 'barrier to justice, unlawful and discriminatory' (UNISON, 2017).

In my experience, the Gibbons review has not led to a change in culture. Our HR policies and management systems are as retributive now as they were in 2007. The outcomes for employees and employers have not improved and the detrimental impact on employee experience is significant. In the decade and a half since the Gibbons review, we have slipped further and further backwards into a self-perpetuating and destructive system which benefits virtually no one.

As a result of this public policy muddle, many of our organizations are unsure what they can and cannot do. They default to a model of retributive justice which to all intents and purposes mirrors the very same dispute resolution regulations which everyone was clamouring to repeal in 1997. It is all very strange and, to be honest, a little depressing. Unless, that is, you are a lawyer.

A critical analysis of the traditional HR policies and management systems

In my first book, *Managing Conflict*, I set out my critique of the traditional grievance procedure. I have updated that analysis for this text. My analysis now covers the suite of HR policies: performance, discipline, grievance, bullying, harassment, absence and conduct. The following critique is offered as a genuine analysis of the problems as I see them. It is not intended to cause offence or to undermine anyone's role.

However, as I said at the start of this book, I shall not dodge the tough questions and I will not avoid calling out the elephants in the room. So, here is my analysis of the management systems and HR processes that are being used in our organizations to address concerns, conduct, complaints and conflicts. The following critique could be extended to cover the entire employee handbook, which, when one takes a step back, reads like a retributive justice encyclopaedia.

My critique of the traditional HR processes and management systems

- The language of the processes is confrontational and divisive. Even their names conjure up a variety of negative terms and phrases:
  - Grievance policy. Loss, blame, betrayal, attack, retribution, feud.
  - Discipline policy. Fault, blame, shame, punish, embarrass, destroy.
  - Performance management policy. Failure, judge, blame, incompetent, ineffective.
  - Bullying and harassment policy. Victim, offender, blame, risk, fear, attack.
- The processes are reactive and are often used at a late stage of a concern, a complaint or a conflict rather than at an early stage. In an entirely counterintuitive way, they drive a culture of reactivity and they impede employees, HR and managers from thinking and acting proactively. Opportunities for organizational learning, personal development and systemic change are impeded or completely lost. They block creativity and innovation, which are critical to business success and economic growth.
- They can become overwhelming for those involved and for those managing the issues. I have heard more than one HR team describe the feeling of 'drowning in formal processes'. Such a disproportionate focus on transactional activity is holding the HR function back and preventing it from becoming an effective people and culture function. In a recent report produced by McKinsey, the authors state: 'The HR function is often overburdened with transactional work and is not well equipped to create value for the enterprise' (Komm *et al*, 2021).
- The favoured retributive justice systems are adversarial and reductive. They pitch people against each other from the outset. The battle lines are drawn, and they try to reduce a complex interaction between two, or more, humans into a neat box: right or wrong; win or lose; black or white. The model is binary and polarizing, and it encourages binary and polarized thinking in the protagonists.

- There are few, if indeed any, opportunities to generate dialogue, empathy and learning. The result being that the parties begin to dehumanize one another and they lose sight of any possible connectedness or common ground that may exist between them (which generally is a great deal). The issues become inflated and conflated. An issue over lateness becomes a lazy employee, a rude comment becomes a bullying manager, or a simple misunderstanding becomes an act of treachery. They all result in an exercise in character assassination. The parties no longer speak to each other and the whole process becomes malicious – the behaviours become more confrontational and the system rolls on. The energy and the time this all requires should be spent on growing the business but instead is spent seeking to destroy each other. It is MAD: Mutually Assured Destruction.

- The processes disempower line managers and supervisors, creating the conditions where they lack the confidence, the competence or the courage to handle people and culture issues effectively. Having received very little training and operating in a complex and emotive space of legal jargon and complex procedures, their responses range from doing nothing (inaction) to responding in an inappropriate or heavy-handed way (overreaction).

- In some cases, a heavy-handed response from the untrained and unsupported manager could lead to an allegation of bullying being made against them, thus resulting in their suspension and an investigation. This sends the message to other managers that doing nothing is a safer option. As a result of the climate of fear created by our retributive justice systems, poor performance persists; poor conduct persists; poor customer service persists. The irony cannot be understated.

- Colleagues who are watching this play out are forced to take sides. 'You're with me or you're against me' they are told. Teams become fragmented, fissures appear, communication breaks down, cliques form, toxicity creeps in and productivity drops. The climate in the team can become one of poor morale, frustration, defensiveness and increasing levels of stress and uncertainty.

- In most cases, informal resolution approaches, including media-tion, are ignored, or they fail to achieve the desired outcome because they sit within, or they are an adjunct to, the formal process.

- The protagonists in the process experience increased levels of stress and anxiety; some may experience even worse symptoms, including trauma and depression (see Jonathan's story on page 127). At the start of this chapter, we saw that the impact on Joanna was so great that she considered suicide. Unfortunately, my team and I are hear-ing more and more real-life stories just like Joanna's and Amul's. With numerous personal accounts and examples of toxic cultures, and a growing dataset which details the damage caused by these processes, Chapter 6 shines a light on just how damaging these toxic cultures have become.

- The processes often take inordinately longer than they should to reach a conclusion. In many of the organizations with which my team and I work, the timescales for managing cases, carrying out investigations, setting up hearings and running appeals are routinely exceeded. In some organizations, this is not simply by days, weeks or even months, it can take years after the original incident(s) occurred. The longest case I have ever personally come across was one where an employee was suspended for six years, on full pay, following an allegation of bullying. It sounds unbelievable, but it is true. It was not until a new HR manager joined the company and asked who the employee was that the issue came to the surface. I was asked to mediate to help draw up a settlement agreement (exit agreement) between the employee and her employer – six years after the original allegations were made (and which were never dealt with). I still cannot quite believe it.

- These processes encourage parent–child interactions which infan-tilize the workforce. The parties are not trusted, so they are not given any control over the process or the outcome. It reinforces the notion that someone else is responsible for the cause of the problem and someone else is responsible for fixing the problem. These processes institutionalize (normalize) the infantilization of the workforce. Thus, the paternalistic nature of the retributive justice model, a model which is so deeply ingrained in our HR policies and management systems, is perhaps one of the most destructive and disempowering of all its features. The retributive justice model, which features throughout our employee handbooks and HR policies, propagates a fear of failure across the organization. And it does so from day one.

- Drawing inspiration from litigation and legal remedies to disputes, our HR policies and management systems are designed for the minority of employees, not the majority. They are more concerned about facts than feelings, evidence than exploration, corroboration than collaboration, mitigation than meaning, rights than responsibilities and process than people.

- They seek to mitigate the risk of future legal action rather than offering a genuine attempt to resolve a workplace issue. All that damage, and all those broken relationships, just to avoid an adverse tribunal ruling which would never come about in the first place if someone had done something, sooner.

The costs and the time associated with resolving issues are so significant and the failure of the process to secure a meaningful outcome is so profound that one must ask, how did it ever get this bad? Retributive justice has become so ingrained into our HR policies and management systems that any sense of humanity, dignity and personal connection has been drained from them.

Critique over. It is now time to offer a few solutions in the rest of this chapter and the rest of this book. It is time for a Resolution Revolution.

How does transformational justice promote dialogue, deliver accountability and build trust?

The solutions to the problems that I have identified are not particularly radical. Here are five that spring to my mind.

1 Listen. Really listen to what the other person is saying. Asking questions, being curious, summarizing back, reframing and reflecting are all examples of listening. When we listen, it gives people a voice

and it tells them that we value them and their contribution. Listening allows people to speak out, to build awareness and to defuse tensions. In all my work, if there was one legacy that would make me feel the greatest sense of achievement, it would be that in some small way I had made the simple act of listening more commonplace.

2 Suspend judgement. This means that we should not judge or evaluate the other person. By acting with objectivity, it creates a high-growth mindset for us and the other person. A high-growth mindset opens a dialogue and it opens possibilities for learning and innovation. When we feel judged or evaluated, it creates a fixed (closed) mindset in both the judge and the person being judged. It makes us defensive, and we know that one of the best forms of defence is attack. By avoiding making judgements and by depersonalizing the situation, you are reducing the risk of the attack/defend dynamic.

3 Put yourselves in the other person's shoes. The ability to be empathetic is a key feature of transformationalism. Empathy can be at a cognitive level or an affective level. At a cognitive level, it simply means that you explain to the person that you are trying to see the situation from their point of view and you ask them to share their story with you. You are trying to understand their thoughts and their perspective. This is often enough to flip a conversation from destructive to constructive. Affective empathy can be even more powerful. This means that you can imagine what it might feel like for the other person and you gain insight into their emotions and can connect with them. This is the kind of empathy that is generated through a restorative justice process such as mediation, facilitation or restorative coaching. Either way, stepping outside of your own reality and trying to understand what is going on for the other person can only ever be helpful and will, in my experience, only have upsides.

4 Be compassionate. Compassionate leaders, managers and people professionals (HR) are concerned about minimizing harm to others. Compassion is about being aware of the harm that our behaviours,

systems and processes can cause and reducing that harm by modifying said behaviours, systems and processes. Compassionate leaders, managers and HR create a psychologically safe space where employees and others can discuss their concerns and reflect on errors and mistakes in a supportive and caring environment. In this way, compassion is not only a kinder and a better way to behave, but compassion can also generate deep reflection, learning and insight – it can drive behavioural and systemic changes. Compassion is the spark that ignites the engines of innovation.

5 Seek out areas of common ground. It is too easy to put other people into a convenient box – bully, nasty, lazy, incompetent, troublemaker, etc. It is much harder, but much more effective, when we stop labelling other people and we start to engage with them as human beings. As we do so we begin to understand that they too have needs, feelings, beliefs, motivations, hopes, dreams, fears and aspirations. The funny thing is this: when we start to engage with people at this level, it turns out that what they feel and what they need and hope for are often very similar to what we feel and what we need and hope for. In my experience (and I have seen some severely broken relationships) there is always common ground – if we are prepared to look hard enough for it.

Some of the benefits of transformationalism

As your organization moves from retributive to transformational justice, you will find that it delivers the following benefits to your organization:

- greater levels of collaboration between key stakeholders. Collaboration builds higher-performing teams and it creates synergies within our teams, divisions and organizations;

- greater levels of transparency and accountability. This ensures that issues can be posted and resolved earlier and that people feel safer speaking up about concerns. It also means that errors and mistakes can be identified earlier – the root cause can be identified and the necessary changes can be made to resolve the issues and to integrate the learning;

- confident, competent and courageous managers who can better predict, spot, resolve and transform complex personal team and organizational challenges;
- enhanced employee engagement, wellbeing and inclusion leading to enhanced EX and CX;
- a generally happier, healthier and more harmonious workplace;
- improved productivity with a more engaging and empowering system for measuring and rewarding performance which drives motivation.

CASE STUDY
Center Parcs – putting its people and values first

Center Parcs offers award-winning family short breaks at six locations across the UK and Ireland, with hundreds of indoor and outdoor activities to enjoy all year round in a unique forest environment. Margaret Mitchell, Director of HR at Center Parcs, has been a driving force in the development of a 'people and values first' approach for resolving workplace issues.

Margaret explains: 'Center Parcs wanted to offer an alternative approach to resolving workplace conflicts and complaints and we felt that most of the issues brought up by our colleagues could be helped enormously with a new approach. We engaged with TCM to provide in-house training for 12 accredited mediators, who would then help us to develop a new resolution policy. We were very encouraged by our previous experiences of mediation; we had some success with a couple of mediations and feedback from the colleagues involved was encouraging. However, the mediation option was not well known, and we had let the number of qualified mediators at each location lapse over the years. Having enough internal mediators to ensure prompt intervention was an issue we were keen to resolve, as was ensuring that mediation became a more prominent feature in our grievance policy.

'We are now reframing our old grievance policy as a resolution policy and intend to launch it as soon as possible when all colleagues are back to work from furlough. We have engaged with HR and other stakeholders, and our HR communities are committed to the "Resolution Revolution". This approach aligns with our People Framework and is on the people roadmap. We see resolution rather than grievance tying in perfectly for the post-Covid-19 world, where the wellbeing of our people is the highest priority for our business.'

The role of transformational justice in modern employee relations

The use of transformational justice and the transformational principles can be integrated into the relationship between unions and management. These principles can be used to drive collaboration and to engender mutual support, respect and trust. These transformational principles encourage unions and employers to engage with each other in a predictive and proactive way.

They enable each party to spot problems and to resolve them before they escalate into collective disputes. This is an exciting and progressive form of social contract – a partnership between unions and management. As explained elsewhere in this chapter, the transformational principles sit comfortably alongside the rights-based models of justice. To that end, the ability of unions to hold employers to account and to create a safe workplace for their members is enhanced rather than undermined by applying restorative principles. A key objective of a transformational culture is to deliver accountability, build trust and protect relationships while reducing the reliance on a retributive model of employee relations.

Simon Sapper is an expert in industrial relations. Director of workplace relations consultancy and podcast specialist Makes You Think, and Commissioner with the Low Pay Commission, he has extensive experience as a senior national trade union official for 30 years. Simon explains that applying the restorative principles in union/management relations can achieve a number of strategic and tactical benefits. 'The benefits of a union/management relationship based on restorative principles make it a no-brainer. Unresolved conflict costs billions and has a devasting effect on productivity and wellbeing. But we need first to recognize and dismantle structural barriers to make progress – an absence of government policy, one-sided flexibility at work, uneven use of technology in favour of low-wage and precarious employment, outsourcing, and the current rash of "fire-and-rehire" initiatives. Can we be confident that businesses adopting the confident, proactive, person-centred approach will be those that survive? I am not so sure, but without a vision of where you want to end up, there's no chance.'

Simon goes on to explain: 'Slowly, it seems, the pieces of a jigsaw are being placed on the table. We do not have the complete picture yet, nor necessarily have any two pieces that link up with each other. But look at the Unions21/SPERI Report (Hunt, 2021) on adapting and growing collective voice, the call for social rights enforceable in law (LCHR) and the "things can't be the same" pitch from new CBI Director General Tony Danker. The "social contract" proposed in this text is in very interesting company.'

TRANSFORMATIONAL THINKING

- What will you do to integrate transformational justice in your own organization?

- What are the potential benefits of this approach?

- How will you secure the buy-in from the following stakeholders?

  o Unions

  o Managers

  o Legal advisors

  o Senior leaders

  o Employees

Conclusion and calls to action

I want to end this chapter by going back to the beginning – how could transformational justice have helped Joanna, Amul and Simon?

Had the organization adopted transformational justice:

- Simon would have been fully aware of the potential for bias in recruitment decisions. He would be trained in fair and inclusive recruitment processes. This would ensure that he understood how to make recruitment decisions on merit, not based on characteristics which have no bearing on a person's ability to do the job.

- The people and culture function (HR) would provide good governance regarding the application of people processes. For instance, recruitment decisions would be routinely evaluated by HR to ensure employees were not being unfairly discriminated against.

- Amul would have felt comfortable speaking out directly to Simon about his concerns relating to the current process. He would have been confident that Simon welcomed feedback, that he would listen and that he possessed the pre-requisite emotional intelligence skills as per the company's values and behaviours statement. Amul could also be confident that the process of raising a concern would not damage his relationship with Simon, or his career prospects.

- Joanna would be trained, as a new manager, to have confident and courageous conversations. This would mean that she possessed the necessary communication and negotiation skills to de-escalate the situation that she faced with Amul.

- When Amul raised a complaint, he would do so making a Request for Resolution (RfR) via the Resolution Framework and the Resolution Unit. His case would be triaged (assessed) using objective criteria (the Resolution Index™) and the most suitable remedy would be sought. In this case, the most likely outcome would be a restorative justice process, such as mediation. This would give both Amul and Joanna the opportunity to resolve their issues in a safe and constructive way and with the assistance of a skilled and impartial third party.

- In any event, had there been a formal hearing and Amul had raised his concerns about the unfair recruitment process, in a transformational culture that concern would not have been ignored by the people in the room. At the very least, it would have opened a dialogue to elicit feedback and learning outcomes for Simon to help him to be a better leader. This might also have led to further coaching for Simon.

I hope this chapter has demonstrated that accountability and justice can be delivered in a way which balances our needs, our rights and our relationships. Transformational justice frees us from being bound by the delusion that we must be proven right or wrong, or that we must win and they must lose. Transformational justice comes from a deeper understanding of the other's truth and it comes from the ability to have our voice heard without judgement or evaluation. Justice can come when the conditions are created where we listen with a desire to understand rather than a desire to defend. It can come when two or more human beings truly understand the impact of their behaviours and the intentions behind them. In so doing, they take full responsibility for the choices they have made and they make better choices for the future. Transformational justice comes when those in positions of authority hand over the power and enable their people to craft and agree outcomes which offer a mutual gain and a shared advantage.

The retributive justice systems offer a mirage of justice and an illusion of fairness. It is time that we recognized the harm that the retributive processes (discipline, grievance and performance management in particular) are doing and the damage they are causing. They do not only undermine good working relationships; the retributive systems of discipline, performance management and grievance erode trust in the HR function and between line managers and their employees. As a result, this lack of trust permeates through the entire employee relations landscape. A lack of trust is the antithesis of a transformational culture, it is toxic and destroys the essence of good working relationships. If we want to build a high-trust organization, we must do so by removing the systems which break it down in the first place.

I work with a great many wonderful organizations and individuals who are desperate to get this right. These people are some of the kindest, most compassionate and most emotionally intelligent people that you could hope to meet. However, the retributive systems squeeze these characteristics from them. If they offer compassion, it is at their discretion. If they choose to be empathetic, it is in spite of the prevailing systems of blame. If they opt to be flexible in how they handle a situation, it can create a risk for them in terms of being called out as inconsistent and unfair. This is not a good way to run an organization.

We need to liberate our leaders, managers, HR, unions and others from the restrictive, complex and bureaucratic systems that we have bound them in. If an organization is going to become transformational, it must be given permission, and the tools, to be human and humane. To put people and values first.

There is no intrinsic benefit in continuing to use these retributive systems. Putting it bluntly, it is not possible to call oneself a compassionate or progressive leader, manager, HR professional or union representative and still wield the destructive and divisive might of the retributive HR policies and management systems. Not when we know that they are so desperately ineffective and to do so will create the most extreme stress, anxiety and trauma for our most important asset, our people.

References

Dekker, S (2017) *Just Culture: Restoring trust and accountability in your organization*, 3rd edn, CRC Press, London

Employment Relations Act 1999, www.legislation.gov.uk/ukpga/1999/26/contents (archived at https://perma.cc/A6EY-DTJ8)

Gibbons M (2007) *Better Dispute Resolution: A review of employment dispute resolution in Great Britain*, DTI, London

Hunt, T (2021) Covid-19 and the work of trade unions: New challenges and new responses, https://unions21.org.uk/ideas/covid-19-and-the-work-of-unions-new-challenges-and-new-response (archived at https://perma.cc/L8GZ-Z43T)

Komm, A, Pollner, F, Schaninger, B and Sikka, S (2021) The new possible: How HR can help build the organization of the future, www.mckinsey.com/business-functions/organization/our-insights/the-new-possible-how-hr-can-help-build-the-organization-of-the-future? (archived at https://perma.cc/9A4S-VYEM)

Liddle, D (2017) *Managing Conflict: A practical guide to resolution in the workplace*, Kogan Page, London

NHS England and NHS Improvement (2019) A fair experience for all: Closing the ethnicity gap in rates of disciplinary action across the NHS workforce, www.england.nhs.uk/publication/a-fair-experience-for-all-closing-the-ethnicity-gap-in-rates-of-disciplinary-action-across-the-nhs-workforce/ (archived at https://perma.cc/H6VP-VLCD)

Orwell, G (2004) *1984*, Penguin Modern Classics, London

Robinson, A (2021) *Blackstone's Guide to the Equality Act 2010*, 4th edn, Oxford University Press, Oxford

Saundry, R and Urwin, P (2021) Estimating the costs of workplace conflict, Acas research, www.acas.org.uk/estimating-the-costs-of-workplace-conflict-report (archived at https://perma.cc/T4JP-Z4W5)

Shapland, J, Atkinson, A, Atkinson, H, Dignan, J, Edwards, L, Hibbert, J, Howes, M, Johnstone, J, Robinson, G and Sorsby, A (2008) Does restorative justice affect reconviction? The fourth report from the evaluation of three schemes. Ministry of Justice Research Series

Simmons, A (2000) *The Story Factor: Inspiration, influence, and persuasion through the art of storytelling*, 3rd edn, Basic Books, New York

UNISON (2017) How UNISON changed the law: The story behind our success, www.unison.org.uk/news/article/2017/08/employment-tribunal-fees-story-behind-success/ (archived at https://perma.cc/UA92-48KV)

Wallis, P and Tudor, B (2008) *The Pocket Guide to Restorative Justice*, Jessica Kingsley Publications, London

Resources

Campaign for Social Rights, www.lchr.org.uk/socialrights (archived at https://perma.cc/5N97-L34Z)

Partington, R (2021) UK should respond to economic crisis with 1945-style reboot, says CBI chief, *The Guardian*, www.theguardian.com/business/2021/feb/03/uk-respond-to-economic-crisis-1945-style-reboot-says-new-cbi-chief-danker (archived at https://perma.cc/4FFL-FEDH)

03

The Transformational Culture Model

*A blueprint for a fair, just, inclusive, sustainable
and high-performing organization*

TRANSFORMATIONAL LEARNING

Within this chapter, you will discover answers to the following questions:

- What are the key components of a transformational culture?
- How does the Transformational Culture Hub work and what does it do?
- What are the eight enablers of a transformational culture?
- What are the benefits of applying a whole-systems approach for driving cultural change?
- How can the Transformational Culture Model be applied in practice?

Introducing the Transformational Culture Model

The Transformational Culture Model offers a blueprint for a progressive, values-based and people-centred organization. It is a blend of interconnected elements which span an organization's entire ecosystem. The model can be used to support the process of designing, deploying and sustaining the necessary changes which will deliver a fair, just, inclusive, sustainable and high-performance organizational culture. The application of the model is supported through enhanced people processes, management systems and leadership strategies and behaviours. While offering a cultural framework, it is not prescriptive. The model is designed to adapt and flex to meet your unique sector, maturity, context, geography, needs and circumstances.

Drawing inspiration from theories and frameworks including systems thinking, nudge theory, positive psychology, restorative justice, emotional intelligence, principled negotiation, appreciative inquiry and non-violent communication (NVC) (see page 286 for definition), there are several defining characteristics which make the Transformational Culture Model unique:

- It makes organizational culture a strategic priority of your organization. By putting your values and your people first, it will enable your organization to achieve the shift from good to great.
- The model is unique – it has been designed to deliver a fair, just, inclusive, sustainable and high-performance organization.
- The model is intrinsically co-operative and collaborative. It is driven by a cross-functional team, the Transformational Culture Hub, which reports directly into the board. Various workstreams (subgroups) provide an enhanced focus on a wide range of topics which are relevant and applicable to your organization. This level of collaborative effort delivers enhanced co-ordination, governance, accountability and impetus.
- It offers a holistic framework comprising eight distinct yet interconnected enablers, each of which is designed to deliver maximum impact for your organization.
- It uses an evidence-based approach in the design, deployment and evaluation of the organizational culture. No more chasing shadows and engaging in guesswork to try to measure and evaluate the impact of your culture.
- It delivers seven tangible benefits which are explored in the following chapter. I call these the 7Cs of transformation.

The Transformational Culture Model

Figure 3.1 summarizes the Transformational Culture Model. This chapter offers a synopsis of the model and a description of each of

FIGURE 3.1 The Transformational Culture Model

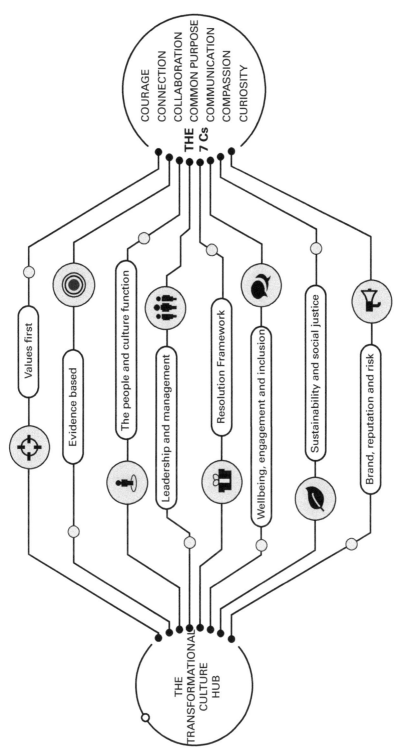

THE 7 Cs

COURAGE
CONNECTION
COLLABORATION
COMMON PURPOSE
COMMUNICATION
COMPASSION
CURIOSITY

Values first

Evidence based

The people and culture function

Leadership and management

Resolution Framework

Wellbeing, engagement and inclusion

Sustainability and social justice

Brand, reputation and risk

THE
TRANSFORMATIONAL
CULTURE
HUB

the different elements and how they work together to form a coherent whole.

The Transformational Culture Model comprises three core elements:

1 The Transformational Culture Hub: this is the cross-functional body which supports the design, deployment and evaluation of the transformational culture.

2 The eight enablers of a transformational culture: these are the elements which drive and sustain a transformational culture.

3 The measurable impact of a transformational culture: these are the 7Cs which result from a transformational culture. They also provide the fuel to turbo charge its integration across your organization. These are described in detail in the following chapter.

The Transformational Culture Hub

To drive successful cultural transformation, and to do so at pace, boards, senior leaders, HR, line managers, unions, employees and other stakeholders need to connect and collaborate in new and exciting ways. The Transformational Culture Hub (the Culture Hub) provides a forum for creating and exchanging ideas. It creates the conditions where stakeholders can plan for change, predict and solve problems, provide the necessary vision, energy and resources, measure impact and create accountability, and it can support the development of a high-growth mindset across your organization.

The overarching purpose of the Transformational Culture Hub is to integrate the principles of transformationalism deep into the organization: fair, just, inclusive, sustainable and high-performing. See page 233 for a practical guide for integrating these transformational principles.

The Transformational Culture Hub should be chaired by a senior leader, typically the chief HR officer, chief people officer or equivalent. This allows for two-way communication and feedback with senior leadership, thereby ensuring that the transformational culture becomes part of the long-term strategic narrative of the organization.

The Culture Hub supports the development of a working partnership between the triumvirate of the modern workplace: management, unions and the people and culture function (HR). This modern form of partnership allows the three members of the triumvirate to prepare their strategy for building recovery, resilience and resolution into the organization.

The Culture Hub provides leadership and governance for the transformational culture. It creates the overarching cultural change strategy, the cultural change programme plan, the impetus, the resourcing and the governance frameworks which support the cultural transformation. In other words, it is responsible for the development, deployment, communication, sustainability, evaluation, review and evolution of the organizational culture. To achieve these objectives, the Culture Hub has several cross-functional workstreams which support the development, deployment and evaluation of the transformational culture.

The question that I posed at the start of this book, 'Who owns the culture?', is resolved through the development of a Transformational Culture Hub: everyone does. Transformational Toolkit # 3 in the Transformational Culture Playbook provides a template for the Transformational Culture Hub and it includes details of the various workstreams which support its work.

To assist with the strategic development and the operational deployment of a transformational culture, the Culture Hub can utilize a set of eight enablers which are designed to help the organization to develop a fair, just, inclusive, sustainable and high-performance culture. The eight enablers of a transformational culture are described in the following pages.

TRANSFORMATIONAL THINKING

- What benefits could a Transformational Culture Hub deliver to your own organization?

- Who will you involve in your Culture Hub?

- How would the Culture Hub fit within the governance structures of your organization?

- How would you ensure that it has delegated decision-making authority?

The eight enablers of a transformational culture

This section explains the eight enablers of a transformational culture. This is the central part of the Transformational Culture Model which drives the fair, just, inclusive, sustainable and high-performance elements of the culture. For ease, the eight enablers are presented in Figure 3.2 operating together to form a whole system.

FIGURE 3.2   The eight enablers of a transformational culture represented as a whole system

© The TCM Group

Enabler 1: values first

Values are the golden thread that runs through an organization and they are central to the development of cultural flow, a term I explore in more detail in Chapter 7. Values bind a transformational culture together by aligning an organization's purpose and strategy with its agreed behaviours and the overall customer and employee experience. Your values should reflect the kind of organization you are and the kind of organization you want to be. In other words, whether written or unwritten, the values of your organization are perhaps one of its most valuable commodities and they should be authentic and aspirational.

Given that they are this important, the values of any organizations should be carefully developed, designed and integrated across the fabric of the business. Earlier, I gave details relating to the role of the Culture Hub and in Transformation Toolkit # 3 I suggest work-streams to assist with developing and sustaining a transformational culture.

To define an organization's values, one first needs to be clear about its purpose. The purpose of your organization defines the reason it exists. Leaders need to think hard about how to make purpose central to their strategy. The purpose should relate to what your organiza-tion does and what it stands for. Avoid generic-sounding purposes such as 'making the world better', 'delivering excellence', 'connecting people' as these are meaningless – they increase rather than lower suspicion that this is a corporate PR exercise.

> 'A good purpose statement needs to be aspirational but not vague. It needs to be precise but not limiting, allowing room for a company to grow.' (Aziz, 2020)

I have seen leaders, managers and people professionals use the organ-izational purpose and values to attract talent and motivate their people. Purpose and values provide a solid foundation to the organi-zation's employee value proposition (EVP). They act as a glue which galvanizes and motivates the workforce, and they provide a pivot point around which changes are delivered. The purpose and values also provide a robust framework from which the organization can define its agreed behaviours and develop coherent rules and processes. Plus, they offer a clear and distinct prospectus to the potential customer and investor and they can provide a valuable component in the branding and the reputation of the organization.

In Chapter 7, I examine the alignment between purpose and values in more detail, plus in Chapter 8 I explore the emerging role of the HR function as the custodian of purpose, values and behaviours.

Enabler 2: evidence based

The use of data and evidence to inform and evaluate a programme of cultural change is central to its short- and long-term success. Without the evidence base, and the necessary data to help us to plan, it is like embarking on a journey in the dead of night, in someone else's car, not knowing where you are going, without a map and with a phone which we forgot to charge. Given the complexities identified so far in this text, at best we will get lost and at worst we may end up in a serious road traffic accident.

To ensure that it has maximum impact, and can be sustained, the design and deployment of a transformational culture require an evidence-based approach from inception. People and culture professionals (HR), managers, leaders, employees, unions and other stakeholders generate an incredible amount of management information, much of which can be applied to a process of cultural transformation.

The data gathered as part of developing a transformational culture can be used as follows:

1 To support the development of a business case for a transformational culture.

2 To identify gaps, hotspots, trends and patterns in your own organization and to allocate resources and act as required.

3 To ensure that your organizational stakeholders have a voice in the development of your organizational culture.

4 To provide valuable baseline data, against which the impact of the cultural changes can be evaluated over the short, medium and long term.

'Evidence-based practice is about making better decisions, informing action that has the desired impact. An evidence-based approach to decision making is based on a combination of using critical thinking and the best available evidence. It makes decision makers less reliant on anecdotes, received wisdom and personal experience – sources that are not trustworthy on their own. It's important that people professionals adopt this approach because of the huge impact management decisions have on the working lives and wellbeing of people in all sorts of organizations worldwide.' (CIPD, 2021)

Enabler 3: the people and culture function

Continually evolving and adapting, the HR profession is perhaps one of the most transformative of all organizational functions. The ever-changing legal landscape, digitalization and globalization coupled with continuous pressure from leaders to recruit and retain the top talent and to achieve more from their 'human capital' has placed greater and greater pressure on the modern HR professional.

As organizations strive to build back better, HR yet again stands at a crossroads. The existing HR orthodoxies are being challenged and the meaning of HR is being hotly debated. HR policies and procedures, which once seemed so solid and reliable, are now being shown to be retributive, damaging and destructive. HR's ability to deliver strategic value and to attract and retain talent is being weakened by persistently low levels of employee engagement and productivity, increasing levels of employee activism, rising levels of inequality, and the existential threats of a climate and economic emergency. HR needs to adapt quickly to this new reality. The HR profession must reject the dogmas and orthodoxies which have acted as a drag on the potential of the HR function for too many years, the greatest drag being HR's reliance on an outdated and outmoded model of retributive justice, which I explored in detail in the previous chapter.

This is a watershed moment for HR. In Chapter 8 I set out a vision and a roadmap to support HR as it transforms into the organization's people and culture function and, potentially, into one of the most strategically important functions in the modern organization.

Enabler 4: leadership and management

Our leaders are integral to the nature of the organizational culture and managers are integral to the climate (micro-culture) within a team or department. The way in which a leader or a manager behaves is perhaps the single biggest factor affecting organizational culture and climate. The way that our CEOs, executives and managers behave creates the unwritten cues and clues for the rest of the workforce. They give tacit licence in terms of the permitted and the expected behaviours.

Many managers and leaders do not realize that through their actions, interactions and reactions (AIR), they are shaping the climate of their teams and the culture of the organization. The AIR that they create becomes the air for others to inhale. Their whispers are amplified to shouts, which echo and reverberate around the organization. When our leaders shout, the roar can be deafening.

A transformational culture offers our managers and leaders a new set of cultural norms within which they can choose to behave and by which they can be held to account for the choices that they make. Within this new cultural paradigm, leaders and managers maximize opportunities for learning, insight and growth.

> 'For those looking to create a workplace culture of employee empowerment and engagement, companies must first re-examine their cultures to ensure they are attracting and retaining the type of talent that will drive business success. Leaders should honestly reflect on the extent to which they're listening to employees, driving cultural values themselves, and recognizing employee performance – all of which are critical to empowering a diverse workforce.' (Baumgartner, 2020)

We need our leaders to show great courage at this time of incredible adversity. Our leaders need to have the courage to trust their people, to listen to them and to empower them to be brilliant, irrespective of their background, beliefs, heritage or personal circumstances. Our leaders need the courage to respond with compassion when the easier answer may be to react with aggression, the courage to listen when the easier answer may be to ignore, and the courage to lead with values when the easier answer may be to lead with control. As Daniel Pink explains, 'Control leads to compliance; autonomy leads to engagement' (Pink, 2009).

Organizational culture (indeed the success of an organization) stands or falls on the influence of our managers and leaders. Their role and their impact cannot be underestimated; the need to engage them in and support them through the process of developing, integrating and sustaining a transformational culture is critical to its success.

Enabler 5: the Resolution Framework

The Resolution Framework epitomizes transformational justice. It replaces an organization's retributive justice systems, including performance, discipline and grievance procedures, with a single, fully integrated structure for handling and resolving, concerns, conduct, complaints and conflicts (Liddle, 2021).

The Resolution Framework comprises several elements which make it a highly effective policy in a contemporary and progressive employee handbook:

- It is values based and person centred.
- Dialogue has primacy.
- Retributive justice has been replaced. Restorative justice and procedural justice have been combined to create a powerful model of transformational justice.
- A cross-functional resolution unit to assist with the management and governance of the Resolution Framework has been developed.
- A new triage process and resolution index are used for assessing the most appropriate route to resolution in each case.
- There is increased use of restorative justice processes, such as facilitation, mediation, coaching and team conferences.
- Warnings are renamed to reminders.
- Performance improvement plans become resolution action plans.
- Hearings become formal resolution meetings.

In Chapter 5, I give a detailed overview of the Resolution Framework, supported by numerous case studies and testimonies from organizations such as London Ambulance Service (LAS), which has adopted this approach. Part Two, 'The Transformational Culture Playbook', also provides a template Resolution Framework which can be adapted and deployed in your organization.

Enabler 6: wellbeing, engagement and inclusion

Employee wellbeing, engagement and inclusion are now so interwoven and so interconnected that I believe they should be considered as a single discipline. These three elements are central to overall EX and as a result they hold the key to delivering great CX.

These three topics are huge and I dedicate an entire chapter to them (Chapter 10), including a fascinating case study from the UK's civil service. I have been involved in the areas of wellbeing, engagement and inclusion all my working life. I have seen policies, strategies and programmes come and go, yet the issues of delivering a happy, healthy and harmonious workforce still elude a great many organizations. The questions I keep coming back to are: a) why is this? and b) what can be done about it?

My first observation is that the issue of managing conflict in our organizations is routinely ignored as a major antecedent to low engagement, poor mental health and exclusion. Whenever I work with conflicts, whether that is on an interpersonal level or a whole-systems strategic level, I am shocked, dismayed and saddened by how little emphasis is placed on this subject. As I have said in this text and in *Managing Conflict* (Liddle, 2017), I have seen better strategies for ordering paperclips than I have for managing conflict at work. The evidence base is threadbare and leaders, HR and managers skirt around the issue and never quite recognize it for what it is – a highly destabilizing function in our organizations. Destabilizing that is, until it is managed effectively. At which point it can become incredibly powerful and a potent driver of individual, team and organizational effectiveness.

As I said at the start of this text, I will not flinch from asking the tough questions and I will call out the elephants in the room. One of those elephants is that the systematic failure by a great many organizations to treat conflict as a strategic priority is a direct cause of low engagement, poor mental health and exclusion at work. Engagement programmes, wellbeing initiatives, HR procedures and zero tolerance policies will not work until the issue of how we handle differences, disputes and dissent effectively is resolved. The irony is that the processes and the initiatives that our organizations deploy, many of which I have listed above, exacerbate the stress, worsen the fear and deepen the anxiety.

It seems that the harder organizations try, the worse it gets. That is often because the organization does not deal with the root cause of the issue, only with the symptoms. The smart organizations, a great many of which are included in this book, are recognizing this and they are doing something about it. They are ditching their retributive and divisive policies, they are opening channels of communication, they are training managers to spot and resolve issues, and they are creating safe spaces for people to engage in adult-to-adult dialogue. To have a healthy workplace, to feel engaged and to be included are basic human needs; we do not need ever more complex and extravagant initiatives to meet these human needs. What we need to do is go back to basics: listen, be compassionate, show empathy, engage, understand and resolve. That means stripping back the complexity, reducing the bureaucracy and putting our people and our values first.

Our efforts to resolve stubbornly low employee engagement levels (Dodge and D'Analeze, 2012), reduce the persistently high productivity deficit (ONS, 2018) and maintain good physical and mental health could be achieved more easily and more quickly if organizations considered the three elements of wellbeing, engagement and inclusion (WEI) as a single, interconnected discipline.

Conflict resolution specialist, mental health expert and award-winning mediator Marie Coombes agrees. She explains: 'Conflict resolution and wellbeing, engagement and inclusion (WEI) are inextricably linked. In every case I have dealt with, WEI is damaged due to how conflict has been handled, with the most significant impact often on an employee's psychological safety. I have listened to employees say how fearful they are of making a mistake at work. Others have said they do not dare to share ideas or opinions as they believe this will damage relationships, resulting in them no longer feeling they belong. Processes such as mediation allow these issues to be raised in a psychologically safe space. Following mediation, what I am told is that the restoration of mutual respect and trust enables them to productively re-engage with their employer and their team.'

Stress and anxiety are major issues which can be resolved by implementing a transformational culture and by aligning wellbeing, engagement and inclusion. Research shows that stress is the number one cause of long-term absence, with average absences due to stress lasting 21 days, according to CIPD research. The research also links stress to higher risk of accidents (CIPD, 2012). My experience has led me to conclude that the root cause of these issues can be resolved when an organization creates a fair, just, inclusive, sustainable and high-performing culture. Where team climate and organizational culture are in flow, where dialogue has primacy and where the purpose of the organization, its values and its behaviours are fully aligned.

Enabler 7: sustainability and social justice

Sustainability and social justice are pressures which have barely appeared on the risk register of most organizations. Virtually overnight, that has all changed – to the extent that these two imperatives will become the defining characteristics of the 21st century.

The pressure on organizations to respond to the threats of climate change is great. Mike Berners-Lee explains succinctly and pointedly that organizations should exist to meet three purposes:

'The first is the provision of useful and worthwhile goods and services – things that stand to enhance wellbeing of people and planet now and in the future. Secondly, they should provide meaningful and fulfilling ways for the workers to spend their days. Thirdly, they need to contribute to the appropriate distribution of wealth such that all people have the resources they need to have quality in their lives. Businesses that don't meet all these criteria should sort themselves out as a matter of priority and those that meet one or fewer should probably simply close down.' (Berners-Lee, 2021)

Creating sustainable, net zero organizations is one of the keys to the reduction of damaging climate change. The BrewDog case study further on in this chapter offers inspiration to anyone who shares their commitment to reducing the impact of their organization on our fragile ecosystems.

In an attempt to secure a position of leadership in the area of climate action, more and more investors are investing in companies which are working to achieve net zero carbon emissions and are committed to environment, social and corporate governance (ESG). Just one example, among a great many, is Aberdeen Standard Investments, which states:

'Investing responsibly is not only the right thing to do, it also helps us to identify opportunities and manage risks. ESG investment is about active engagement, with the goal of improving the performance of assets we manage around the globe. We want to make a difference – for our clients and customers, society and the planet.' (Standard Aberdeen Life, 2021)

Social justice and the development of an inclusive economy is another imperative which has moved off the streets and into our boardrooms and offices. Historically, our workplace cultures have been influenced by forces from within the organization, or from a well-managed group of external stakeholders such as customers, shareholders and investors. However, through long-term lockdowns, we saw a profound shift in society in terms of expectations around social justice. This is perhaps epitomized most by the murder of George Floyd and the resulting Black Lives Matter movement, but also by other prevailing movements such as Me Too, as well as the outrage about the health and socioeconomic inequalities that the Covid-19 crisis exposed. These are the tectonic plates of a society shifting – changing its points of reference, creating new lines of accountability and establishing new expectations of social acceptability.

The impact on company culture must not be underestimated. Employees expect a response from their employer. It is no longer good enough to be non-racist in the workplace. The company is increasingly expected to be actively and publicly anti-racist. Not accepting gender bias, homophobia, transphobia, disability discrimination in the office is not sufficient: our companies are expected to actively support campaigns against prejudice and hate within wider society.

More and more studies, such as one conducted by global opinion research and issues management consultancy Povaddo, support this. They suggest that among employees at US-based Fortune 1000 companies:

- more than 40 per cent say that a company's actions on important societal issues impact their decision to work for it;
- 29 per cent say they would be less likely to continue working for their company long term if it made zero effort to make a difference on an important societal issue;
- 27 per cent of workers at the US's largest companies think employees should pressure their CEOs to be more vocal on social issues;
- 15 per cent are dedicated activists who regularly consume news on politics, expect their CEOs to be more vocal and expect to work for a company that makes meaningful attempts at addressing social issues.

In short, the widespread reorientation of the employee's relationship with the employer, and with society at large, is profoundly changing company culture. Corporate Social Responsibility (CSR) statements and charitable giving are no longer sufficient. The successful organizations of the future will have made sustainability and social justice core focuses of their organization. The successful CEOs and executives will recognize that the culture of their organizations must align with the growing wave of employee and social activism – whether that comes from within or from without.

Enabler 8: brand, reputation and risk

Open any newspaper or visit any newsfeed and it is plain to see that the culture of our organizations, the behaviour of our leaders and way that we treat our employees have a significant impact on the reputation of our companies. Careers are being ended in a blaze of media interest and the impact on the individuals and the firm.

Ed Coke, director at Repute Associates in London, has 25 years' experience of measuring and evaluating corporate reputation and its impact on stakeholder trust in organizations. During an interview with me for this book, Ed explained that reputation is based on the behaviours, competencies, values and communications exhibited by a company. 'Underperform against expectation in any one of these areas and the ultimate outcome – the trust that stakeholders place in a company – can be compromised,' he explained. 'All stakeholders help to shape the overall reputation of a company, which means the perceptions of employees are just as important as those of external stakeholders, such as customers, investors or regulators. Yet among these audiences, the "path to trust" – their expectations and drivers of reputation – will be different.'

Ed perceives the relationship between leadership and culture as being central to an organization's brand and reputation: 'Employees experience the behaviours, competencies, values and communications of leadership daily in their working lives. This constant drumbeat shapes their trust in, and reputation of, a company over time. Although the behaviours of leaders will differ, the pattern of behaviours can loosely be described as culture. At a disaggregate level, leadership behaviours may be judged on such human attributes as openness, transparency and fairness, as well as more rational attributes such as capability of role performance. Many leaders these days are judged by their degree of authenticity – their commitment to a particular behaviour or course of action – which can engender trust as a result'.

One of the key learning points that I took away from my fascinating interview with Ed is that, as we know from elsewhere in this text, clarity, consistency and appropriateness of communication have important roles to play in employees' and stakeholders' assessments of leadership. Taking each of these attributes of leadership and codifying them, whether formally or informally, within a workplace, and – critically – actively and consistently demonstrating these attributes, establishes company culture. And once a culture is lived, it can quickly help stakeholders to form an opinion about the overall behaviours, competencies and values of an organization – and therefore the degree of trust and repute in which a company is held.

I also agree that it is critical for company leaders to seek out and listen to the opinions and attitudes of arguably their most critical stakeholders – employees – to gauge how business decisions may impact employees and the external world (Stewart, 2021).

One organization that is working hard to put its people and its values first is BrewDog. BrewDog is a multinational brewery and pub chain with a mission to make people 'passionate about craft beer'. It employs around 2,000 people across the globe and is the fastest growing food and drink company in the UK. A unique and quirky culture, underpinned by a strong commitment to sustainability, has been key to its continued success. I was delighted when, in April 2021, BrewDog's people director, Karen Bates, agreed to write a case study to highlight the incredible journey that BrewDog has been on to achieve a carbon-negative footprint while ensuring it maximizes its overall employee experience.

CASE STUDY

BrewDog – people positive, carbon negative

People Director Karen Bates describes the BrewDog culture as very different, open, inclusive and non-hierarchical. 'Other people have values, but our culture is defined by five "dogmas",' she explains. These include 'we are a meritocracy' (everyone earns their place on the team) and 'know your numbers'. 'We expect everyone to understand the numbers of the business, not just their own numbers, because we truly believe that if you understand how the business is performing, you can truly engage with it,' she says. BrewDog is also exceptionally fast moving and 'works in Dog Years', which means what a company might normally achieve in a period of seven months, it achieves in one. 'We don't mess around, we make the decision and just go ahead and implement it,' says Karen. 'This also feeds through to our supplier relationships. It allows us to work with small businesses rather than large corporates, because they are agile and can work at pace.'

The fourth dogma is 'be where the action is', which in practice translates into what the business calls 'dogs on decks' shifts. Everyone in the leadership team, for example, is expected to regularly work on the front line, whether that is doing a shift in a bar, going out with the field sales force or working on the production line canning and kegging. 'It means we can make informed decisions because we've been out there, done it and witnessed it first hand,' says Karen. The final dogma is 'challenge everything', with all employees expected to have a voice and speak up. 'It's more of a problem if you don't challenge things in BrewDog than it is to challenge. If something does not look right, people need to say it, so that everyone has the chance to look at what is happening.'

A strong commitment to sustainability is another golden thread that runs through everything the business does. In 2020, after hearing a powerful talk from Sir David Attenborough, founder and CEO James Watt decided to make the business carbon negative with immediate effect.

BrewDog now double offsets the CO_2 across its entire operation, including the supply chain. A new employee benefit, the Carbon Negative Crew, allows employees to measure their personal carbon footprint, which is also double offset, enabling people to become carbon-negative individuals themselves. In true quirky BrewDog style, employees who have a dog can calculate their pet's carbon footprint, so that it can be offset as well.

That would be enough for most businesses. But BrewDog has gone even further by setting a goal to reduce its carbon footprint by 40 per cent on 2021/2022. In pursuit of this aim, it is reviewing its entire business operations, is now powering the Ellon brewery, north of Aberdeen, through a local wind farm and has bought a 'lost forest' near Aviemore, where it will plant trees and create an eco-space available for walking, cycling and kayaking. Employees benefit from an equal profit share scheme, 'the unicorn fund', which has been supplemented by a 'double unicorn' bonus for staff who make sustainable suggestions that are picked up and implemented by the business. 'We have had an amazing response from our crew and becoming carbon negative has also become another unique identifier for us as a place to work,' says Karen. 'If a candidate has two opportunities on the table and they see our sustainability credentials, they are more likely to come and work for us.'

BrewDog has underlined just how seriously it takes its social and environmental impact by recently becoming a certified B-Corp, which commits the business to the highest standards of verified social and environmental performance, public transparency and legal accountability. The process has led it to think about some people-related issues and to review the way it promotes its products. Karen says this commitment to becoming a 'force for good' was made because it felt like 'it was the right thing to do', although it has also brought benefits in terms of employee engagement, talent attraction and brand awareness (BrewDog products now sit in the sustainability section of supermarket online shopping platforms, for example). 'Consumers are very savvy now about where they want to spend their pound and if they have a company that is sustainable versus one that is not, selling the same product at the same price point, they will go for the sustainable option. People have become much more conscious, particularly with the pandemic, about the impact the companies they are buying from are having.'

BrewDog measures the internal impact of its culture in a very public way through the Times Top 100 Best Employers. Initial survey results are already showing an improvement over the previous year against the eight indicators that underpin the ranking. The way the company manages its people no doubt has an impact on the overall employee experience. 'I don't have an employee handbook because I don't believe it's something that is needed any more – we have frameworks rather than policies, because that gives people a structure to work around,' says Karen. 'What's important for us is that we enable people to learn from their mistakes. Yes, there are some mistakes we can't tolerate, and we have to do the right thing, but our approach is that everyone is an adult, and no one deliberately comes to work to do a bad job, so if it's a mistake, let's learn from it rather than being draconian and punishing people.'

Conclusion and calls to action

At this time of great uncertainty and with the need for something solid and tangible to work with, the Transformational Culture Model and the eight enablers of a transformational culture offer a flexible blueprint for a modern and progressive organization. The model can be adapted to meet the needs and circumstances of organizations of any size, within any sector. The model offers a holistic framework, which is neither prescriptive nor directive. The objective of the model is to support an organization on its journey to become person centred and values based. The model will support organizations which are committed to developing a fair, just, inclusive, sustainable and high-performing culture.

For it to deliver a maximum and sustained impact, the model requires fresh thinking on the part of our leaders, managers, HR, unions and other key stakeholders. This is not a model which tweaks at the edges of our organizations, it is a model that drives a new mindset, a new working paradigm and a new set of behaviours. It requires courage and a commitment to change. Doing nothing is not a viable option and hope is most definitely not a strategy. Rising above the challenges that are being thrust upon us, whether they are coming from Covid-19, the resulting economic shock, geopolitical changes, social and employee activism or the pressures of climate change, will require our organizations to be ever more fleet of foot, predictive and proactive.

However, and I really do not want to end on a negative note here, I have seen first hand how poorly many of us respond to and handle change or crises. Turf wars, feuds, power plays, rigidity, fear, toxicity, distress, inertia, dysfunction, mistrust, polarization, division and fragmentation are just some of the outcomes that I work with every day. I am not saying that all change ends this badly, nor that these new sets of challenges will either. However, if we are going to rely on the old paradigms of command and control, misogyny and paternalism, autocracy and power, or status and privilege, there is a risk – some may say a very considerable risk – that things could go badly wrong. It is this knowledge which I believe provides a clear rationale for our organizations to treat the development of a transformational culture as a key strategic imperative.

We need to learn the lessons from the past. If we do not, our competitors will. Put simply, those lessons are that organizations secure the best outcomes when they:

- institutionalize collaboration, particularly between the key stakeholders of leaders, managers, HR, employees, unions, customers, regulators, investors and local communities.
- act courageously to spot and resolve workplace issues constructively and with empathy and to apply a new mode of justice – transformational justice – to replace the tired retributive paradigms of blame, shame and punish;
- create a clear sense of common purpose which aligns all employees and stakeholders;

- ensure that dialogue has primacy and that there are effective lines of communication at an organizational, divisional, departmental and team level;

- integrate compassion into our systems, rules and processes;

- encourage curiosity as a contributor to a happy, healthy, harmonious, and high-performance workplace;

- build and sustain new connections and in particular a specific connection between employee experience and customer experience.

Having introduced the Transformation Culture Model in this chapter, it is precisely these 7Cs which I shall focus on in the next.

TRANSFORMATIONAL REFLECTIONS

- What have you learned in this chapter?

- How will you translate that learning into practical action?

References

Aziz, A (2020) The power of purpose: The 7 elements of a great purpose statement (Part 1), *Forbes*, www.forbes.com/sites/afdhelaziz/2020/02/18/the-power-of-purpose-the-7-elements-of-a-great-purpose-statement (archived at https://perma.cc/P7YB-78ZQ)

Baumgartner, N (2020) Build a culture that aligns with people's values, *Harvard Business Review*, https://hbr.org/2020/04/build-a-culture-that-aligns-with-peoples-values (archived at https://perma.cc/XX8U-ACSW)

Berners-Lee, M (2021) *There Is No Planet B*, Cambridge University Press, Cambridge

CIPD (2021) Evidence-based practice for effective decision-making, www.cipd.co.uk/knowledge/strategy/analytics/evidence-based-practice-factsheet (archived at https://perma.cc/L4GU-57B5)

CIPD (2012) Managing for sustainable employee engagement: Guidance for employers and managers, www.cipd.co.uk/knowledge/fundamentals/relations/engagement/management-guide (archived at https://perma.cc/NF95-9QZH)

Dodge, T and D'Analeze, D (2012) Employee Engagement Task Force, 'Nailing the evidence' workgroup, Engage for Success, London

Liddle, D (2017) *Managing Conflict: A practical guide to resolution in the workplace*, Kogan Page, London

Liddle, D (2021) The Resolution Framework: A fully integrated approach for resolving concerns, complaints, and conflicts at work, www.resolutionframework.com (archived at https://perma.cc/XT2P-K5SF)

Malnight, W, Buche, I and Dhanaraj, C (2019) Put purpose at the core of your strategy, *Harvard Business Review*, https://hbr.org/2019/09/put-purpose-at-the-core-of-your-strategy (archived at https://perma.cc/ARR7-FTEZ)

ONS (2018) International comparisons of UK productivity (ICP), final estimates: 2016, www.ons.gov.uk/economy/economicoutputandproductivity/productivitymeasures/bulletins/internationalcomparisonsofproductivity finalestimates/2016 (archived at https://perma.cc/2LK8-K4FE)

Pink, D (2009) *Drive: The surprising truth about what motivates us*, Canongate, New York

Standard Aberdeen Life (2021) Corporate sustainability statement, www.standardlifeaberdeen.com/corporate-sustainability (archived at https://perma.cc/K7YJ-SZJK)

Stewart, W (2021) The rise of employee activism, www.theceomagazine.com/business/management-leadership/the-rise-of-employee-activism/ (archived at https://perma.cc/X5GT-DEU6)

04

The 7Cs of a transformational culture

TRANSFORMATIONAL LEARNING

Within this chapter, you will discover answers to the following questions:

- What are the 7Cs of a transformational culture?
- How do the 7Cs combine to create a powerful measure of a successful organization?
- How can leaders, managers, HR, unions and employees deliver the 7Cs?
- What is cultural flow and how can I generate it in my organization?
- How does a transformational culture reframe our attitudes to failure and mistakes?

Introducing the 7Cs of a transformational culture

In the previous chapter I set out the Transformational Culture Model and I offered a blueprint for organizations which want to integrate a fair, just, inclusive, sustainable and high-performance organizational culture. I explained the eight enablers of a transformational culture, and highlighted what can be achieved when our leaders have the insight and the foresight to align values and purpose with a commitment to sustainability. In this chapter I explain the 7Cs that arise from and feed into the transformational culture.

My work as a conflict and change strategist has, I believe, afforded me a unique set of insights into the inner workings of our organizations, and the cultures, and the climates, which prevail. My work has enabled me to seek out answers to problems, not from the top looking down, but directly by listening to those people involved in, and affected by, the problems themselves. I have asked a lot of questions and the answers have been revealing. Here are the questions I ask when I am working with people or teams during a conflict or a crisis:

- Why did it happen?
- What did you intend to happen?
- What impact did it have?
- How did you feel?
- What would you do differently if you had your time again?
- What would a fair outcome look like?
- What do you need to happen to allow you to achieve that fair outcome?

I believe that these questions, and their answers, could be at the heart of our recovery, and our ability to build back better. I have aggregated the answers into what I refer to, in something of a nautical fashion, as the 7Cs of a transformational culture: courage, connection, collaboration, common purpose, communication, compassion, curiosity (see Figure 4.1).

Courage

Recent circumstances have required all of us to dig a lot deeper. We have all faced the gravest circumstances, and we have had to contend with the greatest restrictions ever placed upon us. We have, in our own unique ways, shown enormous courage. That is why courage is the first of the 7Cs of a transformational culture – the courage that each of us needs to cope with the changes and the challenges that are required in the future, and to create the conditions for our inner brilliance to shine through.

FIGURE 4.1 The 7Cs of a transformational culture

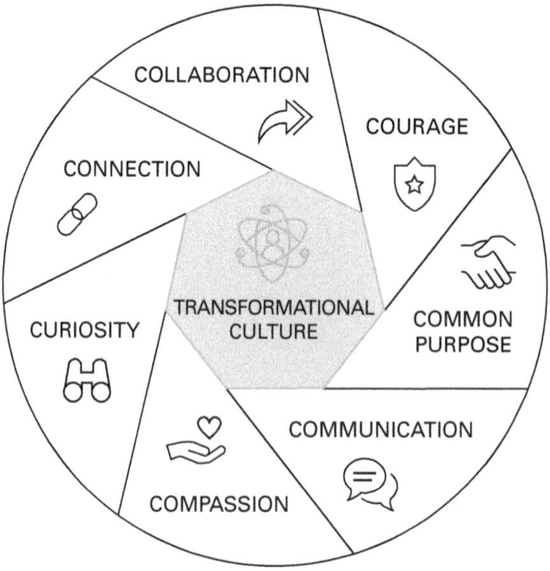

SOURCE Courtesy of the TCM Group

Courage starts by trusting ourselves and having trust in our own beliefs. To have courage we need to challenge ourselves and to challenge others.

> 'The opposite for courage is not cowardice, it is conformity. Even a dead fish can go with the flow.' (May, 1953)

We need our leaders and HR professionals to challenge the conventional wisdom that policies should come before people, and the courage to challenge the orthodoxies of control, power and privilege. We need the courage to reform the systems and structures which foment inequality, division and discord. We need the courage to understand the harm we are doing to our planet, and the courage to value sustainability and social justice as measures of a successful organization.

Each of us requires the courage to reject blame, retribution and intolerance and we need the courage to resolve our differences with empathy, dialogue and understanding. We need the courage to ask for help from others when we need it, and for others to see that as a sign of strength, not of weakness. We need the courage to search within for answers, and the courage to seek insight and wisdom from others, even those with whom we may disagree. We need the courage to utter those most difficult words – 'I am sorry' – and the courage to forgive others when they fail or they fall. We need the courage to accept that we are part of the problem, and we are part of the solution. It is not them; it is us.

We all need the courage to believe that you can't shake hands with a clenched fist; you can't talk with a clenched jaw; you can't listen with a clenched mind (inspired by Indira Gandhi's speech as the Indian and Pakistani armies were confronting each other in October 1971: www.nytimes.com/1971/10/20/archives/indian-and-pakistani-armies-confront-each-other-along-borders.html).

Within a transformational culture we can demonstrate our courage in the following five ways:

1 Our leaders need the courage to listen and to hear what is being said by their people. Not just the people who agree with them and tell them that everything is okay. I mean listening to the difficult people and the rebels. The people who do not conform, who do not agree and whom others label as rebels and troublemakers. Our leaders need to remove the systems which impede rebel voices and remove the stigmatization on them and their barriers to dissent. In so doing, our leaders will unlock the intrinsic innovation and creativity which has been suppressed.

2 HR need to support their leaders and the workforce by having the courage to reject the retributive justice models which permeate through the traditional employee handbook. So laden with rigid rules and processes, the standard employee handbook has become a drag anchor in our organizations. It reduces the opportunities for dissent and disagreement and, in so doing, it undermines the potential for innovation and creativity. The need to build trust and to generate a healthy, happy, harmonious and high-performance workforce is being impaired by its combative tone and the adversarial mindset it precipitates. The traditional employee handbook reminds me of a Haynes Manual. However, this manual will not help me to repair the carburettor in my Mini Cooper; it is a manual for destroying relationships, fanning the flames of conflict, creating stress and generating despair.

3 Our line managers need to have the courage to spot, prevent and resolve disagreements, quarrels and disputes at work before they escalate and relationships deteriorate. Conflict, when managed well, can unlock enormous creativity, energy and productivity. Extensive inaction or expensive overreaction will make matters worse, leading to more difficult and costly solutions down the line. It takes real courage to act but doing nothing is not an option. The way that our managers act is what defines the character (the climate) of our teams. Developing and sustaining psychological safety, being empathetic, encouraging respectful disagreement, promoting open dialogue, actively listening to other points of view – these are all core attributes of courageous managers and they should be the number one criterion on the modern manager's competency framework.

4 Our managers and leaders also need to have the courage to allow the wisdom of others to influence the process. They need to recognize that failure may arise and mistakes will be made. Leaders, managers and HR should reduce the fear of failure, ensure that failures happen fast, that their effect is minimized and that lessons can be learned and implemented quickly. This process is increasingly being known as 'intelligent failure'. As the CIPD's head of learning, Andy Lancaster, explains: 'To drive performance through learning, we must first embrace workplace-based mistakes as they provide some of the most powerful learning experiences. While risks must be managed, we should foster environments that destigmatize and celebrate errors, establish a 'fail fast, learn quick' culture, make room for reflection and leverage mistake-friendly development methods such as simulations and action learning' (Lancaster, 2020).

5 Once the above has been achieved it is incumbent on our employees, unions and representative bodies to have the courage to raise issues and to discuss them openly and honestly. Gossiping, spreading rumours, forming cliques and refusing to speak directly to the person you are arguing with – none of this resolves issues. Engaging in direct dialogue does resolve issues. Employees and unions should recognize that adult-to-adult dialogue has primacy in a transformational culture. To work in a values-based and person-centred organization, opting out of dialogue is no longer tenable.

Connection

The second C of the transformational culture relates to the connections which make our world and our workplaces so rich and so exciting. Covid-19 has shown us how much we need connections. Even the mantra of 'you're on mute' has not dimmed the incredible impact of the video technology that has kept us all connected through the various lockdowns. The emergence of hybrid workplaces – which will enable us to connect to the world of work in a wide range of new and creative ways – is a welcome addition to our dynamic and interconnected world. In building the hybrid workplace of the future, leaders must consider every aspect of the employee's experience. Get it right and employees are going to be successful. Get it wrong and your business will suffer (Teed, 2020).

Within a transformational culture, the connection between purpose, values, behaviours and people is paramount. The top leaders recognize that they need to create flow between the culture and the climate of their organization. This is set out in the Culture Flow System (see Figure 4.2).

For flow to occur within the organization – thereby generating a high level of motivation, engagement, purpose and mastery – values and purpose must connect and be fully integrated into the corporate strategy and the overarching strategic narrative of the organization. The organization's processes (policies, procedures and rules) should connect with the purpose and the values. These processes should therefore balance the needs and aspirations of the workforce with those of the organization. Thus, the processes of the organization are the central pivot point of cultural flow – they provide the vital connection between climate and culture.

FIGURE 4.2   The Culture Flow System

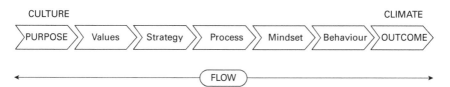

'Flow isn't a nicety. It's a necessity. We need it to survive. It's the oxygen of the soul.' (Pink, 2009)

Within a transformational culture the processes are used to engender the appropriate mindset in the users of the processes – managers, employees, unions, customers and suppliers. These mindsets include the willingness to listen to opposing views, being willing to learn from failure, valuing diversity, engaging constructively, being conciliatory, being willing to apologize and being open to being challenged, etc. These mindsets drive the actions, interactions and reactions (AIR) of managers and employees. These are the behaviours which ultimately deliver the organizational outcomes.

When these factors align, I refer to this as convergent culture flow. The most powerful examples of convergent culture flow that I observe in organizations with which I work include connections between:

- leaders and their people;
- purpose, values and behaviours;
- the organization and the planet;
- EX and CX;
- culture and climate;
- people and process;
- colleagues who share differing views or opposing beliefs and values;
- diverse teams.

Connectivity is a core feature of employee experience, and there are an increasing number of software applications available which claim to enhance the connectivity and employee experience. These applications will play a valuable and important role in the modern workplace of today and tomorrow. However, digital applications such as these should always work with, rather than seek to replace, human-to-human connection. The interconnectedness of the organization should be a consideration for every board and executive committee. Internal communications, while being important for building and sustaining connections, are not sufficient. Each board should have a member who has overall strategic responsibility for ensuring that each of the connections within and without the organization is functioning adequately and resourced sufficiently and that their impact is constantly reviewed.

Collaboration

'None of us is as smart as all of us.' (Blanchard and Bowles, 2000)

Collaboration happens when we co-operate with others to solve a problem or to produce something. Working co-operatively and collaboratively is a fundamental feature of the transformational culture.

Collaboration allows a team to share ideas – it allows diverse and divergent views to be aired and discussed. This diversity of thinking and viewpoints may initiate some early tension but, when that tension is managed courageously (see above), the different viewpoints can begin to yield fresh insights, creativity and innovation. The problem with working collaboratively is that we are often afraid of the initial tension and do not feel confident enough to break through it to begin to secure the benefits of collaboration.

We've all had bad experiences of teams which got stuck in the 'storming' phase and became tense and unpleasant. That creates what I call psychological scarring (memories) which can prevent us collaborating again. However, the scar tissue can be healed (memories can fade) if we keep on going. The other objection I have heard to collaborative working is that it forces us to reach a messy compromise – a kind of 'neither this nor that' outcome. That is a fair point and the leader of the team must be confident to prevent platitudes and pleasantries (group think) interfering with the tougher conversations that need to be had. By asking questions, moving the discussion forward, summarizing and reflecting, the team leader can ensure that the conversation and the team stay sharp.

I have mentioned the need for greater psychological safety a great many times in this text. In mediation we achieve psychological safety by agreeing some basic ground rules. These rules can be incredibly useful for creating a safe space for a team to connect and collaborate:

- Remain civil and respectful at all times.
- Start your sentences with 'I' rather than 'you'.
- Listen to each other – listen to understand.
- The person is not the problem. The problem is the problem.
- Suspend judgement. Be curious.
- Be open to new ideas – and there is no such thing as a stupid idea.
- It is okay to disagree – do so with a smile and with respect.

Common purpose

Purpose is essential to creating energy, pride and passion. It motivates each of us to achieve optimal performance and it underpins our efforts to work in collaboration with others.

> 'Although a higher purpose does not guarantee economic benefits, we have seen impressive results in many organizations. Purpose is not just a lofty ideal; it has practical implications for your company's financial health and competitiveness. People who find meaning in their work don't hoard their energy and dedication. They give them freely, defying conventional economic assumptions about self-interest. They do more – and they do it better.' (Quinn and Thakor, 2018)

When our own sense of purpose is aligned with that of others and our organization, the common purpose that is achieved has the potency to unleash untold riches for people and organizations: passion, innovation, creativity, flow, happiness, harmony, engagement, and individual and team brilliance. Common purpose comes through a connection with our values which unite us in a single coherent objective. You can see it; you can feel it; you can almost touch it. Great customer service, happy employees filled with passion and pride – these are all the outward signs of an organization with common purpose.

Achieving a common purpose does not mean that we all agree; it does, however, mean that when we disagree we disagree well.

Common purpose allows disparate and diverse views to be aired and to be heard. In the context of a transformational culture, our leaders and managers must have the skills to articulate the purpose clearly, to align their people to the purpose, to allow for all voices to be heard and valued, to take the adversity out of diversity, and to handle differences of opinion diplomatically and constructively.

In this way common purpose can be the source of a deeper understanding of problems, co-operative solution design and the maximization of creativity and innovation.

TRANSFORMATIONAL THINKING

- How would you define the purpose of your organization?
- Is that sense of purpose shared across your team, ie is there a sense of common purpose?
- What are the benefits of common purpose to your organization?
- What more can you do to generate a common purpose within your organization?

Communication

Communication is central to any good working relationship, indeed any relationship. It is a core feature of a transformational culture, a culture which is values based and person centred. When communication breaks down, the impact can be significant and severe. It can result in an erosion of trust, it undermines respect and it can damage morale. In all my years working with complex conflicts and disputes, the one piece of advice that I have learned is this: we must always keep lines of communication open.

It is easy enough to communicate when targets are being hit, and everyone is getting along well. It is much tougher, yet much more important, to communicate when we are in tension, when we disagree and when we are under stress. I for one fully appreciate that at those times we may overlook communication; after all, we may feel unsafe and we may be fearful of engaging in dialogue. We may ask ourselves 'what's the point?' or 'why should I bother?'

That is why dialogue – the ability to communicate, as adults, with care, compassion and understanding – has primacy in a transformational culture. Adult-to-adult dialogue involves six separate but interconnected elements:

1 Articulating myself in a way that allows the person(s) I am communicating with to hear and understand what I am saying. That means we avoid attacking, blaming or judging each other.

2 Being open, honest and authentic. This may require each of us to show our vulnerabilities, which is why one of the 7Cs of a transformational culture is courage.

3 Asking a wide variety of open questions to seek out clarification and meaning.

4 Listening to understand, rather than listening to defend.

5 The ability to put oneself in the other person's shoes – to build bridges of empathy.

6 Responding to what we are hearing; not reacting to what we think is being said.

In addition to the above, the best communicators I have met display an innate ability to express themselves in a way which is humanizing, and which protects the self-esteem of the person they are communicating with. I have listened to them carefully and their sentences very rarely start with 'You'. They start with 'I' or 'We'. They aim to draw out meaning, insight and learning during the conversation. They do so by building trust and mutual respect – they also understand that psychological safety plays a critical part in any good communication process. The best communicators I have observed display humility, and they value the feelings of others in a way that creates a powerful and authentic connection. They are authentic and they are safe with their own and with others' vulnerabilities. They also know how to frame the dialogue so that they learn from the past, they can understand the present and they can work together to improve the future.

The best communicators I have met convey their messages in a compelling and assertive way. They know that they can do so without the risk of damaging their relationship and they know that the dialogue will bring them closer together, not drive them further apart.

Compassion

Think of a time when you have experienced compassion. How did it feel? What impact did it have? Compassion is about understanding another person's pain or suffering and taking action to reduce the pain or to resolve the cause of the suffering.

Compassion requires the ability to put oneself into the shoes of another person and to connect with their feelings and their emotions. Research has shown that if people are treated with compassion, they are more likely to stay in the organization longer and work harder for their employer (Kanov *et al*, 2004). Compassion is humility, empathy and vulnerability – it is at the heart of our emotional intelligence. Compassion requires self-awareness and it requires a strength of character. Compassion is not the easy answer; doing nothing is the easy answer. Compassion requires that we act to reduce the pain and suffering of others. In the workplace, one of the greatest expressions of compassion is the action of our managers and leaders to resolve our quarrels and our disagreements, and the action of HR to reduce the heavy toll of their retributive systems of justice.

'When compassion is company-wide, there are systems and practices in place to ensure it is rooted within the organizational culture, so that approaches to recruitment development and reward reflect care for people. Compassion requires leaders to role-model kindness in their behaviours and for the connections between people to be strong, so that networks can be mobilized to provide support.' (Bradley, 2020)

Compassion can also be shown through the policies and the processes of our organization. It is no longer possible to describe oneself as a compassionate or humane manager, leader or HR professional and continue to deploy the stress-inducing and relationship-wrecking performance management, discipline and grievance procedures. True compassion will be achieved when our organizations rid themselves of these policy frameworks, and instead systematize empathy, dialogue-positive engagement, mutual respect, transformational justice and dialogue.

Kindness is not about smiling sweetly and delivering fluffy platitudes. It is about fairness, compassion and having effective and constructive conversations that help employees perform at their best.

Please do not mistake kindness, humility and compassion for weakness; they are signs of great strength.

Curiosity

A few years ago I was training a group of managers and we were exploring the importance of feelings and emotions at work. I was explaining to the group that managers should be curious, and they should not be afraid of asking the feelings questions. In fact, I suggested that their employees would be grateful to them for being interested and for being curious. I explained that opening a dialogue about feelings created a powerful bond of empathy and it seeded deeper levels of insight and understanding. Being curious and asking questions could allow people to be vulnerable in a safe place and being curious acts as a basis for building trust and establishing psychological safety. In that classroom on that morning, I heard something that will never leave me.

It was a question from a delegate. He asked me: 'David, can I just check, are we allowed to ask our employees how they feel?' Now, in my classes there is a rule that there is no such thing as a stupid question, and indeed there is not. While on the face of it this question seems bizarre, it is actually very important. My first instinct was 'Come on, really?', but then the debate began, and it is a debate that has raged ever since. The debate is this – is it the role of the manager to concern themselves with the emotional and psychological needs of their teams?

This is what I have learned about curiosity from my work as a mediator and as a coach – two activities which value curiosity and as such I highly recommend them to anyone who leads and manages others:

- Curious people ask a lot of questions. These include open questions (who, what, why, how, when, where etc), reflective questions (what would you have done differently?), hypothetical questions (if you could go back to your younger self, what advice would you give yourself? Or, if you had a time machine, what would you change to make your future brighter?), empathetic questions (how do you think _____ is feeling today?), closed questions (have you? are you? will you? etc), scaling questions (on a scale of 1–10 how confident do you feel about the task?), future-focused questions (to move one point up the previous scale, what would it require?), learning and insight questions (what have you learned from the past that will help you in the future?) and transformational questions (what changes will you make now that you possess all this knowledge and wisdom?).

- Curious people listen – before they talk. They know that inviting the other person to talk opens both of their minds to new possibilities and new opportunities.

- Curious people know that judging and evaluating closes a conversation down. It hinders the transfer of insight and knowledge.

- Curious people know how to be empathetic. They do so by listening carefully and by imagining that they have shared the experience of the other person. They can't have done so, of course, but the very act of putting themselves in the other person's shoes, and going for a bit of a stroll in those shoes, builds a bridge of shared understanding and deep insight.

- Being curious about another person is a wonderful thing. It allows us to challenge ourselves and each other. It can hold a mirror up to us; it can create the conditions for a powerful dialogue. In addition, if those feelings and emotions that I was talking about earlier are suppressed or ignored, they build up and they manifest as problems with our mental health, physical health and/or the health of our teams. Now I may be going out on a limb a bit here, but we are seeing a huge rise in the focus on mental health at work. Of course that is great, and it is important. However, yet again, as with so many workplace initiatives, it is reactive, and it is papering over the cracks of a fundamental failing in the way that our organizations are functioning and our managers are managing. If we want to improve employees' mental health, to make workplaces safer, to reduce the issues of stress and stress-related absence, we could start by encouraging our managers and leaders to be a little bit more curious.

Curiosity is one of the foundations of a healthy team and a healthy person. You are not prying; you are not sticking your nose in – it is a fundamental part of your role as a manager. And to that manager on my training course, and any other managers who are still unsure about this, you are most definitely allowed to ask your employees how they are feeling.

TRANSFORMATIONAL THINKING

- What changes will you make to help you achieve the 7Cs of a transformational culture in your organization?

CASE STUDY
How the Royal College of Paediatrics and Child Health has transformed its culture

LOUISE FRAYNE IS THE DIRECTOR OF PEOPLE AT THE ROYAL COLLEGE OF PAEDIATRICS AND CHILD HEALTH (RCPCH). I AM GRATEFUL TO LOUISE FOR PRODUCING THIS CASE STUDY FOR TRANSFORMATIONAL CULTURE

The Royal College of Paediatrics and Child Health (RCPCH) is the professional body for paediatricians in the UK. It sets and maintains standards for the education and training of all doctors working in paediatrics and child health, and advocates on child health issues at home and internationally. The College is an evidence-driven body and charity which through a variety of activities influences the quality of medical practice for children in hospital and in the community.

Introducing a new RCPCH people strategy

The RCPCH People Strategy 2019–2021 is the blueprint for changing the way the College approaches staffing so that we can capitalize not only on the existing skills, knowledge and experience of staff but also continue to attract new staff, plan for succession and develop leadership. The People Strategy has six pillars:

1 Diversity and inclusion.

2 Our approach to people.

3 Investing in you.

4 The way we work.

5 Leadership at every level.

6 Living our culture.

Our People Strategy was introduced shortly before Covid-19 and the subsequent lockdown(s). This meant we had to embed the strategy and launch many of the initiatives while working from home, which has meant thinking creatively. To cascade the information, and to promote dialogue, we introduced:

- virtual town hall briefings with presentations and opportunities for staff to ask questions in the chat;

- improvements to the staff intranet 'the Hub' with designated pages on the initiatives, which also allow staff to ask questions or comment;

- a weekly staff bulletin with a host message and spotlight section for teams to talk about the work they do, top tips for maintaining health and wellbeing, and a staff survey to find out how we are doing;

- focus groups with staff on the How We Pay project including FAQs, dedicated pages on the Hub, and supporting documents setting out the proposed changes, etc;

- an employee forum in recognition of the fact that most staff are not union members.

Making the shift to people and culture

We moved from HR to a people and culture function in 2019 as we believe that this is more inclusive and focuses on engagement, consultation, taking people with you, sharing best practice, listening, seeking opinion, etc. We have placed a significant emphasis on capturing lessons learned. This includes celebrating success as well as recognizing when things did not go quite to plan. Each project board has a standard agenda item on lessons learned and the Project Portfolio Board also has this as a standard agenda item. There is also a designated area on the Hub for information to be shared. This is aligned to our values of Innovate and Influence.

1 We introduced Mental Health First Aiders, and flexible working options for those with parental and carer responsibilities in particular. Staff can choose to work between 7am and 7pm to allow time for exercise, etc. We also promoted top health tips. Consequently, we have seen sickness absence fall to below 1.5 per cent, which effectively means our capacity has increased by one full-time equivalent.

2   We introduced the Employee Forum to afford opportunities for the staff voice to be heard through staff representation. Representatives are trained in the role and afforded time off during work hours to undertake this responsibility.

3   We have held actively enhanced communications including Town Hall briefings, staff surveys, focus groups, etc.

We consider this to be critical to RCPCH becoming an employer of choice. Employee experience is woven through everything we do as an organization. We have learned that you can never give this enough time. No matter how much time you have set aside you need to at least double it for engagement to be meaningful. You also need to recognize that one size does not fit all, and you need to deploy various techniques

Introducing a Resolution Framework within RCPCH

Being a very small organization, disputes have the potential to ripple across a whole team and cause discomfort and further tension. Furthermore, there is never a 'winner'. Therefore, in the best interests of the working relationship, and the organization, it is more effective to focus on an informal, no-blame resolution.

We got the union fully on board and ensured we aligned to current best practice from TCM and Acas. To build our business case, we assessed the current costs of grievances both in terms of the investigation, staff abstraction costs, lost productivity, sickness absence, etc. We also referred to best practice case studies, and I qualified as an accredited TCM workplace mediator. Introducing a Resolution Framework and a greater use of mediation has delivered real benefits for RCPCH:

•   A quick resolution of disputes result in minimal sickness absence and minimal workplace disruption. Our employees know that they can raise an issue confident that it will be managed appropriately.

•   A culture of sharing lessons learned openly and honestly with managers and employees has been developed.

•   We have seen better communications, greater understanding and enhanced emotional intelligence – all of which are now seen as organizational assets.

•   Our employees have told us that, if they witnessed discrimination, bullying etc, not only would they have the confidence to report it but they know it would be dealt with.

Conclusion and calls to action

The 7Cs of a transformational culture represent the very best that organizational cultures can deliver. They work as a virtuous circle – the more that they are generated, the more that they give back to the organization. They have the potential to be the magical ingredient which shifts an organization from good to great. The ability to deliver each of the 7Cs, and to combine them in a way which expresses your own unique organizational identity, provides a significant likelihood of driving up innovation, attracting and retaining talent, and delivering enhanced employee and customer experience.

The changes required to adopt these 7Cs will be great. Courage, one of the 7Cs, is at the heart of this cultural change. Sometimes it is easier to do things the way that things have always been done and to accept the status quo.

Our reliance on the corporate systems of retribution, blame, power and privilege, process over people, and so on and so forth are being challenged robustly. These are bad habits that have formed in our organizations over several years. At one time these habits may have served us well, but no longer. Change happens when we understand what is causing the bad habit, when we diagnose its impact and when we make a determined effort to break it.

> 'Habits can be changed, if we understand how they work... Sometimes change takes a long time. Sometimes it requires repeated experiments and failures. But once you understand how a habit operates – once you diagnose the cue, the routine and the reward – you gain power over it.' (Duhigg, 2012)

The biggest threat to a transformational culture is the phrase 'we've always done it this way'. To drive these changes and to embrace a transformational culture – to ensure that our organizations can achieve all that the 7Cs have to offer – changes will need to be made. I have set many of these out already and will continue to do so through this book. Here are just a few:

- Process to people.
- Retributive justice to transformational justice.

- Blame to learning.
- Adversity to dialogue.
- HR to people and culture.
- Power over to power with.
- Fear to flow.
- Failure to opportunity.
- Talking at to listening to.
- Telling to showing.
- Inertia to action.

References

Blanchard, K and Bowles, S (2000) *High Five! None of us is as smart as all of us*, William Morrow & Company, New York

Bradley, A (2020) *The Human Moment: The positive power of compassion in the workplace*, Lid Publishing, London

Duhigg, C (2012) *The Power of Habit. Why we do what we do and how to change*, Random House, London

Kanov, J, Maitlis, M, Worline, M and Dutton, J (2004) Compassion in organizational life, *American Behavioral Scientist*, 47 (6), 808–827

Lancaster, A (2020) *Driving Performance Through Learning: Develop employees through effective workplace learning*, Kogan Page, London

May, R (1953) *Man's Search for Himself: Courage, the virtue of maturity*, W. W. Norton & Company, New York

Pink, D (2009) *Drive: The surprising truth about what motivates us*, Canongate, New York

Quinn, R and Thakor, V (2018) Creating a purpose-driven organization, *Harvard Business Review*, https://hbr.org/2018/07/creating-a-purpose-driven-organization (archived at https://perma.cc/QV7N-2ZAS)

Teed, R (2020) The rise of the hybrid workplace, *Forbes*, www.forbes.com/sites/servicenow/2020/12/22/rise-of-the-hybrid-workplace/?sh=4407ccfe15e7 (archived at https://perma.cc/HN5D-CDJY)

05

The Resolution Framework

A fresh approach for resolving concerns, conduct, complaints and conflicts at work

---

TRANSFORMATIONAL LEARNING

Within this chapter, you will discover answers to the following questions:

- Why are the traditional performance, discipline and grievance procedures no longer fit for purpose?

- Is it possible to have a single, overarching framework which replaces these damaging and corrosive procedures?

- What is a Resolution Framework and how does it work?

- How does the Resolution Framework deliver transformational justice?

- What are the stages and phases for managing cases through the Resolution Framework?

- Does the Resolution Framework work?

- What are the benefits of adopting a Resolution Framework?

Introducing the Resolution Framework

For several years now, there has been a quiet revolution happening in organizations up and down the land – a resolution revolution.

Following the publication of *Managing Conflict* (Liddle, 2017), in which I offered an alternative system for resolving grievances in the workplace, more and more organizations have recognized that their traditional people policies are not working as they should. Evidence is amassing which demonstrates that the traditional HR policies and management systems, which we have relied on for so long – to address concerns, complaints, conduct and conflicts at work – are no longer fit for purpose. Not only are they failing to resolve the issues that they were designed to address, they are also having a detrimental impact on the wellbeing and the overall experience of the workforce, the organizational culture and its precious reputation.

The challenges of dealing with performance, discipline, grievance, bullying and harassment issues at work has perplexed HR, managers, leaders, union representatives and employees for a great many years. Over the past 40 years or so, we have seen a slow yet inexorable shift towards a retributive system of HR policies and procedures, where process trumps people and punishment trumps learning. During that time, our policies have become more onerous; they have become more complex, more rigid and more adversarial.

The humanity which underpins the human resources profession, and the compassion which we need to make our workplaces work, have slowly been drained from our HR policy frameworks and associated management systems (with a particular reference to discipline, grievance and performance management). Each iteration of these policies is designed to deliver one primary objective: protect the company from an adverse tribunal ruling. Each iteration takes the policy further away from its real objectives – keeping people safe, driving performance, making our people and our organizations brilliant.

It is like a haunted carousel in a horror movie, that no one knows how to stop. We know, we feel, we see that the current systems are wrong and that they are not working. We know that no one ever seems happy with the outcome. We can feel the stress and trauma they create. We can see that managers are afraid or unable to administer them properly. Good organizations end up losing good people. Relationships are destroyed. Trust is eroded. There must be a better way.

There is a better way

I fully accept that our HR systems have been designed for a purpose and that no one goes out of their way to create stress and uncertainty for their employees. However, if something is not working, it needs fixing, and our HR processes are not working. I have spent 30 years working with the fallout of these processes and I have seen the heartache and the misery that they cause. I have laboured in the basements of our organizations, sweeping up the debris caused by their broken systems. Sometimes, I have dared to look upwards for answers, and what I have seen is an apparatus of despair and destruction.

At times I have felt powerless to do anything about it. I have felt that I must be the only person in the world who can see this awful impact. But of course, it is not just me, and I am not powerless. That is why, in this chapter, and supported by powerful testimony from organizations which have had the courage to change, I propose a radical reform to the way that organizations handle concerns, conduct, complaints and conflicts at work.

The imperative for change is compelling and powerful. I hope you have been persuaded (or at least have an open mind to the possibility) that this moment in time presents a wonderful opportunity to reinvent our organizations' rules, systems and accompanying policies. Research tells us that organizational cultures which are based upon trust and respect and which include working practices such as transparent communication, empathetic leadership and favourable HR policies are conducive to a compassionate culture (Banker and Bhal, 2018).

The HR policies and the management systems of the successful organizations of the future will integrate their purpose, their values and the needs of their people into their workplace policies and procedures. They will reject retributive justice and they will integrate the restorative principles to deliver an exciting and progressive model of transformational justice. As a result, their policies will be less rigid, less complex and less bureaucratic. Benefiting from a more co-ordinated and collaborative approach in their design and deployment, the impact on employee and customer experience will be immense.

Such a policy framework already exists. It is a fully integrated, legally compliant and tried and tested alternative to the performance, disciplinary and grievance procedures. It is called a Resolution Framework.

TRANSFORMATIONAL THINKING

- What words or phrases would you use to describe your current discipline, grievance and performance procedures?

- Are your HR policies based around your organization's purpose, your values and your people?

- Do you measure the satisfaction of the people who use these processes? If not, how can you be confident that they work? If you do, what does the data tell you?

What is a Resolution Framework and how does it work?

I have spent a great many years developing, testing and refining the Resolution Framework. To date it has been integrated into banks, global insurance companies, airlines, numerous blue-chip companies, numerous hospitals and universities, councils, police and law enforcement agencies, and government departments and NGOs.

The first iteration of the framework, the Resolution Policy™, was launched at the Law Society in 2013. It featured in my book *Managing Conflict* (Liddle, 2017) and it has been adopted by many hundreds of organizations. However, after my book was published, more and more HR professionals, leaders and unions reps contacted me to tell me it was a great idea but it did not go far enough. Why stop at just reforming the GBH (grievance, bullying and harassment) procedures, I was asked. The problems of mistrust, suspicion, division, stress and frustration could equally be applied to the traditional disciplinary and performance procedures as to the GBH policy suite. Never one to walk away from a challenge, I set about creating a new version of my Resolution Policy, which was subsequently extended to become the Resolution Framework™ (Liddle, 2021).

The design of a single, fully integrated and legally compliant framework which spans the areas of concerns (performance), conduct (discipline), complaints (grievances) and conflict (disputes) was a mouth-watering challenge. I decided that the best way to proceed would be to rip up the old policies and to start over (see Table 5.1).

TABLE 5.1 Old policies vs the Resolution Framework

Traditional discipline, performance and grievance procedures	The Resolution Framework (transformational justice)
• Blame has primacy	• Dialogue has primacy
• Facts based and retributive	• Person centred and restorative
• Blame and punish	• Just and learning
• Adversarial	• Non-adversarial
• Win/lose or lose/lose outcomes	• Win/win outcomes
• Didactic	• Adult-to-adult dialogue
• Increase stress	• Builds resilience
• Confusion and atrophy	• Insight and growth
• Reductive	• Expansive
• Uncaring and unkind	• Compassionate
• Promote exclusion	• Promotes inclusion
• Fixed mindset	• Growth mindset
• Unfair and inequitable	• Fair and equitable
• Fight or flight	• Flow and flourish

In developing the Resolution Framework, I sought to balance a) the restorative principles (do no harm, follow our values, listen to learn) with b) the needs and legal duties of the organization and c) the needs and legal duties of its employees. I came up with an initial structure which would then become the glue that held the Resolution Framework together.

One Tuesday morning, I was approached by London Ambulance Service NHS Trust (LAS), which was seeking an innovative approach for reducing the incidence of incivility, for resolving conflicts, for addressing conduct and for driving up employee engagement. LAS is responsible for operating ambulances and answering and responding to urgent and emergency medical situations within the London region. I had worked with LAS previously to help them to integrate an internal mediation and dispute resolution programme. We spoke, and we agreed that LAS would be a perfect organization to pilot this new approach. The organization is complex, highly regulated, unionized and has proven to be welcoming of innovation and open to new ideas. Garrett Emmerson, chief executive, gave this modern approach for resolving complaints concerns and concerns at work his full support:

> 'I am delighted that LAS has designed and introduced this new Resolution Framework. As a single, very up-to-date, integrated approach, we aim to move our organization from the more formal processes contained within traditional grievance and disciplinary policies to focus on resolution that supports our commitment to create a just and learning culture. Our focus is directed on negotiated round-table discussions and learning to address our people issues. I saw this as a real opportunity to positively change and enhance our culture, across all areas of our organization.'

The following case study represents one of the most radical shifts in HR processes and management systems that I have ever witnessed in an organization of this scale and this complexity.

CASE STUDY
London Ambulance Service secures an alternative to its grievance and disciplinary procedures

London Ambulance Service is breaking new ground by becoming the first health sector organization to use the Resolution Framework to manage conduct-related issues, as well as workplace conflicts, complaints and concerns.

Like all NHS organizations, LAS had a tumultuous 2020 at the front line of the Covid-19 pandemic. With staff under tremendous operational and personal pressure, cracks were starting to appear in workplace relationships and the number of disciplinary and grievance cases had grown substantially, to the point at which the HR team was becoming overwhelmed.

'Cases were not getting resolved quickly and this was causing distress for both staff and managers,' said Kim Nurse, Interim Director of People and Culture at LAS. 'We recognized there had to be a better way of us having more mature conversations and giving our staff the opportunity to reflect, look at different choices they could have made and actually learn from the issue rather than just having an adversarial conversation.'

The Resolution Framework, with its emphasis on resolving issues early through dialogue rather than formal policies, was a perfect fit for LAS's People and Culture strategy, the aim of which is to create a fair, open and inclusive organization with an engaged and collaborative workforce. As the organization examined the framework more closely, it became clear it could also help the service take a fairer and more compassionate approach to the way it handled conduct and performance issues.

Chief executive Garrett Emmerson gave his full endorsement for the shift to a new approach, as did the executive team. An intensive period of stakeholder engagement then followed, with unions, HR and operational managers fully involved in developing the framework template and language to meet the service's specific needs. 'I am pleased to say that we have clearly made progress, but we know that we cannot be complacent. We need to continually reflect and challenge ourselves to ensure everyone is treated fairly and build a culture of openness and transparency to ensure we are doing the right thing by our people. This Resolution Framework is a significant step to building on that commitment and I hope contributes to our ambition of becoming an exemplar of good practice in this area,' he said.

Support for the move to a resolution-first approach has been widespread throughout LAS. 'Everyone in the organization wants a quicker resolution process, and the current arrangements are so stressful for everybody that there really wasn't a good reason why people would want to hold on to them,' said Kim Nurse.

A comprehensive programme of training has been developed to support implementation of the Resolution Framework. The HR team and union representatives have had in-depth familiarization sessions, and a cohort of resolution advocates, who will support managers and staff through the process, has also been trained.

An illustration of just how welcome the approach has been came in the shape of the response to an open invitation to staff to put themselves forward to become internal mediators. More than 50 people applied, with a group of 16 initially being allocated places on the accredited National Certificate in Workplace Mediation run by the TCM Group.

Looking ahead, there are plans for all staff to be trained on the resolution-first approach, which will become a key part of essential training for managers and eventually be developed into a mandatory e-learning program.

'Giving our people the right education and training to use the Resolution Framework effectively is so important,' says Kim Nurse. 'Being able to equip managers with the tools to problem-solve and come up with solutions which are fair, just and reasonable is going to be really key to the success of this initiative.'

A full internal communications programme was also put together to support the launch, with everything from drop-in sessions and briefing meetings through to roadshows and interviews on the London Ambulance Service Live TV channel.

An evaluation programme was put in place right from the start, to give LAS the opportunity to assess the success of the initiative as it unfolds and to make any adjustments that may be necessary. There are plans for a six-monthly review involving all stakeholders, with data also being collected from a range of sources including a quarterly staff satisfaction survey, turnover and job stability metrics and exit interviews. An important indicator of success will be a reduction in overall levels of disciplinary action and grievances and the time spent managing the caseload.

Moving forward, Kim Nurse believes the impact of the Resolution Framework will be felt in all corners of LAS. It has been fully embedded into key workstreams such as people and culture, diversity and inclusion, training, talent management and health and wellbeing, to ensure a joined-up approach.

The availability of a framework against which managers can base their decisions will also help to ensure fairness and consistency across the service, in the way it deals with everything from conduct issues to relationship breakdowns or concerns that may be bubbling under the surface.

'The Resolution Framework will help us get to resolution in a more agile manner, but it also sets the tone for the way we want to work with colleagues in the organization,' Kim says. 'With traditional policies, sometimes the stress of the process rather than the actual issue is an inhibitor to creating a good outcome. We need to come out of issues having both learned and taken responsibility for our own part of the resolution process. That is a much more powerful outcome than going through a very stern, formalized process which can scar people for life.'

How does the Resolution Framework work in practice?

The LAS case study has demonstrated how the Resolution Framework combines the existing performance, discipline, conduct and grievance, bullying and harassment procedures into a single, fully integrated framework (see Figure 5.1). The framework is the first workplace policy of its kind which blends procedural justice with restorative justice to create a new model of organizational justice, which I am calling trans-formational justice. It is thorough and comprehensive; it covers every possible eventuality and scenario.

The language of the framework has been carefully designed to be less adversarial and threatening. Dialogue has primacy and it is designed to deliver constructive and collaborative outcomes, wher-ever possible. However, procedurally, it is also extraordinarily robust. It is proportionate and it allows for due process, with the ability for the employer to apply a sanction, up to and including dismissal in cases that merit such action. The Resolution Framework meets and exceeds the minimum standards set out in the Acas code of practice

FIGURE 5.1   A summary of the Resolution Framework

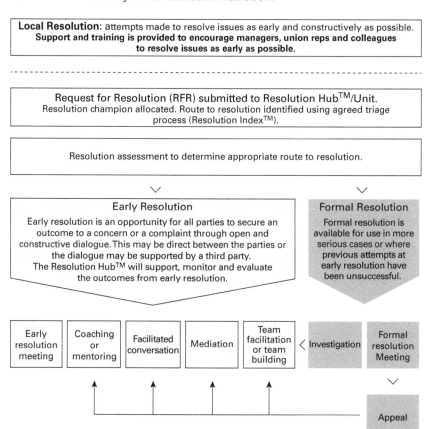

on disciplinary and grievance procedures (Acas, 2015), and it has been successfully defended in an employment tribunal by a large London hotel group when an employee brought a claim of unfair dismissal. The claim was not upheld and the tribunal judge, when summing up, acknowledged the efforts of the hotel to bring about a constructive resolution.

Local resolution

This is the stage where employees and managers resolve issues at a local level. At this stage, resolutions can be sought, action plans can be agreed and the manager can issue either a first or a second reminder. The manager and/or the employee can access support and resources, including coaching and checklists, from the Resolution Unit to assist with the local resolution process.

Request for resolution

This is a short form that is completed by either the employee or a manager. The form is sent to the Resolution Unit. The form is designed using appreciative inquiry and positive psychology, it is therefore solution focused, human centred and constructive. If a complaint letter or an email is received, the Resolution Unit will work with the individual(s) to ensure that the RFR is completed correctly.

Resolution triage and Resolution Index™

This is the process of identifying the most appropriate route to resolution in each case. The case is assessed against an objective set of five indices and given a score from 1 to 5. When aggregated, the combined score (out of 25) suggests the most suitable remedy in that case. In some situations, particularly more complex cases, the triage may be undertaken by two people, a triage panel.

The Resolution Index™ considers five factors:

1 Severity and complexity.
2 Previous attempts to resolve the situation.

3 The stated needs of the parties.

4 Risk to the organization.

5 Risk to the individuals.

The Resolution Unit may wish to speak to the parties involved to assist the triage process and the application of the Resolution Index.

Early resolution

This stage involves a range of restorative processes ranging from direct dialogue between the two parties (early resolution) through to facilitated conversations, mediation, coaching and team conferencing. Further details of each of these stages are given in Part Two: 'The Transformational Culture Playbook'.

Formal resolution

This stage includes the options to investigate the case and for a formal resolution meeting to be convened (this is the new name for a hearing). The formal resolution meeting is chaired by a suitably trained and senior manager. The process, while formal, still applies best practice from the transformational principles, thereby ensuring that it is just and restorative. The chair of the formal resolution meeting has the authority to:

- refer the case back for a restorative justice process such as mediation to develop a resolution action plan;
- apply a third reminder (the final reminder);
- dismiss the employee (with or without notice depending on circumstances).

The employee has the right to be accompanied to the formal resolution meeting. In addition, the chair of the meeting may opt to meet the parties separately and to arrange for them to meet each other as part of the process, the objective always being, wherever possible, to protect the working relationship and secure a constructive and lasting outcome. The Resolution Unit will support the chair of the formal resolution meeting, and wherever required, additional support can be sought, including legal advice and so forth.

Suspension

We know that suspending an employee is not a neutral act and great care should be taken to ensure that it is fair and proportionate. The decision to suspend an employee should never be made by just one person. It should always involve two people (generally, the manager and someone from the Resolution Unit) who must agree that suspension is necessary and proportionate. The suspension process is explained more in the playbook (see page 253).

Right to appeal

The employee has the right to appeal the outcome of the formal resolution meeting in the normal way.

Resolution champions

This is a new role that has been designed to support the application and implementation of the Resolution Framework within larger organizations. Organizations that integrate a Resolution Framework will develop a small cross-functional team of resolution champions who will be allocated to a particular case at the point where a request for resolution has been received. The role of the resolution champion is to provide support to the parties in the stages leading up to and for a period of up to one full year after the resolution process has concluded.

These roles are a vital part of building confidence in the resolution process and sustaining any outcomes which have arisen during the process. Resolution champions act impartially and the same resolution champion works with both parties. While they will offer coaching and mentoring, they do not offer mediation or facilitation. They are there to guide and advise the parties and to provide support at any point after the resolution has concluded. They act as an early warning system in case problems begin to reappear or the agreements begin to unravel. The resolution champions report to the Resolution Unit and they are accountable to that unit.

In the Transformational Culture Playbook, I have provided detailed guidance to support organizations that wish to implement a Resolution Framework. My team and I are always on hand to support, and we provide extensive resources such as white papers, webinars, podcasts and workshops to support organizations looking to introduce this new approach. The Institute of Organisational Dynamics has a Resolution Framework workstream called 'The Tapestry Project', which is developing best practice in the areas of transformational justice and HR policies.

User evaluation

It is important that feedback from users of the Resolution Framework is sought at the conclusion of each case. This analysis can be used as part of the quality assurance and governance, which I explain below.

Ensuring accountability and good governance

I am often asked, how did I ensure due process, efficacy and governance were built into the Resolution Framework? For my new framework to be credible in the eyes of unions, lawyers, HR, managers and employees, I needed to ensure that it would be fully legally compliant and would balance employee rights with employee responsibilities while delivering fair, equitable and just outcomes.

In addition to these overarching principles, I ensured that the framework would:

- align the resolution process to an agreed values and behaviours framework (see Chapter 7 for more details and examples of a values and behaviours framework);
- fully consider the employee experience throughout the application of the process. As you will read further in this chapter, the users of the Resolution Framework are treated as customers and their satisfaction with the process will be sought and acted upon as part of a new resolution quality and governance system – the Resolution Unit;

- remove the legalistic and retributive language of the traditional policies and processes. This included some significant language and structural changes:
  - replace the traditional grievance form with a Request for Resolution (RfR). The RfR would be used to trigger an intervention from the Resolution Unit. The RfR is used in all cases, whether the case is initiated by the line manager or by the employee;
  - replace warnings with reminders (Grote, 2006);
  - replace hearings with formal resolution meetings;
  - replace the dreaded performance improvement plan with a new resolution action plan (RAP);
- integrate psychological safety and reduce the risk of harm, stress, anxiety and trauma to the participants during and after the process;
- draw from sound theoretical models and frameworks such as nudge theory, appreciative inquiry, positive psychology, emotional intelligence, non-violent communication, restorative justice and transactional analysis;
- use data and evidence to develop and deploy a range of predictive, proactive and reactive remedies to concerns, conduct, complaints and conflicts;
- actively promote respect and civility throughout application of the process and thereafter;
- ensure that action up to and including dismissal could be taken in serious or complex cases;
- encourage compassion, empathy and self-awareness by all stakeholders at each stage of the informal or formal resolution process. This was particularly important in the management of serious and complex cases including the stages of suspension, investigation, dismissal and appeal;
- deliver accountability, insight and learning which have the power to drive behavioural change;

- foster adult-to-adult dialogue between the parties and maximize opportunities to use restorative justices processes such as facilitation, mediation and team conferencing;
- engender a fair, equitable and inclusive process and deliver fair, equitable and inclusive outcomes.

I also knew, from working with some of the biggest firms in the UK and globally, that consistency, proportionality and fairness in the application of these processes was a major concern for both employers and employees. So, in addition to the above, I sought to reduce the risk of bias or partisanship in the way that the Resolution Framework was applied, and to ensure that it would deliver a consistent, proportionate and legally compliant response in each case. I was also concerned to ensure that the process protected the mental and physical (pastoral) needs of all the parties.

To achieve these objectives, I ensured that my Resolution Framework included a set of objective criteria (which became the Resolution Index) to assess the merits of each case and to ensure that the appropriate route to resolution would be applied. The Resolution Index was trialled with a major global bank and was rolled out successfully across its global whistleblowing operation.

To deliver the prerequisite co-ordination and governance of the Resolution Framework, I developed a multidisciplinary team which became known as the Resolution Unit or the Resolution Hub. I also ensured that an evaluation of user satisfaction and an ongoing evaluation of the outcomes that the Resolution Framework achieved would be core features of the new approach.

How does the Resolution Framework deliver transformational justice?

In Chapter 2, I set out the arguments in favour of integrating transformational justice into an organization's HR policies and management systems. The various case studies and the stories have demonstrated that it is entirely possible and desirable to balance the rights of the employee, the needs of the employer and the ability to achieve outcomes which are fair, just, inclusive and sustainable. I have also made several links between these outcomes and enhanced individual, team and organizational performance.

As I did in *Managing Conflict*, I feel compelled to take a moment to dispel a common myth. There is no legal, statutory or moral duty on an employer to have a policy called discipline, grievance or performance. The legal duty to have these policies was abolished in 2008 following the Gibbons Review. In his now famous review, Michael Gibbons stated:

> 'Fundamentally, what is needed is a culture change, so that the parties to employment disputes think in terms of finding ways to achieve an early outcome that works for them, rather than in terms of fighting their case at a tribunal.' (Gibbons, 2007)

To recap what I explained in Chapter 2, what we have now is a mess – a complex and confusing muddle of public policy coupled with opaque and outdated guidance. As the case study from Imperial College Healthcare NHS Trust on page 141 highlights, the current situation is doing more than causing a few sleepless nights. People are dying.

However, the case studies and examples throughout this book, from organizations as diverse as TSB Bank, MAPS, Center Parcs, Aviva, the *FT*, the BRC, Hounslow Council and the RCPCH, among many others, give us all cause for hope. There can be a change, and the change comes when we put our people and our values first. This is not a soft option, this is real justice, delivered by real people.

The Resolution Framework far exceeds the requirements of the law and existing equality and human rights legislation. It has the backing of an increasing number of lawyers, one of whom, Laura Farnsworth, and her colleagues explained in *Managing Conflict* that 'incorporating a requirement to engage in principled negotiations to resolve a dispute before the commencement of formal legal proceedings has been shown to be a more effective approach. In this regard, the way forward may be to replace an employer's grievance and disciplinary policies with one resolution policy that incorporates a more holistic approach to dispute resolution' (Farnsworth *et al*, 2017).

That is precisely what the Resolution Framework offers. It does not tinker at the edges of the discipline, grievance and performance management processes. It tears up the retributive orthodoxies and corrosive dogmas, replacing them with a fresh and modern approach for resolving workplace issues. In so doing, it far exceeds any remedies currently available in the UK or elsewhere.

Aviva Insurance is another company that has made the shift towards a Resolution Framework. Anthony Fitzpatrick is the Head of Colleague Experience and Employment Policy at Aviva. Aviva launched its Resolution Framework in 2018. Since that time, the organization has seen a dramatic decline in the number of cases requiring formal action and a substantial increase in the cases settled through early resolution and mediation. The company has moved from a costly, lengthy, complex traditional grievance process involving multiple stakeholders to now dealing with circa 60 per cent of cases through coaching, facilitated conversations and mediation.

Anthony reflects on his experience of developing a Resolution Framework within Aviva:

'The introduction of our Resolution Framework changed the whole concept and dynamic of managing conflicts and complaints within the workplace. Culturally, the change in language and emphasis has been so important. We aren't focusing on being aggrieved, we are focusing on resolution and that is a fundamental difference. We have seen that the vast majority of cases are settled either at triage or through a facilitated conversation. This means that for the cases where a formal meeting or a mediation is required, we have more time to dedicate to that. If colleagues can feel that the outcome was swift, easily managed and resolved, it allows everyone to focus on their job and increases morale and motivation, which is good for personal wellbeing; it's good for the business and it's good for the customer, too.'

What are the differences between the Resolution Framework and the traditional HR policies?

Some of the main differences and similarities between the Resolution Framework and the existing HR policies and management systems are listed in Table 5.2.

TABLE 5.2 Differences and similarities between the Resolution Framework and existing HR policies and management systems

What's different?	What's the same?
• Dialogue has primacy • Resolution Champions support parties throughout and beyond the resolution process • Links to your values and behaviours • Transformational rather than retributive justice • A collaborative approach – The Resolution Unit • Use of reminders rather than warnings and Resolution Action Plans replace PIPs • Triage process and the Resolution Index offers objective and consistent approach • Greater emphasis on the restorative justice processes: mediation, coaching, facilitated conversations and team conferencing • HR, unions and managers work together to drive and sustain the outcome	• Fully compliant with Acas code of practice • Due process: ability to suspend, investigate, and dismiss in serious cases • Gross misconduct may still result in dismissal, with or without notice • Managers expected to take responsibility • Employees remain accountable for their actions • Right to be accompanied to the formal resolution meeting • Right of appeal

CASE STUDY
Redefining resolution at the Money and Pensions Service (MaPS)

CASE STUDY PRODUCED FOR TRANSFORMATIONAL CULTURE *BY LAURA CALVERT, EMPLOYEE EXPERIENCE MANAGER*

The Money and Pensions Service (MaPS) brings together three respected financial guidance bodies: the Money Advice Service, the Pensions Advisory Service and Pension Wise. MaPS is an arm's-length body sponsored by the Department for Work and Pensions, established at the beginning of 2019, and also engages with HM Treasury on policy matters relating to financial capability and debt advice.

Our culture promotes personal responsibility and a framework for managing concerns, rather than lots of rules that are policed by HR. The resolution approach fitted well with our culture. Even just reframing the policy from grievance to resolution helps to shift mindsets from focusing on the issues to a solution-oriented approach. There are so many other benefits – most conflicts go through a lengthy investigation with witnesses, expanding the conflict and creating stress for a wider group of people, ending with an outcome that includes mediation. It makes sense to reduce the number of people involved, time and resources to bring mediation up front.

We drafted our Resolution Framework and built in three informal stages followed by a formal stage, which aligns with the Acas Code of Practice but is still termed a resolution rather than a grievance. The informal stages are:

1 Early conflict conversations where the individual could receive coaching from their line manager, colleague rep or HR business partner.

2 Facilitated conversation – this is like a 'mini mediation' with all the elements but shorter in duration, led by trained line managers.

3 Mediation.

Colleagues determine which stage they feel is appropriate guided by their manager or HR business partner. We aim to resolve issues at the lowest level, but this isn't always appropriate, and we don't remove the right to raise a formal resolution request. This approach puts the individual in control of the choice that feels right for them and they have support at every stage.

We used guidance and documents from TCM. They have a very well-tested approach and have been innovators in transforming how workplaces resolve conflict. We consulted on our new policy and our staff reps and colleagues were very happy with the proposed change.

I knew that in theory the resolution approach sounded like a huge improvement, but would it work in practice? I felt a huge sense of responsibility for colleagues' wellbeing. If resolution didn't work, the formal process was still there to fall back on, and I learned that you have to trust in the process. The mediation training and ongoing support from TCM helped with this challenge.

The wider cultural benefits were key to our decision in this change. Moving from a blame culture to one that promotes personal responsibility and support is key. Consultation, communication and training – all ongoing rather than a one-off approach.

Conclusion and calls to action

The Resolution Framework offers a fresh approach for managing the most challenging areas of leadership, management, HR and employee relations. For 40 years we have been slugging it out, trying to make the tired old systems work. It has often felt like pushing water up a hill, but still everyone has persisted (predominantly because no one has yet come up with a better option). However, the past 40 years have been one of the most draining and demotivating periods in the history of labour relations – thankfully, the winds of change are blowing. Yes, we have seen a reduction in industrial action and strikes, but the individual stories of pain and anguish must never be ignored again.

> 'Like prisoners held in a dungeon too long, we want to get out, but the prospect frightens us. We have grown accustomed to a static system in which no one, including us, has to take responsibility.' (Howard, 2011)

What I have sought to do with the Resolution Framework is balance the needs of the employer with the needs of the parties by creating an environment where procedural justice and restorative processes can be combined. By delivering this exciting and modern form of trans-formational justice, the Resolution Framework underpins exceptional employee experience, which in turn assures the highest levels of customer experience.

As the various examples and case studies in this chapter have shown, the Resolution Framework works – it integrates well into a modern and progressive workplace. It has been designed to meet, and exceed, the very highest standards in terms of equality legislation and the requirements set out in the Acas code. As this book demonstrates, two of the most regulated sectors in the UK, financial services and healthcare, have been the early adopters of the Resolution Framework, thus demonstrating that the process is robust and stands up to scrutiny.

The only real barrier, then, to adopting a Resolution Framework are the vested interests that surround the status quo. These I fully understand. As I have said elsewhere, an entire industry has been created in relation to our traditional retributive HR systems and management processes.

Attitudes to resolution are changing rapidly. While I was researching this book, I had the good fortune to interview Simon Robinson, co-founder of Robinson Ralph Solicitors in Leeds. He is a well-known and outspoken employment solicitor and I asked him what he thought about the shift from traditional HR processes to the Resolution Framework:

> 'Do it. Stop talking about it and just do it. It is not difficult. But a lot will not, because in my experience, the most toxic people are the most senior or the most profitable. Some employers would rather put up with bad behaviour than fire the golden goose which, for me, is a false economy. I would like to see a much less adversarial approach for resolving workplace issues. What would be useful would be a more collaborative approach internally, and a much more collaborative approach externally amongst employment lawyers.'

To help with the transition to a Resolution Framework, my best advice is to engage with all stakeholders and give them a voice in its design and development. Invite them to be part of the Resolution Unit and any workstreams that you might generate to design and roll out the framework. Ensure that they can contribute to the design of all the underpinning systems and processes, including the governance and the means of delivering accountability and governance.

We will all need to be courageous and tenacious to deliver this new vision. It is not possible to make a change of this magnitude without meeting some naysayers, sceptics and cynics along the way. Embrace them and listen to them. But whatever you do, do not be put off by them.

References

Acas (2015) Code of Practice on disciplinary and grievance procedures, www.acas. org.uk/acas-code-of-practice-for-disciplinary-and-grievance-procedures/html (archived at https://perma.cc/EUJ2-EUH9)

Banker, D and Bhal, K (2018) Understanding compassion from practicing managers' perspective: Vicious and virtuous forces in business organizations, *Global Business Review 2018*, https://journals.sagepub.com/doi/10.1177/0972150917749279 (archived at https://perma.cc/3CBC-X67A)

Farnsworth, L, Smith, C and Mills, L (2017) Chapter 2 of *Managing Conflict: A practical guide to resolution in the workplace*, Kogan Page, London

Gibbons, M (2007) A review of employment dispute resolution in Great Britain, March DTI, page 38

Grote, D (2006) *Discipline Without Punishment: The proven strategy that turns problem employees into superior performers*, Amacom, New York

Howard, P (2011) *The Death of Common Sense: How law is suffocating America*, Random House, New York

Liddle, D (2017) *Managing Conflict: A practical guide to resolution in the workplace*, Kogan Page, London

Liddle, D (2021) The Resolution Framework: A fully integrated approach for resolving concerns, complaints, and conflicts at work, www.resolutionframework.com (archived at https://perma.cc/P8L8-N4PJ)

06

A very uncivil war

The toxic culture (and what to do about it)

TRANSFORMATIONAL LEARNING

Within this chapter, you will discover answers to the following questions:

- What is a toxic culture and why do they exist?
- What are the signs and the symptoms that a culture has turned toxic?
- What is the impact and what are the costs of a toxic culture?
- Is there a cure for a toxic culture and if so, what is it?
- How can HR, leaders, managers, unions and employees detox their cultures by institutionalizing kindness, compassion, empathy, dialogue, learning, inclusion and collaboration?
- How can transformational justice be used to transform toxic cultures?

What is a toxic culture?

If you have read my first book, *Managing Conflict* (Liddle, 2017), you will know that I am a huge fan of conflict. Not the destructive and toxic kind of conflict that causes harm and distress, but the constructive and functional kind of conflict that can bring people together and which, when managed well, can release our inner and collective brilliance. The kind of conflict that can engender dialogue, promote insight, harness learning and enhance working relationships.

In this chapter, I will get under the skin of the toxic culture (this term is used to describe both organizational culture and climate). I examine how toxic cultures happen, why they happen and the impact that they can have. I will explain how to get a grip on the toxic culture, and I provide guidance and practical tips to help you transform a toxic culture into a transformational culture. I will also explore ways in which an organization can harness the incredible power and energy that are unleashed when the culture shifts from toxic to transformational.

Imagine working in a team where you fear being humiliated by your manager or your colleagues. Where team members barely talk, and when they do it is in hushed tones. Where teams are divided and alliances are more complex than a *Game of Thrones* box set. Where people are afraid to speak out, and where innovation is quashed and creativity is sneered at. Imagine working in a team where fun seems like a foreign word and any achievements that you make are not credited to you. Where people abuse their positions of power, and status is everything. Where rules and procedures are so rigid you need to be a lawyer to understand them, and the unwritten rules are a code that only a chosen few understand. Where failure provokes attack and weakness is seen as fair game.

You have just imagined a toxic culture.

Getting a grip on the toxic culture

Toxic cultures are damaging and harmful. They belch out discord, fear and mistrust, with little concern for the destructive powers they unleash. As surely as the carbon-emitting towers poison our skies, toxic cultures poison our teams, and our souls. They are no longer being tolerated by the many who have fallen foul of the destructive, divisive and often discriminatory or misogynistic behaviours from colleagues, managers, leaders, customers or services users.

In a toxic culture, retribution is deeply ingrained in the psyche of the organization. Risk taking and failure are frowned upon, blame is rife, conflict is stifled and mishandled, difference leads to confusion and exclusion, leaders tell rather than show, and open dialogue is treated with disdain.

It is no wonder that so many of the teams and organizations that I have worked with over the years have existed in a kind of cultural purgatory, where employees' experiences drain them of their good will, their motivation and their passion. The impact, of course, can be one of paralysis and stress, where HR and managers spend more time trying to mitigate the impact of the toxic culture and protecting the reputation of the firm than they do growing a successful organization.

There is no doubt that the threat of the toxic culture should be taken seriously; it should feature in the risk register of every organization. However, looking at the growing amount of literature and the numerous posts appearing online, most of the proposed remedies to the toxic culture sit firmly in the retributive box (blame, shame and punish).

I do not want to appear to be understating the impact of the toxic culture, nor do I believe that those responsible for creating or perpetuating a culture which harms people should not be held to account. However, I also do not believe that the call for increasingly retributive systems is the right way to go about resolving the toxic culture, or any problematic behaviour in the workplace for that matter. I am sure it won't be long before I read a social media post suggesting that we should take the 'narcissist manager' or the 'sociopathic colleague' – whatever those terms mean – and we should 'hang em and flog em'. I am not going to go down that route, for therein lie further sorrow and misery. Retribution breeds toxicity, which breeds retribution – the classic vicious cycle. As seductive as the idea of retribution (which is often mistaken for justice) may be, this chapter does not advise it, nor does it advocate hanging or flogging. It proposes a mature, respectful and civilized approach for delivering accountability, for restoring trust and for addressing the root cause of something which is complex and challenging.

I have been working with toxic cultures all my career. It is one of the most enjoyable and satisfying parts of my job. I have a passion for working with individuals, teams and organizations in distress and helping them to find a way through it. At the outset, I am often met with disbelief, blame, anger, frustration, fear, stress, anxiety and, in some cases, pure hate (not towards me, I hasten to add!).

Toxic cultures can have a devastating impact on our bodies and our minds

A toxic workplace can be a powerful trigger for deep psychological and emotional pain and trauma. I have seen the impact of this for 30 years, as I have gone about my work as a mediator, helping people to redress the issues that caused, and were caused by, the toxic workplace.

> 'The outcomes of destructive workplaces are devastating, harming work teams and individuals alike. For example, in a multi-study effort, my colleagues and I discovered that abusive climates negatively impact a work group's collective efficacy, which indicates that the team has lost its confidence to adequately perform a given task. Furthermore, abusive work environments destroy important bonds between team members, which further results in reduced performance and citizenship behaviours, meaning that employees are less likely to help and support each other. Toxic workplaces also impair the lives of individuals beyond the work realm. Employees report feeling emotionally drained, experience lower well-being, and even increased conflict at home.' (Priesemuth, 2020)

Figure 6.1 shows how our mind reacts in a toxic culture, producing cortisol and adrenaline, which gives rise to the fight, flight, freeze or fall responses. I explore these reactions and the neuroscience of conflict in *Managing Conflict*.

What does it take to shift from toxic to transformational?

Transforming a toxic culture takes courage and it requires tenacity. It calls for compassion and it necessitates dialogue. In this chapter we will learn that toxic cultures can kill, and they can generate untold distress for anyone working within one. The good news is

FIGURE 6.1 The neuroscience of conflict model

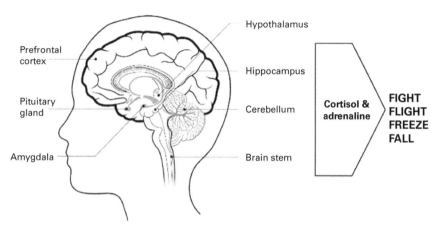

© The TCM Group. Image used with permission

that however bad it has become, it is always possible to transform a toxic culture into a culture which is fair, just, inclusive, sustainable and high performing – a transformational culture.

The process of shifting from toxic to transformational requires three key elements:

1 An acceptance by the whole team, including line managers and senior management, that the culture has turned toxic and that this needs to be resolved.

2 A recognition that it is everyone's responsibility to resolve it and everyone needs to play their part.

3 The courage from every member of the team to choose to engage in a process of open and honest dialogue, constructive engagement and lasting resolution.

When any of these factors is absent, it can be hard to detoxify a team or a department. In fact, even if the issues are somehow resolved, the outcomes can be superficial and short lived. However, when all three of the above factors are present, the team has the potential not only to resolve the underlying issues but to grow, modernize and enhance their motivation and their productivity. The energy that is released when toxic turns transformational can be quite incredible. The best way to describe it is like splitting an atom, also known as nuclear fission. As the toxic culture is resolved, the energy that has been devoted to fighting – to avoiding confrontation, mistrusting colleagues, building and sustaining alliances, finding fault and someone to blame, worrying in bed late at night, fractured relationships with loved ones, and the regrets and the guilt – is released.

Boom! With a blinding flash, all that energy is transferred from toxic to transformational. It is channelled into dialogue, learning, insight and understanding. It provides the fuel that can heal the divisions, repair the harm and release the energy which can propel the team forwards and towards even greater things.

In my experience, no other factor in an organization, barring the most inspirational leader, can generate as much positive energy and have such a unifying effect on a team as a toxic culture can have – at the point that it becomes transformational. Carrying on with the splitting the atom metaphor, converting a culture from toxic to transformational is not rocket science. But it does need someone to have the wisdom, the fortitude and the desire to challenge the status quo. Of course, when people are cowering in their metaphorical trenches, that is easier said than done. In the next section I explain what a toxic culture is and I share with you the story from someone who has survived one.

TRANSFORMATIONAL THINKING

- Have you ever seen or been part of a toxic culture?
- What did it feel like and what impact did it have?
- Was it resolved and if so, how?
- What have you learned as a result?

What is a toxic culture and why do they exist?

So, the scene is set and the challenge has been laid down. Now we need to know what is happening and why. I must warn you, this is not for the faint of heart, and for some, this may be (thankfully) unrecognizable and even grotesque. However, from over 30 years in the fields of conflict resolution and culture change, I know that the toxic culture is very real. A toxic culture can exist across an entire organization, within a department or a division, or within a work or a project team.

There are many types of toxic culture. However, experience has taught me that one, or some, of the following characteristics can be found when the culture becomes toxic.

Rigid

In a toxic culture there is very little desire to change or to adopt innovation or new working practices. 'We have always done it this way' is a generally accepted norm, and people are reluctant to offer new ideas or solutions at the risk of getting shot down or humiliated. If one considers an agile team – a team which is healthy, where different ideas lead to dialogue, where diverse thinking is a source of celebration, and a team that is resilient and able to adapt to circumstances – think of the toxic team as being the polar opposite of that. In a toxic team, even when new ideas and innovative practices are encouraged, generally they run out of steam or someone sabotages them. 'See, I told you it wouldn't work!' is a regular refrain in the toxic culture. Frustration, despair and disappointment swirl around the toxic team, creating a thick and chilling fog.

Communication scarcity

In a toxic culture, the normal systems for communicating become damaged and disrupted. Team meetings and briefings feel frightening and slowly they stop happening, people stop speaking up in meetings, emails become contentious, and the day-to-day office hubbub becomes whispers at the water cooler and stolen conversations after work. Communication during periods of change, crises and uncertainty can be tough enough. In a toxic culture, good quality communication (the kind that is open, transparent and respectful) becomes virtually impossible.

Imagine working in a high-stress environment with no clarity or communication from your managers and leaders, where the only stories you hear are from disgruntled colleagues. We know that nature abhors a vacuum, so we begin to fill in the gaps in communication with assumptions and preconceptions. These then become the narrative of the toxic culture. Rumours become facts and assumptions become truths.

Fear

Cortisol levels are running high in a toxic culture. Unease, apprehension, worry, anxiety are all signs that we are fearful that something bad is going to happen. Our antennae are up, we can feel the tension crackling like electricity. A fist banging a table, a sarcastic comment, a rude remark, a side eye, they all have the effect of switching our amygdala into overdrive. The limbic system is taking over, it is fight or flight. The hormones swirl around our bodies, our stomach flips, we can feel the nausea rising, we become lightheaded. 'Not again! why today? Why me? Why?'

We may try to make ourselves invisible, or we may try to get people to notice us. Either way, we feel increasingly sad, vulnerable and tired. This is not the way to get the best out of a team. This is the fastest way to crush a team. People start to vote with their feet. The ones you want to leave stay, and the ones you want to stay leave. The resources, knowledge and expertise – that have taken so long to build up – are decimated. And for what purpose?

Blame

'It is not me, it is them.' 'They are the ones who are being toxic.' 'It's all their fault.' Blame and toxicity work hand in hand. The divisive nature of a toxic culture lends itself to a divisive mindset and divisive language. And what better form of division than pointing a finger? Blame is the preferred strategy of a great many people when they are caught up in a toxic culture. Blame acts as a blanket of protection that people can wrap around themselves. 'If it is their responsibility, it can't be mine.' Blame is a way of making us feel better about ourselves. It enables us to avoid taking personal responsibility for the choices we may have made and the actions we may have taken. Because after all, blame means 'it is them, not me'.

Our organizations love blame. Blame means fault and our retributive HR and management systems can only work if there is fault. If blame is not apparent or obvious, the organization's GBH procedures soon ensure that blame and fault come to the fore. Some call it 'due process', I call it 'pouring fuel on the fire'. In some cases, particularly where there have been serious allegations made, it is right that the organization conducts an effective investigation in order to ascertain the facts and take the necessary action. However, if you are reading this and you have been there, you will know that it is virtually impossible to do this without making matters much worse. So many investigations are badly set up, poorly administered and undertaken by investigators with very little, if any, training. It is tantamount to throwing a grenade into an already fragmented and divided team. And to what end? It is rare, very rare, for any of these GBH procedures to find fault or deliver a meaningful outcome to a toxic culture. The only real fault is the process itself, but no one seems to investigate that. It walks away, free from any assessment of its own impact. If there was an investigation, the GBH processes would have had to pick up their P45 a long time ago.

In all but the most severe cases (and even then, I would urge caution), the worst possible way to address a toxic culture is to go searching for someone to blame. This is what blame does to a toxic team (to any team):

- People become defensive, and it perpetuates the attack/defend dynamic. Given that attack is often the best form of defence, it is clear where that is likely to lead.

- It fuels divisive, corrosive and, in my view, dangerous language such as 'narcissist', 'psychopath' or 'sociopath'. This language is inflammatory and there is no room for it in a transformational culture. As smart as we might think we are being by using this kind of language, and how credible we think we become by using such impressive-sounding clinical terms, the only real outcome is further toxicity. The only people who should use these terms are trained and qualified experts. The rest of us should refrain from doing so.

- It causes honest people to become dishonest, to cover their backs and their tracks. This adds to the stress, the guilt, the trauma and the anxiety of a toxic culture. People understand that being found 'to blame' for a toxic culture can destroy their career, so they will do everything they can to avoid that happening. Who wouldn't? What a waste of time and energy, when an acceptance of responsibility, an expression of remorse, an apology and an agreement to behave differently could so much more easily resolve the issues.

- People are forced to take sides. The fissures and the fractures that appear when blame is being sought can break a team in two (see below).

- While giving the appearance of holding people to account (which does not happen often – see Chapter 3), blame rarely identifies the root cause of an issue. Going in search of blame and fault does not tell us why the problem occurred in the first place, nor what is required to prevent the issue reoccurring. Therefore, the process of seeking someone to blame inhibits the ability to learn and to gather insight which can precipitate healing and growth.

Alliances

In a toxic culture there is safety in numbers so we often seek out others who we hope will agree with us or take our side. We form small cliques and we forge coalitions. We are told that the collective voice is so much stronger than the voice of the individual and, in truth, it does make us feel a little safer. However, we do not take account of the fact that we are not homogeneous, we do not agree on everything. Someone in the group wants to launch an attack on the other side. I'm hesitant. 'It is a do or die situation, I am told.' 'You are either with us or you are against us.' The threat is not well veiled.

These alliances and coalitions generate fissures and fractures in the team. The team is now splitting and fragmenting, and the problem will become much harder to resolve. It will require well-developed negotiation skills, ingenuity and a high level of diplomatic acumen to bring it back from the precipice of doom. Where are these skills when you need them?

Autocratic

The one-day communication skills training that the manager attended in 2006 has long since been forgotten. They are making it up as they go along. They are using their wits, their instincts and whatever management strategies they were able to glean from the last season of *The Apprentice*. Of course, in the swirling fog of despair and the cortisol-enriched workplace, wits and instincts will not get them very far. 'People just won't listen to me. They don't even respect me.' This is an impossible situation. It is time to turn on the only strategy that they know works, it is time to 'take back control'. The issue here is that the manager has power and feels undermined. They are going to assert their power and authority to re-establish their sense of status. This is going to go badly.

> 'When the person of little status has real power over you, it can lead to some very dark places and go far beyond rudeness.' (Wallace, 2017)

Bluster, frustration and micromanagement will not work, but they do not know that yet. Pointing fingers, getting cross or dividing and conquering – these strategies are going to fail also. They are going to come back as allegations of bullying, harassment and discrimination; they are going to damage careers and real people are going to get really hurt. Sickness levels are increasing. The team is running hot. The culture is turning toxic. The answer? Shout louder. Micromanage even more. Start firing people. No, get HR in, get them to start firing people. Okay, get a lawyer in, get them to start firing people. 'Why can't we just fire someone?' 'Why is management so hard?' And breathe. 'I am stuck. I cannot cope. I do not know what to do. Can someone please help?' At last, progress.

Shining a light on the toxic culture

By shining a light on the issue, and by offering some alternatives, we can improve the working lives of hundreds if not thousands of people. People like Jonathan, whom I had the privilege to interview for my book. Jonathan had experienced working in a toxic culture for several years; like so many, he left before the potential for a transformation.

With over 25 years' experience in a large public sector organization, Jonathan had progressed through the ranks and now held a senior management position. He found himself leading a team that was progressing a new area of work, with strong government interest and pressure to deliver tangible outcomes.

Jonathan explains what happened next. 'The team had already established an in-crowd, which I was not part of; it was clear that I was not welcome. My relationship with my manager deteriorated quickly and I experienced ongoing bullying and gaslighting. After they were promoted, the behaviour continued with my new manager who had been promoted from the "in-crowd". This led me to experience extreme trauma, stress and anxiety, which I am still recovering from to this day. When I raised it with a senior manager (as stipulated in our policy), they failed to take action to protect me, or to address the bullying behaviour or the prevailing toxic culture. I encountered DARVO (Deny Attack Reverse Victim Offender), a methodology I was to learn was a common experience of targets complaining of workplace bullying. It could have been so different. I was broken and I wanted to be heard with empathy and be reassured that my concerns would be examined objectively.'

I asked Jonathan to describe what he learned from his experience. 'My experience showed me that a toxic culture occurs where there is a failure in leadership and often an abuse of power and authority. This abuse of power often leads to psychological assault in the workplace. Those in charge often exploit or worsen the situation by partaking in, enabling or ignoring abusive behaviours. In a toxic culture, transparency is lacking, confused policy exists and guidelines enable the toxic practices. Toxic culture is often evidenced by an atmosphere of collusion, secrecy, and an environment where there is fear to speak up and challenge. This culture is reinforced by bystanders and lack of challenge, which perpetuates to become the accepted normality.'

Jonathan described the impact a transformational culture could have for people in a similar situation. His words are a powerful call to action for every leader, manager and HR professional. 'I see a transformational culture as a place where all employees feel included, supported, listened to and safe; there is respect for diversity and fairness. Its leaders are emotionally intelligent, inspiring, empowering, encouraging, supportive, facilitators and willing to listen while respecting the safety and wellbeing of all. A place where everyone is valued as an essential element of a team that is inclusive and where hierarchy does not impede people's ability to question and challenge ideas, processes and behaviours. In a transformational culture, the leadership not only sets a positive culture but goes on to maintain it through living it and reinforcing it through their own behaviours. Employees are trusted, encouraged and empowered rather than micromanaged. A workplace community exists where all feel membership of and engaged in a team, where support from all colleagues exists and a fear of others' behaviour does not exist.'

Jonathan's story reflects the story of many hundreds, indeed thousands, of hard-working and loyal employees across our lands. The next section considers how it has come to this. That is followed by practical tips and hints to help turn a toxic culture into a transformational culture.

How did it get to this?

I work with extraordinarily smart and fair-minded HR professionals, managers, lawyers, union representatives and leaders who resolve hugely complicated business challenges every day. These are experts in their fields. Experts who organize and run businesses which are so interconnected and so complex it makes my head spin. I am in admiration of them. However, and it pains me to say this, I am still desperately searching for an answer to the following questions when I encounter a toxic culture in their organization:

- Why are they so blindsided by the negative impact that their complex rules and divisive procedures are creating? With their intrinsic need to blame and find fault, these rules and procedures promote the worst kinds of bad behaviour and they fan the flames of disharmony.

- Why can they not see that the propensity to blame others, to promote confrontation and to seek retribution when things go wrong creates a climate of fear, defensiveness, stress and anxiety? It perpetuates toxicity.

- Why do they wait for a situation to erupt into a violent conflagration before meaningful action is taken?

- Why do they not recognize, after all this time, that failing to invest in their managers and leaders – building their confidence, competence and courage to manage their people effectively – is allowing relatively low-level issues to escalate into catastrophic crises and toxic cultures?

- Why do they avoid the most powerful remedy of all, ie listening to their people to understand what is happening and what needs to change?

- Why can they not see that rewarding the wrong behaviours, turning a blind eye to 'high achievers' who harm others, and accepting unfairness and inequity in their recruitment processes, talent management programmes, bonus schemes and rewards programmes will, in turn, create a culture which is divided, frustrated and toxic?

- Why can they not see that putting out slick messages about inclusion and engagement or promoting zero-tolerance policies for this and for that, then not acting to address the behaviours which are at odds with those statements, makes those statements at best rhetorical and at worst deeply hypocritical? They seed mistrust and frustration which, over time, will turn toxic. It is for that reason that I have a zero-tolerance policy for these kinds of zero-tolerance policies.

- When the human and the financial costs are so obvious and so acute, why do they fail to measure the true cost of a toxic culture, and why do they fail to treat toxic culture and conflict as an organizational risk and a strategic priority? As I have said elsewhere, I have seen better strategies for ordering paperclips than I have for managing conflict at work.

Is there a cure for a toxic culture and if so, what is it?

There are no easy cures for a toxic culture and of course, prevention is worth a pound of cure. If organizations focused on developing a transformational culture, ie a culture which is fair, just, inclusive, sustainable and high performing, the likelihood of a toxic culture developing would be dramatically reduced. If a toxic culture emerges in a team or a department, it will be easier to spot and simpler to resolve.

When a toxic culture becomes transformational:

- rigid transforms to agile;
- communication scarcity becomes candid, open and honest dialogue;
- fear transforms to psychological safety;
- blame transforms to accountability;
- alliances transform to collaboration;
- autocratic transforms to empowering.

The importance of psychological safety

Nicki Eyre is an anti-bullying advocate and founder of Conduct Change, an organization which offers advocacy, campaigning, education and awareness raising about workplace bullying. Having experienced bullying in a previous organization, Nicki knows first hand the impact of a toxic relationship. Since that terrible time, she has dedicated her career to raising awareness of the impact of bullying as well as offering practical and pragmatic solutions to organizations that want to improve the way they handle bullying and toxic behaviour. Nicki is an advocate of building a workplace which is psychologically safe. In a discussion with me while I was undertaking research for this book, Nicki explained how the way in which workplace bullying complaints are currently handled directly undermines the concept of psychological safety.

When people are brave enough to speak up against bullying behaviours and place their trust in the policies and procedures, in HR and the leadership, they expect to be heard, acknowledged and supported.

In reality, most bullying complaints are not upheld and the complainant usually ends up leaving – or being forced out of – their job. The costs to the individual – psychological, physical, emotional, behavioural, financial – are high, to the extent that they often cause trauma and leave that person unable to work, sometimes for life.

Witnesses and bystanders to these events see that speaking up puts them at risk. People who have engaged in an act of vulnerability by challenging what they see as bullying behaviours have been punished. That extends into other areas – employees no longer feel safe to speak up about anything: safety, ethics, compliance or behavioural issues. They don't feel safe to challenge the status quo, to own up to mistakes, to ask for feedback and help. Productivity drops as discretionary effort is withdrawn.

Imagine if that person had been made to feel safe instead. Imagine if both parties had been acknowledged and supported to change their behaviours and relationship. Imagine if the leaders of the organization never hid behind title, position or authority; never allowed blame and personal attacks but instead modelled behaviours of inclusion and acceptance, gratitude and appreciation.

Everyone plays a role in creating psychological safety through their own behaviours and words, but leaders and managers in particular must model value-driven behaviour. Observation is where learning starts and how behaviours become entrenched in an organization. As a leader, that might mean having to hold up a mirror to your own behaviour first, improve your own behaviours and develop your own emotional intelligence.

Psychological safety is not just about inclusion and harmony, a moral position of 'doing things right', it's also an environment that allows you to share ideas and challenge constructs without fear of humiliation or reprisal. It's about recognizing that conflicting ideas and views are drivers of creativity and innovation. It's about being able to disagree about a subject without making it personal. It's about bringing curiosity to every situation, exploring mistakes and continually learning.

Most importantly, it's not an initiative. There must be relentless behavioural change, taking workers beyond engagement to being the driving force of the organization – together.

Three simple steps to make toxic transformational

If you find yourself trying to address a toxic culture, I have provided a three-point plan to help address it constructively and efficiently:

1 Treat the process of addressing a toxic culture just like any other complex project. It requires planning, resourcing, clear terms of reference and agreed objectives. The best approaches that I have seen for tackling a toxic culture or a toxic team climate have involved multiple stakeholders (HR, managers, unions, employee reps, etc) working collaboratively to design the process for detoxifying the team and ensuring that the project is delivered well. Always start with the end in mind – be clear about what your objectives are. The project team is also responsible for sustaining the gains made and ensuring that the team develops resilience in the face of ongoing stresses both from within and from without.

2 The project team set up in stage 1, above, will appoint a facilitator(s) who may be internal or external to the organization. The vital factors are that the facilitator is objective and impartial, they are skilled at handling inter- and intra-group conflicts, and they understand how to work with strong emotions and rigid positions.

3 Be transformational. This means applying the restorative principles to achieve a successful resolution. Restorative justice processes such as mediation are highly effective remedies for a toxic culture and should be used as early as possible:

   a. The process will be managed by a trained and objective facilitator.

   b. The process will be fair to all.

   c. The process will be psychologically safe.

   d. Mutual respect and civility are prerequisites.

   e. All parties need to be open and honest.

   f. There cannot be retaliation for anything that is said in the process.

   g. The process is future focused and solution oriented.

My toxic culture three-step plan delivers psychological safety, which is critical to resolving a toxic culture. As renowned author and Novartis Professor of Leadership at Harvard Business School, Amy Edmondson, explains, 'Whenever you are trying to get people on the same page, with common goals and a shared appreciation for what they're up against, you're setting the stage for psychological safety' (Edmondson, 2019).

Conclusion and calls to action

The toxic culture is diametrically opposed to a transformational culture. Prior to and through Covid-19, movements such as Black Lives Matter, #MeToo and others have shone a light on toxic behaviours and toxic cultures. This is a zeitgeist moment; the tectonic plates of our society and our organizations are shifting. This is a moment of great societal change. Individuals and communities, who have for so long been disempowered and disenfranchised, are standing up, as one, to the toxic behaviours and toxic cultures which have shackled them for so long and in so many cases have destroyed lives.

These movements have shown that the bright light of transparency can have a powerful disinfecting impact. Over the past few years, behaviours and attitudes which were once acceptable and, in some cases, rewarded are now being challenged publicly and in an organized way. Bad behaviours are no longer so easily hidden and the impact is no longer so easily brushed under the carpet.

The prevailing norms of extensive inaction, or expensive overreaction, are being challenged. The dial is turning towards action. Action speaks so much louder than words. Action is so much more powerful when it is led from the top and in an inclusive and joined-up way:

- action to call out bad behaviours and to render them unacceptable;
- action to create systems of accountability which build trust, which protect relationships and which deliver transformational justice;
- action to resolve our differences and disagreements in a constructive and supported way;

- action to build cultures where our dignity is preserved, our diversity is celebrated and where dialogue has primacy.

The best action that an organization can take to resolve a toxic culture is through a restorative process such as mediation. Mediation delivers on all the above, in an extraordinary and effective way. It is the most powerful and the most successful remedy for a team in distress. Mediation is safe, empowering, robust, challenging and highly effective. Mediation gives dialogue primacy. It engenders a solution-focused and safe space to resolve issues and for teams to agree a new way of working. Mediation works!

TRANSFORMATIONAL THINKING

- Have you got a toxic culture or a toxic team climate in your organization?
- If so, what impact is it having?
- How will you resolve the toxic culture/climate, having read this chapter?
- Has this chapter given you any ideas about how to prevent a toxic culture from happening?

References

Edmondson, C (2019) *The Fearless Organization: Creating psychological safety in the workplace for learning, innovation, and growth*, Wiley, New Jersey

Liddle, D (2017) *Managing Conflict: A practical guide to resolution in the workplace*, Kogan Page, London

Priesemuth, M (2020) Time's up for toxic workplaces, *Harvard Business Review*, https://hbr.org/2020/06/times-up-for-toxic-workplaces (archived at https://perma.cc/XM85-FTJM)

Wallace, D (2017) *F*** You Very Much. The surprising truth about why people are so rude*, Penguin Books, London

07

Aligning people, purpose, values and behaviour

TRANSFORMATIONAL LEARNING

Within this chapter, you will discover answers to the following questions:

- How can values act as a golden thread in our organizations?
- How can organizations calibrate culture and climate?
- What is the Culture Flow System™ and how does it work?
- What happens when purpose, values and behaviours are not aligned?
- Why are values the alchemy for the 21st century?
- How can HR put values, people and culture first?
- Does focus on people and culture present a renaissance opportunity for HR?

What have I observed, heard and learned?

I have worked as organizational development (OD) and human resources consultant, a trainer and a mediator with thousands of amazing organizations, spanning every sector imaginable. In my work, I have observed, I have listened and I have learned. It has been a privilege (but it has not always been easy).

I have observed that the most inspirational leaders, the most creative teams and the highest-performing employees have all had something in common. They have all felt a deep alignment to the purpose of their organization. They share a common purpose which drives their passion and their pride. They believe that the values of their organization provide a route map to success, and they feel valued and appreciated by their colleagues and customers. I have observed that in the most successful organizations, leaders, managers and employees align their behaviours to the organization's values in a way which delivers personal and collective accountability. This builds trust and mutual respect, thus reducing the need for formal and complex rules and policies, which in turn means less red tape, greater freedom, increased autonomy and empowerment. Within these organizations, I have observed that managers and leaders understand that they are role models – they display great self-awareness, and they recognize that their actions, interactions and reactions (behaviours) contribute directly to the climate and culture of their organization.

I have listened to people at times of conflict, crisis and uncertainty. They have told me that they feel lost, vulnerable, disengaged and unhappy because their working lives lack meaning, their relationships have broken down, and trust and mutual respect have all but evaporated. They have told me, sometimes between sobs, that they have no clear sense of purpose, and the values of their organization are a distant and opaque concept with little meaning to their real lives. The only values that they see being lived are 'keep your head down', 'get on with your job' and 'don't rock the boat'. They have told me that they feel undervalued and underappreciated, and they see misalignment between the behaviour of their leaders and managers and the organization's stated principles. They have used terms such as 'hypocrisy', 'out of touch' and 'untrustworthy'. I have heard them say they feel confused and disconnected from the culture of their organization and they feel overwhelmed by the toxic climate in their teams. I have heard them complain about complex and adversarial procedures which pit people against one another. The impact of all this, they have told me, is that they are less engaged, they feel disempowered and are less likely to perform to the highest standards. Some have told me that their mental and physical health is damaged, they are deeply unhappy and they have deeply unpleasant thoughts.

I have learned that stories and narrative are the key drivers of an organization's purpose and values, not buzz words stuck on a lobby wall. I have learned that it is the organizations with a clear, shared sense of purpose which are the ones that benefit from the passion and the pride that fuel growth. I have learned that organizations whose values are woven, like a brilliant golden thread, through the workplace are the ones which deliver the best employee experience and, as a direct consequence, the best customer experience. I have learned that when the behaviours of leaders, managers and employees are aligned to the values, it quickly builds trust, promotes mutual respect, and drives inclusion, collaboration, innovation, creativity and enthusiasm. I have learned that rigid policies and procedures do nothing to create or sustain a values-based and people-centred organization.

Generating alignment between culture and climate – the Culture Flow System

As I explained in Chapter 1, the culture of the organization is an amalgam of numerous micro-cultures (climates). Creating flow in an organization is a powerful way of connecting our organizational culture with the climate within a team, a department or a division. However, as seen later in this chapter and elsewhere in the book, creating a positive convergence between culture and climate can be challenging, particularly in large organizations or those made up of disparate and disconnected units or divisions.

In organizational culture terms, I refer to this as convergent culture flow (aligned and harmonious). Conversely, in organizations where there is dissonance between the purpose, the values, the strategy, the procedures, the behaviours, the mindset and the outcomes, I refer to this as divergent culture flow (disconnected and discordant).

'Cultural flow' is a term I have devised in my work as a transformational culture architect. It can be defined as a state where the purpose of the organization is aligned to a set of clearly defined values which, like a golden thread, are woven through the entire organization, as set out below:

- The purpose and values are fully integrated into the organization's strategy and into the strategic narrative of the organization.
- They are enacted through the behaviours (actions, interactions, reactions) of the organization's CEO, executives and senior leaders.
- The values and purpose form the foundation of the organization's policies, processes, and procedures. These procedures, which shift from retributive to transformational, reflect the needs, goals, aspirations and beliefs of the wider workforce. In so doing, they promulgate a mindset across the workforce which links directly back to the organization's purpose and values.
- This mindset defines the character of our teams (climate) and it defines the behaviours (actions, interactions, reactions) of managers and employees. The climate of the team and the outcomes achieved by the team are directly aligned to the strategic objectives, the purpose and the needs of the organization.

This process of creating flow also travels back up the organization via systems of feedback, dialogue, data analytics and positive engagement. Flow is non-linear; however, it can forge a useful linear connection between culture and climate. This linearity can act as a beneficial tool which helps leaders and managers to codify and evaluate the culture of their organizations and the climate of their teams. It can also be used to ensure that the organization's purpose reflects the outcomes of the teams, and vice versa. It allows for modifications to be made to any of the seven areas of the Culture Flow System (see Figure 7.1) and for their impact to be carefully measured and evaluated.

In a healthy organization, there is flow between culture and climate – the two feed into and they feed off each other. In these organizations, culture and climate work together in harmony – in equilibrium. This equilibrium yields what I refer to as the 7Cs of the

FIGURE 7.1   The Culture Flow System

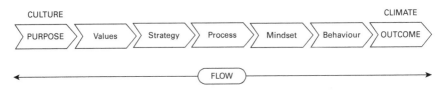

transformational culture: courage, connection, collaboration, common purpose, communication, compassion and curiosity (see Chapter 4 for more details of the 7Cs). In addition, convergence of culture and climate drives motivation and engagement.

I believe passionately that creating cultural flow could be one of the most exciting tasks for a new-style Human Resources function. In the next chapter and then throughout this book, I explain why I believe it is time for HR to transform itself into a modern and outwards-looking people and culture function. I will explain why I believe that HR sits at a crossroads, and why a rethink of the role of HR could mark one of the most exciting periods in its history – I would go as far as to say that a focus on people and culture could mark a renaissance for the Human Resources profession and everyone involved in or with HR.

TRANSFORMATIONAL THINKING

Using the Culture Flow System as a reference, where is your organization experiencing:

- convergent culture flow

- divergent culture flow?

What steps will you take to resolve the issues of divergence?

When values are not aligned – tragedy strikes

These lessons all play out in the following case study. By way of context, in 2016 a registered nurse, Amin Abdullah, who worked at Imperial College Healthcare NHS Trust, took his life in the most tragic circumstances. He had been suspended by the Trust and suffered from mental health issues because of ongoing delays in the way that the disciplinary case was handled. The case shook the NHS. It resulted in a major review of the way that the NHS manages disciplinary cases, with new guidance provided for all Trust chairs and CEOs in May 2019 (Harding, 2019). The following case study explains how the Trust has recovered and illustrates how the Trust's values are now central to how it will handle disciplinary issues in the future.

CASE STUDY

How a focus on people and values has helped a major NHS Trust to recover following the tragic death of an employee

CASE STUDY PREPARED FOR TRANSFORMATIONAL CULTURE *BY FIONA PERCIVAL, DIVISIONAL DIRECTOR, IMPERIAL COLLEGE HEALTHCARE NHS TRUST*

Following his dismissal from the Trust in December 2015, nurse Amin Abdullah tragically took his life in February 2016. We commissioned an independent consultancy, Verita, to carry out an investigation, the findings of which were accepted in full by us. Inevitably, as a large employer, there are times when we need to follow formal procedures, but in all circumstances it is essential that we treat people with dignity and kindness in line with our values. We fell short of that commitment in Amin's case. Opportunities to resolve the issues informally were missed. We are enormously grateful for the commitment and continuing input from Amin's partner, Terry Skitmore, who provided robust but constructive challenge in the subsequent review of the Trust's disciplinary policy and more generally on how we have responded in the wake of Amin's tragic death.

We are also committed to combatting any bias or discrimination in our employment and management practices, but like many NHS Trusts have been deeply concerned by the disproportionate number of BAME employees who have been subject to disciplinary procedures in the past. This was something we needed to address. Allegations of misconduct in the Trust are approached differently now. We immediately implemented a range of measures to ensure cases are thoroughly assessed before any investigation or formal procedures are initiated, and expanded our pastoral support for employees. We should always be asking ourselves whether our actions are proportionate and justifiable and whether managing situations informally achieves a more productive outcome.

Following the introduction of these measures we have reduced formal disciplinary investigations and hearings by a third. We have also reduced the likelihood of staff from a BAME background being subject to a disciplinary hearing to the same level as that of their white colleagues. We know we cannot be complacent. We need to continually reflect and challenge ourselves to ensure everyone is treated fairly, and build a culture of openness and transparency to ensure we are doing the right thing by our people. As part of that, we have invested in resources to develop a holistic, people-focused resolution framework at the Trust, building on existing wellbeing and support interventions, ensuring that we manage all conflict and issues in the workplace in a way that is consistent with our values – kind, collaborative, expert and aspirational. This work is ongoing at the time of writing; we hope to implement the framework during 2021–2022.

Our values are at the heart of everything that we do. In late 2018 we launched the 'Leading change through vision, values and behaviour' programme. There is persuasive evidence that a simple, shared and compelling vision – in our case, 'better health, for life' – plus a commitment to meaningful values and behaviours will help our organization be a great place to work and enable us to do our best for our patients and local communities.

More than 2,000 staff took part in activities designed to explore themes around our vision, values and behaviours; their views and insights fed into work to develop our organizational strategy and to define our priorities. This feedback also helped co-design a 'behaviours framework', setting out clear examples of the behaviours that demonstrate when we are living our values and those that show when we are not. We then sought wider feedback anonymously from colleagues about the draft framework and what they thought were the priorities for us to address. This feedback reassured us that the behavioural framework was the right one for us and helped us to identify key areas for action going forward. We also enlisted around 150 'values ambassadors' across the Trust, championing the values and behaviours and supporting the rollout of the values programme.

Our CEO, Tim Orchard, has been instrumental in role modelling and personally driving the values and cultural change, as has Kevin Croft, our Director of People and Organizational Development. Our executive meetings always end now with someone in the group being asked to feed back to their colleagues about the behaviours and values demonstrated. We recognize that real change only happens when we are all willing and able to hold that mirror up to ourselves, and that has to start at the very top.

It also helps that we have constructive and collaborative relationships with our trade union and staff-side partners and they are wholly supportive of the cultural change, as are our staff network leads. These groups are key stakeholders in the work that we are doing to continue to improve how we resolve conflict at the Trust.

Our values were shaped and decided by our people and the response to the values has been overwhelmingly positive; we strive to ensure that the values underpin everything we do. But we recognize that changing an organization's culture is one of the most complex leadership challenges to tackle and we are at the start of the journey at Imperial College Healthcare Trust.

We have a number of quantitative and qualitative measures in place to help us to evaluate how we are progressing – our annual staff survey is a good way to monitor employee engagement and experiences of working at the Trust, and to identify potential hotspots where we may need to work harder to embed cultural change. We closely monitor the themes and issues being raised in informal complaints and grievances, and by our Freedom to Speak Up Guardians, trade union colleagues and in our mediation referrals.

We have learned a great number of lessons as a result of this tragic case and we are confident they could and should apply to all employers, not just in the NHS but across all sectors:

- Be open and honest about what the problems are and where we have fallen short in tackling these.

- Avoid the narrative of badging individuals as 'difficult' employees.

- Recognize the potential influence of bias – unconscious and conscious – in all of us.

- Recognize that Human Resources (or People & OD, as we are at Imperial) has a crucial role in driving and embedding cultural change – and the importance of investing in the right people at the right time to do so.

For us right now, reset and recovery is all about supporting the health and wellbeing of our people as we shift our focus from Covid-19 to the future. It's an opportunity to think about our team dynamics and how we can re-establish our connections and rapport. Many of our people will have been working for months outside of the teams they are used to; others may be returning from a prolonged period of absence or shielding.

As teams reform and colleagues come back together, we are encouraging our people to reflect on how they behave towards each other. We know that it's not unusual to experience feelings of anger or irritability both during and following a crisis situation, and we need to work together to ensure we treat each other with the same kindness and empathy that we reserve for our patients, and not allow incivility to creep in.

Longer term, we are committed to a more people-centred model of resolving employee relations matters, taking a proactive and preventative approach and supporting people with having courageous conversations to nip conflict and other issues in the bud. We will do this by developing the capability, confidence and compassion of our managers and providing supportive interventions that are accessible to all. We are confident that this will lead to better relationships, a further reduction in formal cases and a kinder and truly inclusive workforce.

Values – organizational alchemy for the 21st century

When my clients embrace their values, it is like alchemy, alchemy being the medieval forerunner of chemistry, concerned with attempts to convert base metals into gold. Their values can convert the base metals of their organizations into gold. The base metals are:

- corporate and people strategies;
- the employee handbook;
- WEI strategies and activities;
- agreed behavioural frameworks;
- recruitment and induction processes;
- customer experience and customer value proposition (CVP);
- employee experience and employee value proposition (EVP);
- environmental, social and governance strategy (ESG) and activities;
- branding, PR and reputation management systems;
- framework for resolving concerns, complaints and conflict at work;
- management and leadership competency framework;
- performance management, reward and benefits systems;

- systems for resolving collective disputes and promoting good employee and industrial relations.

To maximise their potential impact, each of the above documents, processes or systems (the base metals) should refer explicitly to your agreed organizational values. They should also include a summary of how the values impact on that area of the business and what steps your leaders and managers will take to deliver them. For instance, in your ESG strategy, by explaining your core values you can also explain how you are ensuring that the sustainability principles are being applied across your workplace and how they are being embedded into your organizational culture and agreed behaviours. In so doing, your values bring the commitment to life and give it meaning.

Without doubt, each of these base metals can work without values being integrated into them. However, when the base metal is mixed with values, they become the elixir that can move an organization, at pace, from good to great.

TRANSFORMATIONAL THINKING

- What are your organization's core values?

- Are they written or unwritten?

- How do your values manifest themselves through your organization?

- Do you measure the return on your values (ROV) and if so, what impact do your values have?

Values are the greatest of all the potential competitive advantages

> 'All companies need a values culture in order to attract the best people and compete effectively.' (Rhoades, 2011)

Values provide the structure which acts as a bedrock to our organizations. However, they cannot be superficial PR statements or inconsequential jargon which has no relevance to people's everyday working real lives. Those are not values – those are words stuck on a lobby wall. It is vital that we do not get the two mixed up.

The successful organizations understand that their values are a key part of their brand and their reputation; they can create powerful connections between employees and between an organization and its stakeholders and its investors – values such as creating an inclusive workplace, treating people with respect, being fair and just in the way that we solve problems, celebrating our diversity, being flexible enough to allow everyone to participate, having the courage to challenge, working together to unleash our inner and our collective brilliance, and acting in a way which is sustainable and which reduces our impact on the planet.

For the avoidance of doubt, I am not suggesting that values should not be stuck on a lobby wall – it suggests that the organization is striving to be values based. What I am suggesting is that if they are going to be the golden thread in our organizations, the lobby wall cannot be the only place that we see them. Adding values to email signatures, onto mugs, into the frosting in meeting room windows and onto posters in toilets does not count either, I am afraid.

Values, at their best, are inclusive, they are empowering, and they evoke a sense of common purpose across even the most disparate business. They generate a sense of belonging and, most significantly of all, they provide a powerful system by which we can hold ourselves, and others, to account. They are the basis for us to build trust, mutual respect and confidence. In that regard, organizational values form the basis of the social and the psychological contracts. These contracts define the character of our organizations and they impact the people who work within them, the suppliers who trade with them and the customers who buy from them. Having a clearly defined and widely owned set of values is one of the most important elements of a transformational culture. Values-driven cultures are products of a values-management process and/or the result of inspired leadership, they are the highest-performing culture (Barrett, 2006).

These are the values which underpin a transformational culture. Values which deliver the alchemy essential for turning base metals into gold. The outcomes of the alchemy are measured in terms of fair, equitable and inclusive workplaces, delivering just and restorative outcomes to workplace concerns, underpinning a commitment to sustainability and driving higher performance.

TRANSFORMATIONAL THINKING

If you were able to design your organization culture from scratch and you were given two options, which would you pick?

Option 1: Let my organizational culture develop organically.

Option 2: Use a set of clearly defined and agreed values to help shape my organizational culture.

Which option did you pick and why?

Aligning values with behaviours

In a great many of the organizations with which I work, there are often vague and opaque statements about which behaviours are acceptable and which ones will not be tolerated. In most cases, these are presented as a list of behaviours in a disciplinary procedure which would constitute gross misconduct, thereby warranting dismissal from the organization.

My experience has led me to believe that this lack of clarity about desirable and undesirable behaviour is one of the most significant causes of toxicity, entropy, distress and general dysfunction in our teams. This is exacerbated by a lack of support for line managers and a failure to provide them with the tools that they need to hold themselves to account, to hold their people to account, to recognize and reward the right behaviours, and to modify the undesirable behaviours with confidence and courage. In a transformational culture, managers use processes such as nudge theory, emotional intelligence, appreciative inquiry, principled negotiation and positive psychology to promote the desirable behaviours and to ensure that undesirable behaviours are challenged and modified.

As a result of the lack of clarity and consistency, managers must engage in guesswork (often at a time of heightened emotions and tension). To mitigate the impact of all this guesswork, HR creates more and more complex rules and processes to plug the gaps created by the lack of clarity and consistency. It does this rather than trying to figure out the root cause of the lack of clarity, and consistency and resolving the problem at source.

Interestingly, the defence I often hear in favour of these rules and processes is that they create clarity and they offer consistency. They do not. They paper over the cracks created by a systemic lack of consistency and clarity. If HR and leaders explained to employees and managers exactly what the expected behaviours are, they would not have to engage in guesswork, which in turn would create consistency and clarity, thus reducing the need for more and more policies, processes and procedures. Without a baseline understanding of the desirable and undesirable behaviours, all the rules and processes do is promote confusion and distress, and the vicious cycle continues.

For the past few years, I have been helping organizations such as the BRC (see case study below) to develop frameworks which align values and behaviours. These values and behaviours frameworks are designed in such a way that they explain clearly which behaviours are desirable and which are undesirable. These behaviours are directly aligned to the organization's values. This is a core element of achieving cultural flow convergence (see page 139).

The values and behaviour framework looks something like the one in Figure 7.2.

FIGURE 7.2   The values and behaviour framework

Value 1		Value 2		Value 3	
Desirable	Undesirable	Desirable	Undesirable	Desirable	Undesirable
Behaviour	Behaviour	Behaviour	Behaviour	Behaviour	Behaviour

Once the values and behaviours framework has been developed and agreed, management competencies can be shaped. Developing a set of values based competencies will ensure that managers are confident and competent to promote and reward desirable behaviours and they have the courage and the competence to transform undesirable behaviours. Managers should receive training and be equipped with the skills and the strategies to hold themselves and their people to account and to 'nudge' their people from undesirable to desirable behaviours.

Some practical steps to integrate values and behaviours

Organizations integrate their values and behaviours framework into their organizations through the following means:

- on their websites and through other promotional content;
- in recruitment materials and during recruitment processes;
- in the employee handbook and as a key feature of the EVP;
- through leadership and management competencies and associated leadership and management development programmes;
- to support coaching and mentoring programmes;
- as a baseline for performance reviews and bonus and reward schemes;
- to assist with the management of change;
- as a diagnostic tool for evaluating conflicts within and between teams;
- as a basis for managing concerns (performance), conduct (discipline), complaints (grievances) and conflicts at work;
- as a mechanism to secure cultural alignment during or following a merger or an acquisition (M&A).

In this way, the values and behaviours framework becomes a 'living and breathing' part of the modern organization. It can also be valuable for aligning purpose, strategy, behaviours and the climate in teams, as the British Retail Consortium (BRC) found out recently.

CASE STUDY
How the BRC aligns its values with its corporate strategy, its purpose and its agreed behaviours

I have worked with the British Retail Consortium for several years and I have been impressed with the way in which the organization has put its values and its people first. I was privileged enough to have the opportunity to interview their HR Director, Carolyn Hawley, for *Transformational Culture*.

David Liddle: Why did the BRC decide to give focus to its values/what was the catalyst?

Carolyn Hawley: One of the catalysts was a change in our organization when we sold part of the business. Prior to this we had a different set of values which straddled two different types of business. We were prompted to think about what was right for the BRC – our identity and purpose as well as our employees and members. We asked all of our employees for their ideas, and this formed part of an Away Day Workshop a few years ago. The outcome was a couple of iterations of our values, culminating with the ones we have today: Welcoming, Collaborative, Passionate, Visionary, Trusted.

DL: How did you integrate your values into the BRC and what difference has it made?

CH: Because it was a 'bottom-up' approach, it was easier to integrate our values as it wasn't something which was imposed. It is still a work in progress, but we have taken some positive steps. We realized that we needed to bring our values to life with examples of behaviours, so we held several workshops (together with TCM) to explore what our values really meant in practice to our employees – positive behavioural indicators and contra-behaviour indicators. This enabled us to give some real examples around expectations.

DL: Can you say a few words about how the BRC values were integrated into your corporate strategy and any benefits that this delivered?

CH: So, we have an overarching visual of our BRC mission and current three-year strategy, with member value at the heart and then our five BRC values come next in the centre of everything we do (see Figure 7.2). We will be renewing our three-year strategy from July 2021 and our BRC values will still form a core part of what we do and how we work, both internally with each other and externally with our members.

DL: The alignment of values with behaviours set an interesting baseline for building accountability and for reinforcing the right behaviours across the BRC. Could you explain how this works and the benefits?

CH: We are still on a journey, for sure. However, we have integrated our BRC values beyond our strategy into various other areas of our business. What is noticeable is that while our BRC values may not be referred to constantly in our dialogue with each other, they act as an unwritten rule which people have an awareness of. Luckily, we have not needed to refer to negative behavioural indicators very often, and we look for ways to celebrate the right behaviours. We have 'shout-outs' in our weekly internal newsletter of positive things our colleagues have done, and we also hold our Values Awards twice yearly, where nominations can be put forward by anyone at the BRC, and together with the shout-outs we recognize our colleagues in each of our values' categories. Everyone then has a chance to vote for their winner. Winners are given a sum of money to contribute to a charity of their choice. Usually this is combined with a company 'Away Day' but due to lockdown this was held virtually in 2020 and employees received a care package to say thank you and to recognize hard work.

DL: Are there any other areas that the BRC values have been integrated into?

CH: Our BRC values form part of job descriptions, and performance reviews are based not only on 'what' is achieved but also on 'how', which is where the values come in. We ask employees to think about their strengths and areas where they could focus more on a particular BRC value from a developmental and stretch perspective. There is lots more we could do here. We are looking at how we can improve employee recognition, particularly with a digital focus now that we are not physically seeing each other so much, and we will incorporate our values into this.

DL: What has been the benefit of giving your values focus at the BRC?

CH: We are still learning; however, by giving more focus to our values, we have been able to recognize our people within this framework and been more able to be specific about the great work that our people are doing, while underpinning what is important to the BRC. We have a Values Team whose role is pretty broad and is represented across the organization, which helps with communication channels. We have been making a particular effort around engagement and connection ideas, especially since working remotely for the last 12 months, as this has made things more challenging, and we've needed to give this more focus, adapt and learn.

DL: What tips and lessons could you share with others who may wish to follow in your footsteps?

CH:

1 Start bottom-up and involve everyone, with sponsorship from the senior team.

2 It is never finished; there is always a gap which can be filled.

3 Listen well to everyone's input, thoughts and challenges.

4 It takes hard work to keep values alive and current.

5 Constantly ask the question about how else and where else values can feature in a business, its people and how it works.

6 Keep talking about your values and celebrate them!

FIGURE 7.3   The BRC corporate strategy

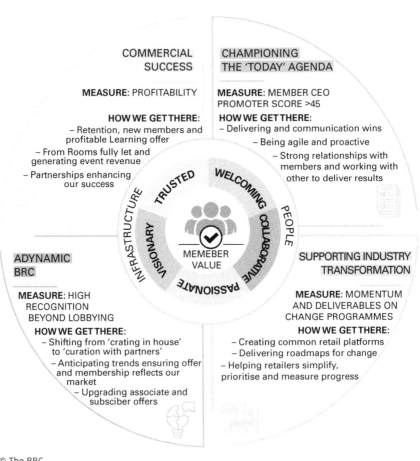

COMMERCIAL SUCCESS

MEASURE: PROFITABILITY

HOW WE GET THERE:
– Retention, new members and profitable Learning offer
– From Rooms fully let and generating event revenue
– Partnerships enhancing our success

CHAMPIONING THE 'TODAY' AGENDA

MEASURE: MEMBER CEO PROMOTER SCORE >45

HOW WE GET THERE:
– Delivering and communication wins
– Being agile and proactive
– Strong relationships with members and working with other to deliver results

ADYNAMIC BRC

MEASURE: HIGH RECOGNITION BEYOND LOBBYING

HOW WE GET THERE:
– Shifting from 'crating in house' to 'curation with partners'
– Anticipating trends ensuring offer and membership reflects our market
– Upgrading associate and subsciber offers

SUPPORTING INDUSTRY TRANSFORMATION

MEASURE: MOMENTUM AND DELIVERABLES ON CHANGE PROGRAMMES

HOW WE GET THERE:
– Creating common retail platforms
– Delivering roadmaps for change
– Helping retailers simplify, prioritise and measure progress

TRUSTED   WELCOMING   PEOPLE   COLLABORATIVE   PASSIONATE   VISIONARY   INFRASTRUCTURE

MEMEBER VALUE

© The BRC

Conclusion and calls to action

This chapter has, I hope, demonstrated that cultural flow can be achieved when an organization aligns its purpose with its values, with its behaviours and with its people. The benefits are clear, and the impact is potentially significant.

However, this flow does not happen by accident. It needs to be planned, designed, executed and evaluated with perseverance, tenacity and energy. In the next chapter I propose that a new people and culture function is created in our organizations. This new function can support the development of a transformational culture, it can generate cultural flow and it can support leaders, managers and other stakeholders to create the conditions where employee experience and customer experience can become far more closely aligned.

Acting as the golden thread of our organizations and delivering a wonderful, modern form of alchemy, values must underpin and inform everything our organizations do, from recruiting, selecting and inducting new employees to the way that we handle an employee's exit from the organization. Organizations must think about how their recruitment and selection approaches move more towards being values driven and how they could take steps to place as much emphasis on the alignment of the individual's personal values with those of the company as they typically do on the individual's career history and their specific skills and/or qualifications.

In other words, our purpose and values should be integrated into the entire employee life cycle.

References

Barrett, R (2006) *Building a Values-Driven Organization: A whole system approach to cultural transformation*, Routledge, London

Harding, D (2019) Letter to NHS Chairs and CEOs, https://www.england.nhs.uk/2019/06/provider-bulletin-5-june-2019/ (archived at https://perma.cc/M8TA-QPHJ)

Rhoades, A (2011) *Built on Values: Creating an enviable culture that outperforms the competition*, Wiley, San Francisco

08

Putting the human into human resources

The emergence of a modern people and culture function

TRANSFORMATIONAL LEARNING

Within this chapter you will discover answers to the following questions:

- What role does HR play in the development and deployment of a transformational culture?

- What is the HR paradox and how can it be resolved?

- How can HR transform into a modern people and culture function?

- What are four pillars of the emerging people and culture function?

- Why is it more important now than ever that HR puts people and values first?

- What five changes must HR embrace in order to become a people and culture function?

- How can a people and culture function align employee experience with customer experience?

Resolving the HR paradox

In Chapter 1 I explained why a transformational culture requires the HR function to transform itself into an overarching people and culture function – a function where it can become purpose, people and values led and it can release itself from its perceived proximity to management. In so doing the people and culture function can transition the organization from a reliance on retributive justice to a modern and progressive model of transformational justice (a balance of due process and restorative justice). To do this HR must relinquish its reliance on retributive policies, processes and procedures which are proven to generate adverse outcomes such as the traditional grievance, discipline and performance procedures.

In Chapter 5 I explained how the HR function, as is, can develop and deploy an overarching Resolution Framework for addressing concerns, conduct, complaints and conflicts in the workplace. This includes integrating collaborative, inclusive and constructive remedies to people issues. As a result, organizations will benefit from a reduction in the paternalistic and risk-averse nature of the HR profession and will reap the rewards from a culture of empowerment and adult-to-adult dialogue.

In my first book I set out what I referred to as the HR paradox and it is worth revisiting this paradox in the context of organizational culture. Over the past four or five years the HR paradox seems to have become even more pronounced. While HR has played a pivotal role supporting people through Covid-19, the systems which HR deploys, particularly when things go wrong, have remained a divisive and toxic feature of the modern workplace.

There are now so many models of HR that it has become quite confusing, and the HR profession appears to have become caught up in a continued search for meaning and relevance: Next Generation HR, Ulrich 2.0, the People Value Chain, HR Delivery model and so on and so forth. A new model of HR appears on the feeds of social media at least once a week.

While blissfully ignorant to these musings within the HR profession, many employees view HR as the custodian of a policy suite which promotes blame, division, confrontation, negativity, fear, betrayal, stress and resentment. This is particularly so among those who have a complaint, are having their performance managed, who feel bullied or harassed, who are subject of a disciplinary investigation, who have been overlooked for promotion, who are experiencing conflict with a colleague, or feel that a manager is not as positive or strategic as they could be.

'I will go to HR' or 'I will take a grievance out against you' is still used as an existential threat against a colleague or a manager. HR, in these cases, becomes the Sword of Damocles hanging above people's heads. As I explained in *Managing Conflict*, for many employees the HR function is seen as the controlling parent, the police officer or the authoritarian arm of management. Therein lies the HR paradox. On the one hand, HR is an enabler and a strategic partner. On the other hand, HR, and its associated rules and processes, is seen to be complicit in the devastation of people's lives and the destruction of relationships at work.

At the heart of the HR paradox lies the very suite of HR systems which have been designed to resolve issues in the workplace: performance management, conduct, absence, discipline and those awful GBH policies, grievance, bullying and harassment procedures.

These policies are the antithesis of a fair, just, inclusive, sustainable and high-performing organization. They are neither values based nor are they person-centred. As such, the function which is the custodian of these processes is, unfortunately, viewed in the same way by a great many of the workforce and this perpetuates mistrust and suspicion.

TRANSFORMATIONAL REFLECTION

Undertaking an evaluation of your HR policies, processes
and procedures

Starting with your discipline, grievance and performance policies please rate each policy against the 10 statements in Table 8.1 – 0 is low confidence and 5 is highly confident.

TABLE 8.1   Rating discipline, grievance and performance policies

Statement	Your score
The policy is clearly aligned to our purpose and values.	
The policy empowers managers and colleagues to resolve issues constructively.	
The policy actively promotes restorative processes such as mediation, coaching or facilitation.	
The policy has been designed to reduce the release of stress hormone cortisol and facilitate the release of the 'happy hormones': dopamine, serotonin, oxytocin and endorphins.	
The policy draws from best practice in the areas of nudge theory, emotional intelligence and principled negotiation.	
The policy identifies and resolves the root cause of issues or concerns.	
The policy seeks to protect working relationships.	
The policy seeks to protect the mental health of all parties.	
We routinely seek and act on feedback from colleagues and managers who use the policy.	
We measure the medium- and long-term impact of the policy in terms of employee wellbeing, engagement and inclusion.	
Total	/50

Your aggregate score can highlight which steps you may wish to consider taking:

0–20. Rip it up and start over.

21–40. Needs a root and branch review to bring it up to date with best practice in human relations, organizational dynamics, neuroscience and positive psychology.

Over 40. This is a good score. It reflects a policy which is working.

I believe that the HR paradox is an existential threat to the very HR function. Unless HR becomes less protective of its policy frameworks and less resistant to innovation and creativity in the way that it deals with complex people issues, the role of HR will slowly be eroded. This is not a great future for such an important function. I agree with Ben McCormick when he says:

'By owning and communicating culture, ensuring that it is embedded yet constantly evolving and by acting as the intermediary that aligns those at the top with those lower down the chain, HR can affect significant change at every level and enable the delivery of results that empower and engage the entire organization.' (McCormick, 2019)

This moment in time represents a golden opportunity for HR to transform itself into a modern and progressive people and culture function, one which plays a pivotal role as one of the most strategically important functions in the modern organization. In this new role HR will deliver cultural flow within organizations and could become one of the most (if not the most) strategically important functions in the modern firm – the people and culture function.

The new people and culture function should operate around four broad pillars:

1 People.
2 Culture.
3 Justice.
4 Strategy.

On page 161 I describe four pillars which I believe will shape the emerging people and culture function.

There are numerous examples of organizations which are embracing the shift to people and culture. To test the water I ran an online poll and the response was interesting. Of the 50 people who responded, over half said they had either adopted the title people and culture or were considering doing so in the future. Only 20 per cent of respondents rejected the idea, saying they had no plans to make the shift from HR to people and culture.

If there was ever a time to be led by our values, this is it. When the tills are ringing and everyone is happy it is not too difficult to bring the values that organizations espouse to life. But it is when the going gets tough that our values come into their own – acting as a beacon and shining a light on the way we should act, interact and react with each other. That time is now.

There is an opportunity here for HR to come into its own – coaching and supporting managers on how to handle difficult situations, have good-quality dialogue and build resilience in their teams. It is a chance for HR to remind managers of the values the organization holds dear and to nudge them towards the type of behaviours and open adult-to-adult interactions the organization wants to see.

The new people and culture function needs to press home the message that compassion is not something soft and fluffy that just gets rolled out when something bad has happened. Compassion needs to underpin every action and decision that managers take about their people. It is about them listening, putting themselves in the other person's shoes and being able to come to a collaborative, joint decision about a set of circumstances or a problem. These principles are the beating heart of a transformational culture and the new people and culture function should protect them with every possible effort.

The best managers do this with authenticity, and also have a strong awareness of their own needs. Managers and leaders should be hired against these competencies and they should be fully trained in them. Compassion for others starts with self-compassion. The new people and culture function needs to encourage managers to take time out for themselves, to reflect, breathe and notice how they are feeling and responding – because if they can take a calm and mindful approach, they are going to be better equipped to handle other people's problems.

An exciting future for HR

This is an opportunity for the people and culture function to bring diverse stakeholders together and to align purpose, values, people and strategy. To be successful in the future, HR must be viewed as an impartial role which identifies and resolves issues across the organization using modern and effective means. HR should give dialogue primacy in the workplace and should champion dialogue and reject retribution at every opportunity. HR should adopt the principles of nudge theory to drive behavioural change, and should actively promote the principles of nudge and the other restorative principles across the organization.

To assist with the achievement of these objectives, HR must embrace five critical changes:

1   HR should be champions of the transformational principles and they should support managers to deliver transformational justice through recruitment processes, training, coaching, mentoring and mediation. HR should create and administer robust systems of accountability and foster and sustain good relations with a wide range of stakeholders.

2   HR should promote and sustain a culture of open dialogue, inclusion, restorative justice and learning. These should be balanced against the needs of due process and meeting the requirements of regulators and any statutory duties on the employer. This will be a tough balancing act. However, as the case studies in this text have demonstrated, it can be achieved when HR is creative and innovative. It will require many in the HR profession to think deeply and to embrace radical change. To help achieve this HR must, as a matter of urgency, relinquish its reliance on retributive justice and its destructive and damaging policies and processes. By putting people and values at the centre of the HR universe, HR should reconnect with its employees and other stakeholders at every level of the organization, and should make wellbeing, engagement and inclusion strategic priorities.

3   HR must become a standalone and objective function in the organization, with no vested interests and with a mandate to become predictive and proactive. The term 'business partner', which reinforces the perceived alignment of HR with management, should be dropped from the HR lexicon.

4   HR should seek to align employee experience with customer experience and should become the people and culture partner to enable this objective to be met. Users of HR processes should be viewed as the customers of HR and employee feedback should be

sought and acted upon. Employees should, as any good customer services manager knows, have a voice in the development of systems and processes they are using. In other words, HR needs to listen to its customers.

5 HR should act swiftly to reduce tensions between unions and management which define the traditional pluralist workplace. HR should drive transformationalism into the traditional employee relations processes and procedures. To achieve this, HR must become the enabler of a new and exciting partnership between unions and management, and should support the development of a new social contract based on mutual respect, accountability, trust and dialogue. HR should be the broker of reconciliation and diplomacy when problems and disputes arise, trusted by all sides to be fair, proportionate and just.

The terms non-partisan, proactive, neutral, impartial, fair, just, inclusive and enabling need to become the key words which describe the future of HR. It is no longer tenable for HR to seek to sit at the 'top table' while disregarding the harmful and divisive impact that its policies, processes and procedures are having across the workforce. A transformational culture offers a more balanced and nuanced model of HR, a culture which puts the human back into the profession and where HR is driven by a focus on, and a passion for, people and culture.

The people and culture function – the four pillars

The following text describes the potential roles and priorities for a transformed people and culture function. The model centres around four thematic areas: 1) people, 2) culture, 3) justice and 4) strategy.

Pillar 1: People

- The employee handbook balances the strategic needs of the organization, its values and the needs of the workforce while ensuring legal compliance.

- Recruitment processes ensure that people are hired and promoted on merit and the risk of unconscious bias is reduced.
- Ensures that the purpose and the values of the organization are integrated into the employee life cycle and the employee value proposition (EVP).
- Takes responsibility for shaping and evaluating the organization's values in partnership with key stakeholders
- Employee relations processes apply the principles of 'transformationalism'.
- Designs and delivers wellbeing, engagement and inclusion programmes and measures their impact.
- Adequate training, coaching and mentoring are delivered to line managers to equip them with the skills and capability to manage people and culture issues and to create the required climate in their teams and divisions.
- Supports and delivers organizational change programmes and ensures that people, values and culture are key considerations during organizational change.

Pillar 2: Culture

- Ensures that the culture of the organization is fair, just, inclusive, sustainable and high performing.
- Sets up and leads a cross-functional transformational culture hub which supports stakeholders to drive the necessary culture changes to develop and sustain a transformational culture.
- Data and evidence are used to design and measure the culture, the climate within teams and divisions, and the impact of the people (human capital) within the organization.
- Possesses skills and expertise in the areas of systems thinking, positive psychology, emotional intelligence, nudge theory, restorative justice, principled negotiation, non-violent communication and appreciative inquiry.

- Measures the impact of the culture across various axes:

  - brand and reputation;
  - wellbeing, engagement and inclusion;
  - EX and CX;
  - business performance.

Pillar 3: Justice

- Embraces transformational justice and ensures that the fair, just and inclusive principles are integrated across the organization.
- People policies and ER processes apply the transformational principles, ie they are restorative in nature, and they focus on protecting relationships and delivering robust outcomes which build trust and accountability.
- Ensures that the organization's values are integrated into all management systems and organizational processes.
- Creates and sustains the organization's values and behaviours framework and ensures adequate support and training are provided to make the framework a reality.
- Integrates learning from the application of the justice processes and ensures that insights and improvements are integrated. In other other words, justice becomes a driver of organizational learning and continuous improvement.

Pillar 4: Strategy

- Develops the people and culture strategy which supports the organization to deliver its purpose and strategic objectives.
- Acts as a people and culture partner to support the deployment of the strategy to line managers.
- Acts as key enabler of corporate strategy by providing data and evidence from the people and culture function.
- Ensures that the organization is agile and its people can adapt quickly to changing internal and external landscapes such as digitalization, hybrid working, social justice movements, the climate, and economic emergencies.

CASE STUDY

Putting people and values first at Cheshire and Wirral Partnership NHS Foundation Trust

CASE STUDY PREPARED FOR TRANSFORMATIONAL CULTURE *BY DAVE HARRIS, DIRECTOR OF PEOPLE AND ORGANIZATIONAL DEVELOPMENT AT CHESHIRE AND WIRRAL PARTNERSHIP*

Cheshire and Wirral Partnership NHS Foundation Trust (CWP) was formed in 2002. We provide health and care services for local people, including mental health, learning disability, community physical health and all-age disability care – including the provision of three GP surgeries. The prevailing culture at CWP is one that is person-centred and values based. Feedback we get from regulators, partners and new colleagues is that our caring and compassionate culture is a tangible feature of CWP. That said, we know that we are only part way there. We know that teams, especially in such a dispersed organization as ours, can develop their own cultures often shaped by leadership and unwritten rules within the team. Our aim is to ensure that wherever you go in CWP you will find that same person-centred, values-based experience.

We are a living community made up of a diverse range of people, each with their own unique contribution to make. It is our fundamental values that shape how we enable those people to come together to connect their different contribution. The care we deliver, and the care people receive from us, hinges on those relationships, on the interactions between human beings. We are a living organism not a mechanical construct and our business is people and what matters to them. Our values and our focus on people lie at the centre of a model and approach we have developed, which we believe has widespread application and which we are using to shape our organizational culture, purpose and outcomes.

In quality terms those outcomes are about safety, effectiveness and experience. Lots of attention is already given to the first two but we are now really focusing on experience: what people can expect their experience of working (or volunteering) for CWP to be. That has an important behavioural component to it and something on which we are looking to engage with all our colleagues by using pen-pictures. It is these behaviours and day-to day interactions that ultimately shape our culture and how we care for others.

Utilizing a person-centred and values-based culture shapes the environment within which our people can make their contribution. It defines what expectations we can have of ourselves as individuals and of each other and so helps define the experience of working within CWP. We know that if we provide a great experience for those delivering care then those receiving that care are also more likely to have a great experience. We believe this is what has enabled us to be rated as 'outstanding' for care by the CQC.

Being person-centred and values-based means we start with what matters to individuals and how we can involve them in shaping their experience, whether as a colleague or a patient. Our policies, processes and pathways should be shaped around that desire, not the other way round. Ultimately, the work that we do is all about how what we do meets the needs of those we serve.

We are reshaping our policies and processes in order to deliver our strategic objective to be a person-centred, values-based organization. In particular we are focusing on resolution and learning and so ripping up our 'big 4' policies on discipline, attendance, grievances and dignity at work. As for recruitment, CWP has always placed a big emphasis on values and cultural fit when it comes to selecting people. We have values-based recruitment in place and when it comes to board member positions, values make up a crucial part of the selection process and final decision. We have a range of people with different backgrounds, perspectives and skillsets on our board, but what unites us is our shared common values and purpose. Board decisions set the tone and direction for the rest of the organization, so we see board behaviours as crucial to safeguarding the culture of CWP.

My advice for other organizations is to be clear about your values – what you stand for, what matters to you as an organization. Be clear what your common purpose is and align everything to that. Transformational change can take time. It's unpredictable, messy, complex and confusing. You need a level of honesty and humility – you cannot totally control it. What you can do is nurture its growth; create an environment where each person is clear what is expected of them and feels safe and confident to make their best contribution to the common purpose you are all striving towards.

TRANSFORMATIONAL THINKING

- Is your organization ready to embrace people and culture?
- If so, what changes will need to be made to achieve the transformation?

Conclusion and calls to action

In its current form and as the custodian of the retributive and destructive employee handbook and HR policy suite, the HR role seems increasingly less relevant in a modern workplace. As a result, HR appears increasingly out of touch with the needs of a diverse and ever more vocal workforce.

HR must ensure that values inform all the elements of the employee life cycle. This will help to 'normalize' them and move values from being unconsciously applied to consciously applied.

HR needs to modernize, and to do that must be less defensive of its policies and more open to listening and engaging with its employees and other stakeholders. The transformation of the traditional HR policy framework does not present an existential threat to the role of HR. The numerous case studies in this book have demonstrated that quite ably. On the contrary, if the HR function can transform itself to focus on people and culture and can become the custodian of the transformational principles of fairness, justice, inclusion, sustainability and high performance, the modernized HR function could become one of the most strategically important roles in the modern organization.

To achieve this objective, as explained in this chapter, the new people and culture function will need to:

- put people before process and become less risk averse and less rigid. This will mean that the traditional employee handbook will need to be transformed to ensure that it aligns to the purpose, values and culture of the organization;

- embrace data and an evidence-based approach to underpin the development and deployment of its people and culture strategy;

- reconnect with employees at every level of the organization – engage in big conversations and organization-wide listening exercises to understand what employees need;

- actively promote transformational justice and become the function that is responsible for securing learning and improvements from the application of justice;

- develop a transformational culture hub which will become the enabler of a new and exciting partnership/social contract between unions, management and other key stakeholders;
- work closely with colleagues in customer experience to align with employee experience;
- work closely with key stakeholders to ensure there is an adequate talent pipeline to meet the short-, medium- and long-term needs of the organization.

Sadly, if HR is unable to achieve at least some of the above, it may become increasingly marginalized and the HR function could become little more than an administrative one in our firms. Without some serious soul-searching and a radical reform of its purpose and modus operandi, I predict HR will become ever less transformational and ever more transactional.

Conversely, if HR can grasp this opportunity to transform itself, this could represent a watershed moment. With courage, energy, tenacity and perseverance, this could become a moment where the new people and culture function becomes one of the most strategically important functions in the modern organization.

Reference

McCormick, B (2019) 5 ways HR can drive company culture change in the boardroom, www.raconteur.net/the-hive/5-ways-hr-drives-culture-change (archived at https://perma.cc/BT95-896N)

09

Engage leadership

Leadership, management and the transformational culture

TRANSFORMATIONAL LEARNING

Within this chapter, you will discover answers to the following questions:

- How do our leaders and people managers influence organizational culture?
- How does our leaders' and people managers' behaviour create the climate of their teams and the AIR that we all breathe in?
- What role do leaders and managers play in a transformational culture?
- How can leaders and managers use coaching skills to unlock our inner brilliance and to manage performance?
- What is radical listening and how does it support leadership?
- What will be the new leadership orthodoxies for the 'new normal'?

The big questions about leadership

'Everyone thinks they know what leadership means until, that is, they have to do it themselves.' That is what a good friend once told me; it has stuck with me ever since. Leadership is the definitive example of an art, a science, a craft. This chapter will explore the meaning of leadership and management in the context of a transformational culture. I explore the role that leaders and managers – who, I must stress, are also leaders – play in developing, maintaining and aligning the culture and the climate of their organizations. I also offer practical tools and tips to support leaders and managers as they adapt to this exciting new cultural reality – a culture where values and people come first.

I am often asked what makes a great leader, and I am asked which leader inspires me the most. Given that leadership is probably the most widely written about of all the business topics, I do not have the perfect answer to the question of what makes a great leader. However, I have learned this along the way: true leadership comes from being the best version of ourselves, during the good times and the bad. Great leaders recognize, amplify and celebrate the inner brilliance of others. They understand they do not have all the answers, so they build teams with divergent ideas, backgrounds and viewpoints. They listen to them, they value them, they show them and they empower them. Some of the best leaders that I have met possess a significant predilection for coaching, mentoring and diplomacy. While they love success and they relish winning, the best leaders I know are also compassionate, collaborative and humble. They also have a good sense of humour and they do not take themselves too seriously.

'Leaders must take a role in developing, expressing and defending civility and values.' (De Pree, 2004)

To the question of which leader inspires me personally, I am inspired by a great many leaders from a wide spectrum of people in the fields of sport, business, community leadership and, dare I say it, occasionally politics. The leader who is inspiring me the most right now is a political leader, Jacinda Ardern, Prime Minister of New Zealand. Ever since the tragic massacre in Christchurch, in which terrorists attacked two mosques, killing 51 people, Jacinda Ardern has demonstrated some of the best possible leadership qualities. These have also been demonstrated through her handling of Covid-19. Below is one of my favourite quotes from Ardern, from an interview with the BBC. In it, she highlights her commitment to empathy and compassion in

leadership and the courage to be true to her beliefs. While she is refer-
ring to political leadership, I do not think it takes too much of a leap
to apply this quote to virtually every other form of leadership –
including leadership within an organization.

> 'It takes courage and strength to be empathetic, and I'm very proudly an
> empathetic and compassionate politician. We teach kindness, empathy,
> and compassion to our children but then somehow, when it comes to
> political leadership, we want a complete absence of that. I am trying to
> chart a different path, and that will attract criticism, but I can only be
> true to myself and the form of leadership I believe in.' (Ardern, 2018)

TRANSFORMATIONAL TAKEAWAY

- Which leader or leaders have inspired you, and why?
- What changes will you make to your leadership style to be more like that
  leader?

Climate, culture and the air that we breathe

The responsibility that executives, leaders and managers have for
creating, influencing and perpetuating the culture and the climate of
their organizations cannot be underestimated.

> 'For better and worse, culture and leadership are inextricably linked.
> Founders and influential leaders often set new cultures in motion and imprint
> values and assumptions that persist for decades.' (Groysberg et al, 2018)

By way of a recap, the culture of the organization is the aggregation
of the purpose, shared assumptions, rules, processes, written or
unwritten values, behaviours and experiences across the workplace.
The culture is global, ie it operates within and across the entire
organization's ecosystem.

The climate tends to be more localized; climate can adapt and flex more easily. Climate centres around a team, a division or a department. The climate of a team can be characterized predominantly by the behaviour of its leaders and managers. The climate is particularly sensitive to the way that leaders and managers Act, Interact and React with each other, with employees, with suppliers and with customers. The AIR that our leaders and managers produce through their behaviours becomes the air that we all breathe in – it creates the climate that we work in. This is more acute at times of stress brought on by conflict, change or crisis. Then, the AIR can become thick and choking; the climate can become toxic, destructive and dysfunctional. Or it can be healthy, constructive and functional.

Actions are the day-to-day behaviours of the leader or manager. These behaviours set the tone and the mood of the workplace. Aggressive, irritable, exclusive, divisive or inconsistent behaviours can create and perpetuate a toxic climate which can, over time, develop into a toxic culture. Day-to-day behaviours which are respectful, supportive, empowering, compassionate and empathetic set the tone for a transformational climate and culture. Sprinkle in a bit of fun and these are the leadership and management actions which create a happy, a healthy and a harmonious workplace.

Here are three sets of actions that people tell me they value about their leaders and their managers. They are remarkably simple:

1 They say, 'Good morning' and they show an interest in my life outside of the workplace. Remembering my partner's or my kids' names makes me feel incredibly special. They are intuitive enough to know if I feel a bit down, or fed up, they are not afraid to ask me how I am feeling. And when I answer their questions, they know how to listen to me with empathy.

2 They ask me what I think and feel about a topic, they listen to my answers and they value my input. They never make me feel stupid or inferior, even when my idea is clearly not a good one. They coach me to be the best that I can. They help me to understand myself and to reframe problems into opportunities. They use the information that I provide to predict the future. They use it to plot a path that we will all follow, as we have also helped to shape the path and set the direction.

3 They thank me when I work hard, and they notice when I achieve something. They do not make a big fuss, they tell me, quietly and to my face, that they value my work and they appreciate me. They push me to achieve better things because they want to see me succeed – not to make them look good but to make me feel great.

Interactions describe the way that our leaders and managers engage and interact with others, verbally, in emails, on social media or in meetings. This includes interactions with customers, suppliers, team members, other managers or their bosses. Where those interactions are inconsistent, uncivil, disrespectful, discriminatory, misogynistic, blaming, sarcastic, divisive, rude or disingenuous, those characteristics easily become the accepted behavioural norms in project or work teams, in management teams, across divisions of the entire organization. The manager or the leader has given licence to behave in exactly that way. These interactions strike fear into people's hearts and they watch, in terror, as the interactions unfold.

Where the interactions of our leaders and managers are driven by a sense of personal responsibility, when they are people centred and compassionate, and when the organization's values play a part in shaping the interactions, then that too is an implicit licence for others to follow suit. They are setting the bar.

Here are three sets of interactions that people tell me they value about their leaders and their managers. These, too, are remarkably simple:

1 They use coaching skills every day. They ask questions of me and the person they are interacting with. Sometimes the questions are so simple that they are incredibly tough to answer; they evoke deep thinking and reflection. They are curious and they genuinely want to know what the other person thinks. They give positive feedback, and they feed forward (look ahead to see what needs to be done) to help shape objectives, to give focus and to set realistic goals.

2 They do not rush to judge and they know how to suspend judgement (even when others are trying to get them to take sides). They avoid making disparaging or evaluative comments about other people. They are respectful and they are civil. When they hear others being disrespectful or uncivil in their interactions, they are always willing

to step in and challenge. It makes us feel safe – you know exactly where you stand and you know what the standard of behaviour is.

3 They like a bit of fun and will laugh at or make jokes. However, their jokes are never at another person's expense. They do not play games or get involved in petty politics, and they do not take advantage of others to gain an advantage for themselves. They may be competitive, but they are also collaborative, they play fairly and they expect others to do so, too.

Reactions describe how our managers and leaders respond during times of conflict, change or crisis. At these times, like any human being, the leader or manager can expect to feel mixed emotions and they will experience stress, anxiety, vulnerability and confusion. Their amygdala gets switched on in the same way as everyone else's does, and they can experience surges of the stressor hormones – adrenaline and cortisol. They can, like anyone can, feel triggered, and they can get locked into a fight, flight, freeze or fall state.

At times like this we look to our leaders and managers for guidance. We do not expect them to be saints or to be robotic, or for them to avoid having feelings or emotions. However, when these feelings and emotions take over and the leader or manager loses their grip on them, their reactions to stress set the tone for others. My experience is that our managers' reactions to stress can have a disproportionate impact on organizational climate. Not only is the reaction stressful for others to watch, but they are also fearful of provoking the reaction. The term 'walking on eggshells' is a commonly used refrain in such team climates.

Here are three sets of reactions that people tell me they value about their leaders and their managers. These, much like the others, are remarkably simple:

1 If they are attacked (verbally), they respond calmly and they avoid reacting defensively. They demonstrate great self-awareness and they encourage others to do the same. When they feel triggered or riled, they know how to de-escalate a situation. They manage to turn it around and rather than pointing fingers, they put themselves into the other person's shoes.

2 They are assertive and they present their feelings and their points of view robustly and clearly. They know how to demonstrate their vulnerability without it appearing turgid or pious. They never seek to attack, and they avoid making wild accusations, assertions or evaluations which will hurt the other person. They will not let the situation become personal. They will always allow the other person to speak and to express their feelings and point of view, and they will listen carefully and with empathy.

3 They always seek a win/win outcome. They understand that there are no winners if the reactions are irrational and the interaction becomes polarized or entrenched. They may take time to pause and reflect before they respond. They seek to understand the needs and interests of the other person and they reflect their own needs and interests. They seek areas of common ground and convergence. They have an innate sense of diplomacy – they try to build bridges, not walls.

TRANSFORMATIONAL TAKEAWAY

Having considered the above guidance, what will you do to improve the AIR that you create in your team, division or organization?

• Actions
• **Interactions**
• Reactions

The $64,000 question: how?

Organizational culture and team or departmental climate are the compound effects of the choices that our leaders and managers make every day – some little choices, others much bigger. Culture and climate are not passive, nor are they rigid. Climate and culture can adapt, for better or worse, due to the choices that our leaders and managers make and, in particular, the way they choose to behave.

Clearly, we need them to make the right choices, but that right choice is not always immediately obvious and no one can make the right choice every time – that is an impossible ask when the information that leaders have is so often imperfect.

So, to create a transformational culture and a transformational climate, our leaders and managers need to have better information to make better choices. The $64,000 question is, how do they get this information and how will it help them to make better choices? They cannot get it by surrounding themselves with 'yes' people – colleagues or consultants who tell them what they want to hear. The answer is a lot easier, and a lot cheaper.

There are three things that a leader or a manager needs to do to get the information that they require to make the best possible decisions – the beauty of this approach is that it is completely free (other than the obligatory donuts)!

- Engage: meet your people where they are. Set some boundaries. Create a safe space. Open a dialogue.
- Listen: hear what is being said, ask questions, summarize what you are hearing, check in, clarify, be curious, lead with empathy.
- Act: deliver a clear vision and promote a common purpose. Agree next steps and objectives. Clarify who does what and by when. Go for it.

The answers are there, they lie within. We do not need fancy algorithms, complex formulas and expensive databases. We were given the tools we need to be great leaders at birth; they sit on either side of our head.

Listening for improved performance

Listening unlocks brilliance – it builds trust, it fosters respect and it empowers both the coach and the coached. As I have said previously, I have seen my fair share of disputes between managers, leaders, employees and unions. But I have never read a complaint letter from a disgruntled employee that said the following:

Dear HR Manager,

I would like to complain about my line manager. They listen too hard and they respect me too much. When I talk to them, they try to put themselves in my shoes and they value my input. They are trying to coach me to help me perform effectively in my role. They recognize me for who I am, they empower me, and they ensure that I feel included and supported within the team. All these questions, please make it stop! While my manager may not always agree with me, they do not put me down or belittle me. Can you please take immediate action as this is all too much for me to bear?

Yours sincerely, Dis Gruntled

The above complaint letter is, of course, a joke, but my intention is to convey a serious message. Listening with compassion, demonstrating self-awareness, acting in an empathetic way, empowering others through coaching and valuing their ideas are the answer to the $64,000 question. With this knowledge, we can make new choices about how we act, interact and react, and those choices can transform the climate and the culture of our organizations.

The best leaders go to where their people are

Leaders need to go to where their people are before they can expect their people to follow them. Failure to do so creates dissonance – leaders pull one way and employees either stay put or they pull the other way. I call this relational dissonance. Think of dissonance as a big gap that is desperate to be filled in. In relational terms it is a gap that is created when we are unsure where we stand with a leader. We may ask ourselves: Do I like or dislike them? Can I trust them? Are they genuine or fake? Do they mean to harm me or will they nurture me?

These unanswered questions then create the second level of dissonance – cognitive dissonance. This is the gap that is created when we do not know the answers to the questions that we are asking. This creates an inner conflict as our assumptions, prejudices, beliefs and values begin to collide with each other, creating discomfort and confusion. Mixed with an (un)healthy dose of unconscious bias, the cognitive dissonance fuels mistrust and suspicion. This represents the early stage of conflict. Unless this relational and cognitive dissonance is identified and resolved, the inner conflicts manifest as behaviours which become the antecedents to a worsening and often destructive conflict (Liddle, 2017). The term 'going round in circles' could aptly be applied here.

How do transformational leaders reduce relational and cognitive dissonance?

Transformational leaders understand that being present and engaging with employees and engaging in radical listening is the source of deep and powerful connections. It empowers the employee (gives them agency), and it builds trust and mutual respect and, to my previous points, it engenders common purpose. Below are the five key steps that transformational leaders use when they wish to avoid or resolve dissonance:

1 Take a step back. Have you got all the information you need? If not, it is time to start asking questions and listening to your people. Give them a jolly good listening to. This is radical listening.

2 Challenge your own assumptions. This means suspending judgement about a person or a situation and being aware of how you are feeling and how you are reacting.

3 Name the feelings. Transformational leaders are comfortable with their own and other people's emotions. They know that by naming feelings this results in them becoming easier to work with and it prevents them from being suppressed or ignored.

4 Frame the problem as an opportunity. Avoid personalizing the situation and avoid slipping into a blaming or evaluative mindset or language. The problem is the problem, not the person.

5 Explore what is important to the other person(s) – their interests, values, beliefs and needs. This will create a valuable reference point to help you to resolve the problem. When a transformational

leader operates at this level, it encourages a growth mindset and it becomes much easier to spot the areas of dissonance (divergence) and to spot and generate areas of alignment (convergence). It may also prompt new ideas and creative thinking/problem solving.

A mnemonic that has often helped me to reduce or spot and resolve dissonance is to go SLOW:

Stop talking.

Listen to others.

Observe what is happening.

Wait before responding.

It's time to engage leadership

There can be no doubt that our expectations of our leaders is changing at a blistering pace. The old orthodoxies of autocracy and rigidity, command and control, power and hierarchy are being challenged robustly. To address these orthodoxies, my colleagues and I regularly challenge organizations and leaders to 'Engage Leadership' (TCM, 2021). Connecting people with the purpose and values of their organization produces outstanding results. Teams are extraordinary when they collaborate with focus and energy. This passion to succeed comes from the culture and the climate created by their leaders. To attain this new transformational leadership orthodoxy, leaders must possess the following five competencies:

- Visionary: transformational leaders create a clear and compelling vision and proactively shape and reset the organization for the future.
- Resilience: transformational leaders remain rational in decision making and they build resilience so that they and their teams remain engaged, motivated and creative. They ensure that their organizations, divisions and teams promote psychological safety, are inclusive and their managers possess the capability to manage conflict and change effectively.

- Clarity: transformational leaders read the current reality accurately, translate this and its meaning to their teams, and maintain a clear sense of purpose. They do this through establishing and maintaining clear goals and objectives for their organizations, their teams and their people.

- Agility: transformational leaders take decisions in a timely way, reducing bureaucracy and maintaining key stakeholder involvement to stay proactive and leading the agenda.

- Compassion: transformational leaders reduce the harm to others and to the environment. They use values to challenge and guide decision making, they demonstrate empathy and self-awareness, and they are people focused and balance achievement of tasks with human impact.

The pace of change and these new expectations require a sea change in the way that we recruit, train, support and develop our management and leadership populations. If we thought leadership and management were hard before, they just got a whole lot tougher.

Why is leadership so tough?

In *Managing Conflict* (Liddle, 2017a), I explained how four 'F words' – fear, failure, fights and feelings – can contribute to a worsening of workplace relations. They can impact the lives of those we work with, the lives of those we live with and the lives of those we love. I have recently added a new 'F word' to the list: 'Feedback'. Feedback has become a significant 'F word' which is proving to be the downfall of many a good working relationship. A little word which has become so corrosive that it is precipitating the development of a next-generation system for managing performance.

Individually, these five 'F words' act as a force against the development of a just, fair, inclusive, sustainable and high-performing culture. When combined, they can herald the beginning of the end of a good working relationship, a team, a department or an entire organization. These five 'F words' can undermine good relationships with unions, they can reduce a merger to a petty quarrel, they can knock an acquisition off course, they can cause an investor to turn off the tap, and they can result in an otherwise promising start-up becoming just another statistic.

To enable the transition to a transformational culture, each of the 'F words' must be addressed fully and confidently by our managers and leaders. I will kick off with fear as fear is the most corrosive of all the 'F words'.

Fear becomes flow

Fear is prevalent in so many of our organizations. Fear can be debilitating and destructive. It is a primordial reaction to a threat (perceived or real). It can be a cause, and a symptom, of a profound sense of loss. Fear can be the trigger for individual and group distress, trauma and dysfunction; it can arise from being a victim of, or a witness to, abuses of power by our managers and leaders. Fear can be generated by unfair decision making, concern over damage to our career, or witnessing inequitable allocation of resources with no way to stop it happening. Fear can be produced when we are shouted at or threatened. Equally, it can build quietly and invisibly when we see others being treated unfairly or when others are given opportunities that have not been afforded to us or when we have no way of expressing our frustrations.

In some organizations, employees may experience a fear of retaliation or recrimination for raising concerns or speaking up. They may experience a fear of being judged or victimized because of one of their characteristics, beliefs or values. Amy Edmondson, leading academic and advocate of the fearless organization, sums it up well when she says:

> 'More than just business failure is at stake when psychological safety
> is low. In many workplaces people see something physically unsafe
> or wrong and fear reporting it. Or they feel bullied and intimidated
> by someone, but don't mention it to supervisors or counsellors. This
> reticence unfortunately can lead to widespread frustration, anxiety,

depression, and even physical harm. In short, we live and work in communities, cultures and organizations in which *not* speaking up can be hazardous to human health.' (Edmondson, 2019)

Fear arises from and causes loss: a loss of control, a loss of face, a loss of hope, a loss of perspective, a loss of relationship and a loss of one's sense of self. To manage fear, we need to know what is at stake, what is being lost. To achieve a transformational culture, we need our managers and leaders to have the skills and the courage to reframe the loss and turn it into a gain. The same goes for managing change or conflict. Either of these can create fear.

To manage change or conflict effectively, a manager and a leader needs to have the ability to understand what is at stake, what employees are feeling, what they are thinking, what they need. To do this, the effective people manager must create a psychologically safe space for dialogue; they must lead with courage and compassion. The ability to create psychological safety, engender adult-to-adult dialogue, be assertive yet calm under pressure, listen with empathy, respond non-defensively to criticism, handle strong emotions and understand people's needs are recurring themes within this text.

Failure becomes learning

I am not proposing that our organizations suddenly turn a blind eye to errors or allow mistakes to be made with no accountability. However, the retributive systems of justice, which have primacy in our organizations, seek to identify fault, apportion blame, reduce risk and punish the wrongdoer when an error is made. They deliver accountability in some cases (certainly not all), but often at a great cost.

Within a transformational culture, failure requires accountability and people must take responsibility when problems occur and when errors are made. But that accountability can come from accepting a mistake has been made, taking personal responsibility, where necessary demonstrating remorse, giving and accepting forgiveness, and drawing out insights and learning. On page 80, I explore the meaning behind a new term, 'intelligent failure'.

A transformational culture requires us to reframe our attitude to mistakes and failure. In a transformational culture, failure and errors become valuable assets of the organization. When coupled with a focus on learning and insight, apologies, expressions of remorse and forgiveness, they become powerful mechanisms for driving innovation and accelerating growth. These are even more powerful when they are driven by a leader/manager who can coach and mentor their people and who can foster a fair, just, safe and learning team climate.

The challenge of this new relationship with failure will not be easy, as this extract from an HBR article explains:

> 'While companies are beginning to accept the value of failure in the abstract – at the level of corporate policies, processes, and practices – it's an entirely different matter at the personal level. Everyone hates to fail. We assume, rationally or not, that we'll suffer embarrassment and a loss of esteem and stature. And nowhere is the fear of failure more intense and debilitating than in the competitive world of business, where a mistake can mean losing a bonus, a promotion, or even a job.' (Farson and Keyes, 2002)

In a transformational culture, the organization is open to learning and it handles mistakes and errors in a fair and just way. Some errors are so serious that an investigation and possible sanctions are inevitable. The Resolution Index™ which operates within the Resolution Framework is a useful way to assess severity and risk and to develop a strategy for resolving the issue(s) based on following an objective and robust assessment process. However, most people do not come to work to cause harm. Most errors and mistakes are relatively low level and can be identified and resolved without the threat of a retributive process or the need to attribute blame or fault. Within a transformational culture this wider acceptance of failure and errors and the ability to create learning opportunities and to develop organizational memory permeate through the organization. As a result, HR policies, management systems and cultural norms view failure as an opportunity to deliver accountably, to correct problems, to seek out learning and insight, to co-create solutions and to build and secure trust.

Fights become flow

The way that an organization manages complaints, concerns and conflicts at work is a key indicator of how advanced that organization is in adopting a transformational culture. The more destructive (dysfunctional) the conflict is, the less transformational the culture is. Conversely, the more constructive (functional) the conflict, the closer that organization is to operating a transformational culture. In other words, the way that our organizations handle fights acts as a barometer of the organizational culture. That is why I am still staggered at how little time, energy and resource are allocated to the management of conflicts, concerns and complaints at work.

Conflict at work is still treated with disdain and our organizations' leaders routinely fail to recognize the dire impact that it is having on both employee experience and customer experience. The lack of evidence in most organizations relating to the volume, the causes, the costs and the outcomes from low-level quarrels to full-blown bullying, harassment or discrimination is woeful. A lack of data and evidence acts as a barrier for HR and others to see the urgent and pressing need to drive reform.

I still cannot understand why the vital area of resolution still fails to appear in the top 10 strategic priorities of most firms. In my book, it should be strategic priority number 1. Talking of my book, within my first text, *Managing Conflict*, I explained that conflict can be either 'functional' – constructive and healthy – or 'dysfunctional' – destructive and harmful. I also described numerous causes of conflict, I explained the antecedents and the causes of conflict, and I highlighted five potential reactions to conflict. I advocated for the use of positive psychology and the creation of flow, which can help to reduce the incidence and the intensity of conflict at work. Flow of ideas, of empathy, of dialogue and of insight. All of which are central to the creation of a safe, learning and productive workplace. I asserted that most conflicts follow a distinct and broadly predictable life cycle and I explained how and why the earlier the resolution process can happen, the less of a negative impact the conflict will have (Liddle, 2017a).

In a transformational culture, there is no reason for fights and disagreements to escalate and to become destructive and damaging. Managers and leaders can use a fair, just and inclusive approach to resolve issues. We need our managers and leaders to be comfortable with conflict and to have the confidence and the courage to spot and resolve conflict (or a toxic culture) before it embeds itself into the team. In so doing, they will recognize that conflict at work can present one of the most incredible opportunities to build trust and to gather insights that can enhance the systems, structures and processes in their workplaces. In others words, when managed well, conflict can be the key to innovation and enhanced performance – two of the most sought-after elements in any organization.

Feelings generate empathy and compassion

The ability for managers to handle the 'F word' – feelings – is vital in a transformational culture. Feelings, suppressed, create the heat and the energy which can erupt into fierce and destructive explosions. Alternatively, suppressed feelings can act as a canker, slowly eating away at individuals and teams from the inside.

The transformational leader and manager knows how to listen. They understand the importance of asking the feelings question, 'How are you feeling?', and they know how to respond with care and compassion when the feelings surface and manifest as anger, tears or withdrawal.

They create conversations which enable feelings to be aired and discussed in a safe way. They also know that the feelings represent a set of unmet needs. By seeking to understand what is causing frustration for an employee, they can also begin to explore the necessary changes to prevent the frustrations from happening. This process of reframing feelings into needs allows the manager or leader to adopt a solution-focused approach.

Here is an example of a manager using empathy coupled with a solution-focused approach:

Manager: Steve, I noticed that you weren't yourself at the team meeting this morning. Is everything okay?

Steve: Yeah, I am feeling really frustrated at the moment.

Manager: Thanks, Steve. I understand that you are frustrated. Can you explain why you feel this way?

Steve: It's just that I have been doing the same job for two years and I can't see where the role is going. I am getting bored and I feel deskilled.

Manager: OK. On a scale of 1 to 10, how bored are you at the moment?

Steve: Probably an 8.

Manager: What would it take to get that down to a 7?

Steve: Good question. I would like some more responsibility and maybe an opportunity to work more closely on some of our key customer accounts.

Manager: OK, Steve, let me summarize to make sure I have heard this right. You are feeling frustrated, and you need to feel more fulfilled in your role. To achieve this, one option you have identified is to have more responsibility and to be more active on some of our key accounts. Does that sound right?

Steve: Yes, that's captured it.

Manager: So, if you did have more responsibility and you were working with key customer accounts, how would that make you feel?

Steve: I'd feel really motivated and I'd be grateful for the opportunity to develop my skills. If this could happen, I would score a 1 on the scale that you asked me about.

Manager: OK, Steve. Leave this with me. I'll see what I can do and perhaps we can speak again tomorrow. I'll let you know what I've got in mind. Does that sound okay?

Steve: Great, yes, thanks.

TRANSFORMATIONAL THINKING

Considering the exchange between Steve and his manager:

- How did the manager behave?
- How did they show empathy?
- What solution-focused technique did they use?
- What impact did this conversation have on Steve and on his relationship with the manager?
- What must the manager do next?

Feedback becomes feedforward

'Sue, can I have a word, please?' Sue's heart sinks. 'Sit down. I want to discuss the project that you have been leading on. It is behind schedule and it is haemorrhaging money. You do not appear to have a grip on the operational detail and you seem to have lost the way with your project team. The client is frustrated and you have let them down one time too many. Sue, your job is on the line here, what have you got to say for yourself?'

Maybe this is an extreme example of feedback, but we all know it happens. This is often the case with feedback and traditional performance systems – the feedback is given late, it is retrospective, it comes at you in floods, and it appears to be given with a finger of blame pointing firmly in your direction. In this extreme example, there are no clear learning points or teachable moments; Sue is likely to react, as any reasonable person would, defensively. Of course, not all feedback is this bad, nor is it given in this way. However, even in the best examples of giving feedback, it can still be retrospective and backwards looking and opportunities for deep reflection, insight and learning are lost in the desire to complete a spreadsheet, tick a box and calculate a standard deviation. One of the worst examples being the annual review.

There is a general acceptance that the annual appraisal systems are not working and are broken. Traditional performance management processes are often perceived as burdensome, demotivating and without value (Pulakos and O'Leary, 2011). Bearing in mind that I can barely remember what I had for lunch yesterday, trying to review an activity that happened weeks or many months ago is a fruitless and, for many, wholly dissatisfying activity.

How can feeding forward help?

The first thing to say about this is that the process of feeding forward should sit within a modern performance management system which includes:

- regular and ongoing dialogue (catch-ups) to discuss and review progress and to spot and resolve problems early. This allows for realignments to be made and for areas of tension to be resolved;

- clearly defined short- and medium-term goals which align directly to the values and the purpose of the organization;
- hindsight to drive insight and learning. The catch-up offers the opportunity to reflect and learn from the past in a fair, supported and safe environment;
- looking ahead. This will involve the use of coaching skills from the manager. The learning and insight should then be transformed into drive, purpose, passion and focus.

Feeding forward is about developing short-term achievable goals, then providing support and coaching to help achieve the agreed goals. It is about helping people to explore the positives and their strengths rather than becoming knocked off course by negatives and an evaluation of their perceived weaknesses. Feeding forwards is empowering, supportive and solution-focused. If you do need to look back, consider the past as an opportunity to draw out learning and insight, which will fuel growth and personal development.

TRANSFORMATIONAL TAKEAWAY

How will you change the way that you handle the 'F words'?

Fear

Fights

Failure

Feelings

Feedback

CASE STUDY

The Magical Mushroom Company (MMC)

One organization which is challenging the traditional leadership orthodoxies is the Magical Mushroom Company. MMC is an exciting start-up with a vision 'to be Europe's largest sustainable packaging company, helping business to thrive without causing harm to people or the planet, to rid the world of damaging polystyrene'.

With polystyrene causing immense environmental harm, a commercially viable and practical alternative is essential. Packaging grown by MMC, and licensed from patent holder Ecovative Design LLC, is 100 per cent biodegradable at home and breaks down in soil within 40 days. The process takes the post-processing waste from agricultural products such as hemp, hops, corn and timber and combines it with mycelium, the root system of the mushroom. This living material is then grown to shape using 3D moulds of the packaging design. These moulds are baked, hardening the material and preventing any further growth.

The MMC culture is defined by the following five statements:

- What do we do? We grow natural, sustainable and home-compostable materials for protective packaging, horticulture and interior design solutions.

- How do we do it? We provide a sustainable alternative to polystyrene, comparable in performance and price. We do this with biotechnology using natural materials grown in formed trays in our mycelium plants.

- Who do we do it for? We do it for businesses which are committed to sustainability. This benefits business, the environment and the living things that rely on it.

- What value do we bring? We make a positive impact on the planet and add value to customers' lives by enabling them to replace a planet-polluting polymer with a natural biodegradable alternative and we provide shareholders with a strong return on investment by running an efficient, profitable business.

- How do we keep doing it? We do this by ensuring we do everything through assess-and-plan methodology and the delivery of high-quality processes and systems. We recruit, train, develop and retain a dynamic and diverse workforce as a dedicated employer of choice.

Paul Gilligan, founder and CEO of MMC, brings a wealth of international management experience across a broad range of industries from construction to food retailing. He has experience of managing large teams after spending 14 years at Sainsbury's in a range of senior roles, winning several industry awards. 'The term "we" is very important,' Paul explains. 'The MMC values (we challenge, we protect, we deliver, we respect and we imagine) are at the heart of everything that we do. My objective is to drive collaboration and interconnectedness across the business and to create an organizational culture where our values make a real difference.'

This is not just a fanciful idea: the company's values are clearly integrated into the DNA of MMC. For instance, Paul and the MMC board have set out to put their purpose and their values at the heart of their operational and strategic activities. 'Our values have been designed to make everyone's lives easier and to embed the right culture and the right systems to drive growth. Our values benefit everyone. The board's role, and my job as a leader, is to ensure that the roles are designed correctly, that the right structures are in place, that everyone has the right tools that they need, and the organization has the necessary interconnectedness which will make the business succeed,' explains Paul.

To drive a culture of high performance, and to ensure that the MMC board can be both proactive and predictive, Paul and his team have developed an innovative scorecard for measuring the progress of the strategy and its impact on the MMC people and culture. MMC runs regular employee engagement and pulse surveys to ensure there is an alignment with the MMC values. 'These help us understand where any problems are arising, and it gives us the ability to predict and resolve issues effectively. As a board, we are constantly looking for an alignment between our values, our culture, the scorecard and the engagement of our employees. We believe that this alignment is the key to our future success.'

Agility, learning and the transformational culture

One of the key facets of a transformational culture and one of the five competencies of transformational leadership, as described earlier, is the ability for our managers and leaders to act in an agile way and to create and sustain a learning organization.

Coaching, mentoring and diplomacy skills should feature at the top of the leadership and management competency framework, for it is these skills which allow managers and leaders to adapt and to develop their agility, and that of others. There is absolutely no question that employees who receive or are offered coaching, who have the attention of leaders and managers and are able to raise concerns in a confidential and safe environment, are better able to perform at the required level, will be more productive. They will have a higher level of morale, will have fewer limiting factors and are less likely to end up leaving the organization (Jones and Gorell, 2018).

In an agile and learning workplace, team members are encouraged to engage with each other regularly and routinely. The conditions exist for them to share ideas and to express their views openly, knowing that they will be valued and respected for doing so. Managers understand that diversity of thought leads to better decision making, and that a flexible team structure and working conditions enable the full and active participation of a broader and more diverse workforce. In an agile workplace, fear of failure is replaced with a desire to fail fast and to learn and implement the lessons learned. 'Failing to fail is the real failure' (Edmondson, 2019).

In the following list, Edgar Schein neatly describes the role of leadership and the learning organization (Schein, 2017):

- The world can be managed.
- It is appropriate for humans to be proactive problem solvers.
- Reality and truth must be pragmatically discovered.
- Human nature is basically good and, in any case, mutable.
- The best kind of time horizon is somewhere between far and near future.
- The best kinds of units of time are medium-length ones.
- Accurate and relevant information must be capable of flowing freely in a fully connected network.
- Diverse but connected units are desirable.

Agility, especially when it exists in a transformational culture, brings people, processes and technology together to drive business success. John Mark Williams, CEO of the Institute of Leadership and Management in Tamworth in the UK, believes passionately that what he describes as 'pre-emptive agility' will enable leaders and managers to predict and prepare. I have been working with John and his team to help them establish a Resolution Framework to replace the Institute's traditional grievance and disciplinary procedures. I was thrilled to have the opportunity to interview John for this book. The interview is fascinating; in particular, the comment that John made about the first and most important act of an aspiring great leader being humility. John challenges the very essence of leadership which for so long has been defined by power, authority and control.

AN INTERVIEW WITH JOHN MARK WILLIAMS, CEO OF THE
INSTITUTE OF LEADERSHIP AND MANAGEMENT

David Liddle: What role do leaders play in creating the culture of an organization?

John Mark Williams: Every organization is a dynamic organism, not a static one – the 'culture' we see now is constantly changing in small and important ways. Consequently, the role of a leader in determining, creating and perhaps changing the culture of an organization is limited to time and place and situation – in other words, context.

DL: If culture is dynamic and leadership is situational, how can leaders make a positive difference?

JMW: Leaders can play a role in modelling behaviours, rewarding others' behaviours and allocating capital in support of positive behaviours – all three of which are vital. At the same time, the influence this will have on culture needs to be supported by tangible actions. If the culture needs changing, restructuring will need to happen – culture never changes without lines of accountability changing, and this is one of the most challenging acts for a leader. If the culture needs merely 'tweaking', the leader can nudge things in the right direction by 'reward for the right things'.

DL: Why do some leaders get it so wrong, and what could they do better?

JMW: The first and most important act of an aspiring great leader is humility; it is as fundamental to leadership as breathing is to life. The most effective leaders are those who can observe, analyse, assimilate and then play back the signals within the organization, in such a way as to align organizational behaviour with optimum outcomes. G.B. Shaw said, 'The reasonable man adapts himself to the world. The unreasonable man tries to adapt the world to himself. Therefore, all progress depends upon the unreasonable man.'

DL: I see fear of failure as a barrier to effective leadership. Would you agree?

JMW: I agree. There is an old saying: All great political careers end in failure. Unrecognized by most leaders is that leadership is a political career. Navigating the vagaries of organizational behaviour is exactly equivalent to managing the affairs of a region or a nation, with the same range of potential ups and downs. The antidote to the almost inevitable entropy inherent in being risk averse and process driven lies in two things:

- Leaders should strive always for the minimum viable outcome. Over-engineering outcomes leads invariably to over-engineered protections and processes. Simplicity is a mighty virtue in achieving organizational success.

- Faced with any risk or any dilemma, leaders should ask themselves the question: 'What would I do if I was not afraid?' It is surprising how often the outcome can be beneficial.

And we should never forget another old saying, 'The things we need to learn before we can do them, we learn by doing them.' It is okay to be uncertain – no matter what situation we are facing, none of us has ever been there before.

DL: Which are some of the most useful models of leadership in terms of organizational culture?

JMW: There are as many models of leadership as there are people with an opinion. The only valid critique I can think of is that none of them works – otherwise there would not be any others. And that says quite clearly that agile leadership – the principle of being able to sense and respond – emerges as a front-runner. I have my own version of that, which is underpinned by my lack of attachment to any other leadership model. None of them seems to see into the future. Instead of modelling 'if this, then that', we should be using what I call 'pre-emptive agility' – seeking to predict and prepare. The idea is that we do not need to see far into the future, just far enough to achieve a competitive advantage. Most drivers can intuitively predict the way traffic patterns work (otherwise we'd be having even more accidents than we do) – businesses passionate about analytics can do the same.

DL: If you had three pearls of wisdom that you could share, what would they be?

JMW: My suggestion for an effective leadership model is to coach the whole organization into collecting, collating, analysing and predicting from data – and preparing for the future ahead of competitors (or, in the case of the public sector, ahead of events).

1 Focus on understanding what really motivates people, at the individual and the group level. Motivated people don't need management – and will display leadership.

2 Recognize that people need challenge as well as support. Growth in confidence, competence and commitment comes when we overcome challenges – supporting our people to do that is enormously beneficial for the person, the leader and the organization.

3 Reward people for the quality of their contribution to the organizational objectives and not for time served or status or self-promotion. Reward for quality of contribution displays recognition, sends positive signals across the organization and motivates others to follow the example of both the leader and the rewarded team member.

And I add two more things which might be relevant:

1 The first is a quote from Marcus Aurelius: 'Waste no more time arguing what a great man is. Be one.' We talk too much about what constitutes great leadership instead of just doing it.

2 The second is a quote from me! I wrote a tweet some years ago which simply said, 'Leadership requires us to apply hindsight with clarity; insight with ingenuity; and foresight with audacity. No wonder great leadership is so hard.' I was trying to illustrate the courage needed to be a leader, so we can allow ourselves permission to feel uncertain sometimes.

Conclusion and calls to action

This chapter has highlighted that effective leadership and management are central to a transformational culture. Our leaders and managers do not need to be perfect; they just need to be able to handle the human beings in their organization like human beings. These are not human resources, they are people, with all the wonderful uniqueness that makes people so special and so brilliant. If we break our people or let our people see us breaking others, it damages them. It breaks their spirit, their motivation and their health. There really is no need for this to happen. I do not think I'm being particularly naïve to believe that most people do not go to work to do a bad job, to cause problems or to do harm. By listening to and engaging with their people, managers and leaders could transform the workplace overnight.

The perennial issues of low productivity, destructive conflict, toxic workplaces, poor engagement and poor mental health could be resolved if leaders and managers adopted the transformational principles set out in this chapter. We don't need more sophisticated and elaborate initiatives and programmes in our workplaces which mitigate poor leadership and management. We need to invest in our leaders and managers to equip them with the basic skills that they need to do their jobs and to run our organizations well.

To recap, I have listed these skills below:

- Walk the talk by role modelling the right behaviours and ensuring that leadership behaviours are aligned to the core values of the organization.

- Listen. Really hear what people are saying.

- Develop a corporate strategy which underscores the development of a transformational culture – a culture which is fair, just, inclusive, sustainable and high performing.

- Be proud ambassadors of purpose and values and recognize that a vital role is to drive these across the organization and to do so with tenacity and courage.

- Align actions, reactions and interactions (AIR) with the values and purpose of the organization, and hold themselves and others to account in a supportive yet assertive way.

- Be confident to handle and reframe, as I did earlier, the 'F words' of the modern workplace:
  - Fear
  - Feelings
  - Fights
  - Failures
  - Feedback.

- Exercise 'power with' rather than 'power over'. This means rejecting the leadership systems of 'autocracy', 'paternalism', 'misogyny' and 'command and control' in favour of a model of leadership which demonstrates humility, is empathetic, values others, is humanizing, visionary, optimistic and pragmatic. This is transformational leadership.

- Engage with and listen to the workforce and then use that information to act. This is the opposite of deciding what action to take and then engaging with the workforce and listening to them as part of a 'consultation process'. People can see that for what it is – a sham.

- Treat issues of conflict, inclusion, wellbeing and engagement as strategic priorities with clearly defined objectives, targets and resources.

Looking back to my interview with John, what I took away from it was the importance of self-awareness for leaders and the need for them to adjust and moderate their style based on circumstances. I welcomed his thinking in terms of 'pre-emptive agility' and the need for managers to have just the right amount of information for them to be able to see slightly further ahead than their competitors. This is the perfect end to this chapter. We live in a competitive, brand-savvy and digitalized world. We are stepping into the unexplored terrain of a post-Covid-19 world teetering on the precipice of an economic and a climate emergency. The ability to be humble, to be compassionate and to be kind are still the most fundamental of the human virtues. Perhaps it is these most basic human principles, much maligned and misunderstood, that will be the key to the successful organizations of tomorrow.

TRANSFORMATIONAL THINKING

What have you learned from this chapter?

- What actions will you take away to promote transformational leadership and management in your own organization?

- How will you integrate the transformational principles into your leadership and management development programmes?

References

Ardern, J (2018) It takes strength to be an empathetic leader, www.bbc.co.uk/news/av/world-asia-46207254 (archived at https://perma.cc/T25L-G2AJ)

De Pree, M (2004) *Leadership Is an Art*, Currency Books, New York

Edmondson, C (2019) *The Fearless Organization: Creating psychological safety in the workplace for learning, innovation, and growth*, Wiley, New Jersey

Farson, R and Keyes, R (2002) The failure-tolerant leader. *Harvard Business Review*, August, https://hbr.org/2002/08/the-failure-tolerant-leader (archived at https://perma.cc/4FMY-BVAR)

Groysberg, B, Lee, J, Price, J and Yo-Jud Cheng, J (2018) The leader's guide to corporate culture. *Harvard Business Review*, January/February, https://hbr.org/2018/01/the-leaders-guide-to-corporate-culture (archived at https://perma.cc/6LSS-2ZQF)

Jones, G and Gorell, R (2018) *How to Create a Coaching Culture: A practical introduction*, Kogan Page, London

Liddle, D (2017a) *Managing Conflict: A practical guide to resolution in the workplace*, Kogan Page, London

Liddle, D (2017b) Do traditional grievance procedures destroy relationships? *Personnel Today*, 18 October, www.personneltoday.com/hr/traditional-grievance-procedures-destroy-relationships/ (archived at https://perma.cc/5S8A-HGPJ)

Liddle, D (2021) It's time to put the 'human' into human resources, *People Management*, 24 February, www.peoplemanagement.co.uk/voices/comment/its-time-to-put-the-human-back-in-human-resources (archived at https://perma.cc/8MAQ-8QUQ)

Pulakos, E and O'Leary, R (2011) Why is performance management so broken? *Industrial and Organizational Psychology: Perspectives on Science and Practice*, 4 (2), 146–164

Schein, E (2017) *Organizational Culture and Leadership*, 5th edn, Wiley, New Jersey

TCM (2021) Engage leadership, https://thetcmgroup.com/engage-leadership/ (archived at https://perma.cc/TS78-5QVG)

10

Wellbeing, engagement and inclusion

The key to great employee experience and world-class customer experience

---

TRANSFORMATIONAL LEARNING

Within this chapter, you will discover answers to the following questions:

- Why should wellbeing, engagement and inclusion (WEI) be considered as a single, unified discipline?
- How can organizations create a happier, healthier, more harmonious and higher-performing workplace?
- What is the employee experience equation and how does it work?
- How can leaders and managers align employee experience with customer experience and what benefits does this deliver?
- How can an organization create and sustain an inclusive workplace?

The way we treat each other defines our character

So far within *Transformational Culture*, I have set out the benefits of shifting from retributive justice to transformational justice and I have argued that organizations should reduce their reliance on rigid policies for managing concerns, conduct, complaints and conflict at work. I have offered a proven framework for managing these issues – a Resolution Framework – and I have proposed a new model of employee relations which underpins a progressive and modern social contract within our organizations.

I have set out the Transformational Culture Model and I have examined the eight enablers and the numerous benefits of a transformational culture – the 7Cs. I have advocated for the development of a cross-functional Transformational Culture Hub and I have set a challenge for HR, leaders, managers and unions to put people and values first.

In this chapter I explore three areas which are very close to my heart: wellbeing, engagement and inclusion. Over the past 30 years, I have worked in various environments as a mediator, a consultant, a coach and a trainer. I have worked in schools, prisons, universities, boardrooms, offices, clinics, wards, depots, shopfloors, warehouses and airports. In my work, I have witnessed the very best of humanity and the very worst of it. One thing that I have learned is that the way we treat each other defines our character and the character of our organizations. Nothing on earth defines our humanity more than the way that we treat our fellow human beings. If the past decade has taught us anything it is this: money, power, influence and status count for nought when we are held to account for our treatment of others. If we treat each other badly, it has a significant and detrimental impact on every aspect of our organization and on the people who work within it. But if we treat people well – I mean treat people with respect, civility, dignity, compassion, fairness, equity and kindness – our organizations will thrive, and so too will the people within, and without, our organizations.

A report published by Engage for Success highlights that even before Covid-19, the global economy lost more than US$ 1 trillion each year due to depression and anxiety. It highlights that depression is now a leading cause of disability, affecting more than 264 million people globally (Nadin, 2021).

One of the contributors to the report, Maggie Williams, explained:

'Workplace wellbeing and inclusivity go hand-in-hand. No-one can be at their best if they feel excluded from the environment they work in or are not treated fairly in employment or life. George Floyd's murder in 2020 shone a spotlight on the different experiences of black colleagues, and the extent to which wellbeing services such as employee assistance programmes (EAPs) were able to support them. Making sure that workplace practices and wellbeing benefits are genuinely inclusive is a priority if everyone is to be able to feel well at work.'

It is not rocket science. However, it does not happen by accident (well, not usually). This commitment to delivering a great human and employee experience requires planning, resourcing and dedication. It requires unflinching leadership to ensure that wellbeing, engagement and inclusion (WEI) becomes, and remains, a core strategic priority for our organizations.

That is one of the primary recommendations of this chapter – to align these three areas of human need into a single coherent business discipline. I will explain why I believe that organizations should create a combined strategic pillar in the people and culture strategy for WEI. The disparate disciplines of employee engagement, equity, diversity and inclusion (ED&I) and employee wellbeing compete against each other for resources, energy, time and focus. Yet, in virtually every possible respect, they complement each other. By bringing them together as a single, unified discipline, they act in a synergistic way, with each area enhancing the other. In so doing, our organizations create a person-centred and values-based virtuous circle, underpinned by the transformational principles of fairness, justice, inclusion, sustainability and high performance.

Moreover, with the integration of a transformational culture, where the focus is on collaboration, connection and common purpose, the area of WEI will become deeply integrated into the organizational activities relating to employee experience (EX) and customer experience (CX). I would go as far as to say that any efforts to enhance EX and CX which do not also include a focus on wellbeing, engagement and inclusion will be undermined and could ultimately fail to achieve their strategic objectives. I spoke to Ben Whitter, distinguished author and employee experience expert, about this and he explained to me:

> 'A world-class employee experience guarantees a world-class customer experience. The very best leaders deliver this outcome by unifying people around a shared purpose, mission, and compelling set of lived values. The result is a truly extraordinary experience for all stakeholders within and beyond a brand.'

WEI is one of the eight enablers of a transformational culture. It drives, and is driven by, a systemic and holistic view of our organizations and the people who work within them, who invest into them, who trade with them and who buy from them. These areas of our organizations are receiving unprecedented attention right now. As highlighted elsewhere in this book, the impact of Covid-19 on our mental and physical health, the rise of social and employee activism, the increased focus on employee experience and so on and so forth have made these three areas of the workplace some of the most discussed and hotly debated topics of our times. There is a big and very exciting conversation going on right now and this is a chance for our organizations to be part of it and to take a lead in it.

CASE STUDY
Creating a fair, just and inclusive culture within the UK Civil Service

THIS CASE STUDY HAS BEEN WRITTEN FOR TRANSFORMATIONAL CULTURE BY JASON GHABOOS, DEPUTY DIRECTOR, CIVIL SERVICE INCLUSIVE PRACTICE TEAM

The Civil Service is committed to harnessing the broadest range of diverse talent in terms of thinking styles, ideas and experience that will help us solve complex problems, innovate and deliver the very best public services. Our 2017–2020 strategy committed to tackling under-representation, building inclusive cultures for all and ensuring systems accountability for progress on inclusion.

We have taken a broad approach to working with culture, based in complexity science and viewing organizations as complex adaptive systems, and used this to develop an innovative culture model for the Civil Service. Our culture model represents the many influences of culture as shared, interconnected and dynamic. It shows us where and how we might intervene in the system to provoke change and shift cultural patterns.

We believe that to work with culture in a meaningful and enduring way we must intervene in all the influences on culture, supporting both the conscious and subconscious processes to achieve change. The Civil Service approach to working with organization culture uses this model of culture as its foundation. We support teams across the system to work confidently with culture through a tested and adaptable enquiry process and play back cultural insight at system level via our Culture Observatory.

We have also developed, in partnership with the Behavioural Insights Team and the CIPD, a robust and validated diagnostic tool for assessing how inclusive our organizations are. The diagnostic is a specially developed survey to understand individuals' perceptions of inclusion. It covers six domains: leadership, fair treatment, psychological safety, belonging, authenticity and organizational citizenship.

Our approach continues to focus on:

- embedding and mainstreaming diversity and inclusion (D&I) across all our workforce activities and processes;
- ensuring the approach is evidence driven, data led, delivery focused and merit based;
- reflecting a broader range of diversity (geographical, social and career backgrounds).

Wellbeing, engagement and inclusion should become a single discipline

As explained earlier, focusing on the areas of wellbeing, inclusion and employee engagement in a divergent rather than a convergent way fragments organizational focus and it undermines efforts to achieve any one of them to their fullest potential.

Indeed, in some organizations, the three agendas of wellbeing, engagement and inclusion compete against each other for resources and strategic leadership support. From the outside looking in, this can appear to be reactive and disjointed. As one strategic lever is pulled, due to the lack of integration with the other two it has a detrimental impact on all three of them, rendering each of them less effective and less successful. This also undermines overall trust and confidence across the workforce by giving the impression of chaotic and discordant decision making in three of the most important areas of our organizations. Where data is gathered, it requires a PhD to be able to triangulate them with each other and to make sense of them. The data are often misaligned, and the issues of causation and correlation are entirely unclear, rendering a strategic-level analysis virtually impossible. The best examples I have seen still involve a lot of guesswork and assumptions.

Of course, a great many of the issues I have highlighted above are cultural, systemic and structural. They require a combined effort to resolve them. I believe that the combined area of wellbeing, engagement and inclusion should be a central focus for the people and culture function, and a core feature of the people and culture strategy, both of which I explored in more detail in Chapter 7.

The EX equation

There is no magic bullet or simple answer to the big questions of improving employee wellbeing, engagement and inclusion. If there was, we would all be doing it and the issues would have been resolved long ago. The emergence of EX is a step in the right direction. However, unless employee experience can actively address the wider issues of wellbeing, engagement and inclusion, it could easily become just another in a long list of failed business fads. That would be a dreadful shame as the EX agenda has the potential to be a gamechanger for our organizations.

Within the context of a transformational culture, I believe we can imagine employee experience as an equation, as shown in Figure 10.1.

FIGURE 10.1   The Employee Experience Equation™

$$\frac{W + E + I}{3P} \times 4H = EX$$

© The TCM Group. Used with permission

The EX equation explained

WELLBEING, ENGAGEMENT AND INCLUSION

At the top of the equation sits WEI, the numerator. This reflects the organization's combined strategic and operational efforts to create and sustain an inclusive, engaged and psychologically safe workplace. A workplace where employees are given a voice, they are valued, their issues are resolved constructively, they are treated fairly and they feel included in making decisions which will impact them.

As part of a transformational culture, the organization's people and culture strategy includes a pillar relating to WEI which ensures that it is resourced, evaluated and reported on effectively. In addition, this is one of the subgroups of the cross-functional transformational culture hub which ensures that the area of WEI receives attention and commitment from all stakeholders. In other words, WEI becomes a shared narrative that cuts across all organizational disciplines.

POLICIES, PROCESSES AND PROCEDURES

These three Ps sit as the denominator in the employee experience equation. The combined efforts for delivering wellbeing, engagement and inclusion at work are divided by the impact of the organization's policies, processes and procedures. When the organization's policies, processes and procedures are aligned to the purpose and the values of the organization, and where the policies are concerned about protecting relationships, engendering resolution, restoration and learning, promoting dialogue and driving collaboration, there is less of a negative impact on the overall EX equation.

Conversely, where the organization's policies, processes and procedures are about risk mitigation, where they draw on the principles of retributive justice, they are reductive, they are destructive, they are divisive and they pit people against each other, the more of a negative impact on the overall EX equation they will have.

The policies and procedures which should be considered in the EX equation include but are not limited to:

- procedures for the recruitment and induction of new employees;
- the entire employee handbook;

- policies for resolving concerns, conduct, complaints and conflicts at work;
- policies and procedures for tackling bullying, harassment and discrimination at work;
- whistleblowing and similar speak-up and/or speak-out policies.

HAPPY, HEALTHY, HARMONIOUS AND HIGH PERFORMANCE

These 4Hs relate directly to the climate in our teams and the felt experience of team members. They also relate to the way that our jobs are designed. When our job design reflects our organization's purpose and the values, it deepens our connection to our organization, to our colleagues and to our leaders. It acts as a catalyst for unlocking our inner brilliance and it empowers us to deliver the best possible customer experience. Where our jobs are designed in this way, it has a net positive impact on the overall employee experience, with the opposite being true – confusing, out-of-date or inaccurate job design damages overall EX.

The climate of our teams is directly influenced by the behaviour of our managers and leaders, ie their actions, interactions and reactions. Therefore, in the EX equation, the impact of the 4Hs is significantly increased when our managers and leaders align purpose with values and behaviour. The greater the emphasis our leaders and managers place on creating a happy working environment, the greater the impact on the overall EX equation. In addition, the impact on the EX equation is significantly enhanced when the following occurs:

- Where our managers and leaders understand that they are role models and their behaviour and language set the tone for the rest of the team.
- Where our managers and leaders are concerned about the health and psychological safety of team members. Where they actively promote and integrate management systems which enhance psychological safety, and they are trained to spot and respond appropriately to any mental health issues which may arise within their teams.

- Where our managers and leaders are empowered to be responsive, flexible, agile and adaptable to the changing needs of the organization and its stakeholders.

- Where our managers and leaders see, harness, amplify and celebrate the inner brilliance of their people. Where they coach their people and act as mentors to support their teams to grow and to develop.

- Where our managers and leaders can spot and resolve disputes early and have the skills and the capability to resolve them constructively.

Some organizations concentrate only on the first three Hs (health, happiness and harmony) but they overlook the fourth (high performance). Their credibility is therefore reduced and the criticism is that the culture of the business is too 'hearts and minds' and it fails to take account of hard business realities. In other organizations, the focus is predominantly on the fourth H. Those organizations believe that high performance can be achieved without taking account of the other three Hs. In those organizations, burnout, low engagement, low morale, high turnover and poor customer service will follow as surely as night follows day.

The key to great EX is to get the equilibrium right.

EMPLOYEE EXPERIENCE

When WEI is divided by the 3Ps and the aggregate is multiplied by the 4Hs, this gives the overall employee experience.

I am going to have to come clean here. This equation is simply an idea – I have never seen an organization that captures all the data that would be necessary to fully complete the equation and therefore to fully assess its overall employee experience. However, as more and more organizations hire for roles that are dedicated to EX, the ability to understand the antecedents of EX and to measure its impact becomes within reach. In this age of rapid digital transformation, we know that the data to measure EX already exists in our organizations, it is about having the courage and the tenacity to go in search of it.

I am not advocating an algorithm to replace good judgement and human wisdom. However, the EX equation can act as a useful tool to evaluate the multivariate data that is available to us and to use the data to map and analyze the current state of our employee experience in our organizations. By applying the EX equation in localities (departments, divisions or sub-brands), it enables organizations to identify patterns and trends and to allocate the necessary resources to support local initiatives to enhance EX. It also allows those areas of our businesses which are delivering strong EX to act as beacons and champions, which can inspire improvements in other areas of the organization.

Happiness, positive psychology and performance

The links between happiness at work and improved productivity and performance are well documented. The areas of positive psychology and neuroscience have been instrumental in raising the profile of the power of happiness and the numerous advantages that happiness can deliver in the workplace and in our lives.

> 'When we are happy – when our mindset and the mood are positive – we are smarter, more motivated, and thus more successful. Happiness is the centre and success revolves around it.' (Achor, 2010)

Happiness is a state of mind that is characterized by positive feelings and emotions such as joy, excitement, fulfilment, gratitude, satisfaction, pride, contentment. Happiness is driven by the achievement of pleasure and/or engagement and/or meaning in our lives. This mindset has the potential to enhance overall employee experience and can drive customer experience.

Using the principles of positive psychology, this alignment between EX and CX creates flow within the organization – a flow of ideas, innovation, insight and learning (all sources of happiness). It can also create a flow between culture and climate (see pages 138–140 for details of the Culture Flow System).

At times of happiness and flow, we experience the release of the DOSE hormones – dopamine, oxytocin, serotonin and endorphins -

widely known as the happy hormones. These happy hormones deliver multiple positive benefits that can improve our mental health and wellbeing. They can help us to regulate our feelings, develop resilience, improve our mood, give us drive and, perhaps most importantly of all, help us to get a good night's sleep.

Aligning employee experience with customer experience

Happiness, therefore, can act a powerful enabler and a desirable outcome of good employee experience and customer experience. Aligning your employee value proposition with your customer value proposition is central to creating an engaged, productive and healthy workforce, a workforce who are aligned to the needs of your customers and who delight in delivering outstanding customer service.

It also gives a coherent meaning and direction to everyone within the organization. Critically, it removes any perception that there is competition for focus, value or resource between the employee and the customer. At a fundamental level, the Transformational Culture Model is predicated on a simple belief: when the employee is happy, the customer is happy and when the customer is happy, the organization is successful.

In 2019, the CEOs of nearly 200 US companies said that shareholder value was no longer their main objective:

'Investing in employees, delivering value to customers, dealing ethically with suppliers, and supporting outside communities are now at the forefront of American business goals.' (Fitzgerald, 2019)

In many of the organizations with which I work, there is a focus on viewing the employee as a customer. This concept is gaining traction, with many HR teams developing their employee value proposition with a clear focus on the employee as customer.

I recently had the pleasure of interviewing Ted Stone, CEO of Customer First. Customer First UK is the awarding body for the

Putting the Customer First® standard, the national standard for customer service. I asked Ted why organizations should align customer experience with employee experience and this is what he told me:

'There is a direct link between customer experience and employee experience. Your employees are the most important asset within your organization. Make sure that you treat them this way. You can have the most fantastic product or service offering in your market segment, but if you have staff who feel overworked and undervalued, it will consistently degrade the customer experience. People buy from people – make sure your staff are valued and they will value your customers.'

The inclusive workplace

Inclusion, and the development of a fair, just and learning workplace, is a central tenet of the transformational culture. Shakil Butt, HR consultant and leadership professional, agrees. Shakil is a long-standing campaigner in the areas of equality, diversity and inclusion. As I was researching *Transformational Culture*, I asked Shakil for his views on the current state of WEI in our workplaces. He explained to me that for it to have any significant impact, it must be treated as a core strategic priority:

'Equity, diversity and inclusion have been advocated for decades, but apart from a few strands of difference, organizations remain mostly unchanged. This is because very often it has not been owned by everyone internally and paid only lip service by senior leadership teams. It gets passed down the line to HR or a D&I lead to resolve as a "fait accompli". Worse still are those organizations that establish employee resource groups and expect them to resolve the very problems they are suffering from. Systemic issues that lead to marginalization are multilayered and complex, so simple fixes will not work and the complete employee journey, the products and services and wider ecosystem all need to be considered to bring about meaningful change. This requires investment and accountability in the same way that any strategic change programme is managed.'

In support of Shakil's perceptions, the CIPD in its 'Building inclusive workplaces' report highlights some troubling statistics (CIPD, 2019):

- FTSE 100 CEOs in 2018 were more likely to be called Dave or Steve than be female, meaning male and female experiences of workplace progression aren't equal.
- If the current rate of progress remains the same, FTSE 100 companies won't meet targets for BAME board representation until 2066.

Given these statistics, and considering recent events, it occurred to me that this book presented a great opportunity to develop an inclusive workplace pledge. The pledge offers some guidelines for employers and employees about how to create and sustain an inclusive workplace.

The inclusive workplace pledge

An inclusive workplace is one where we can be the best version of ourselves, free from others judging, condemning or excluding us because of our age, race, gender, class, physical ability, mental health, sexuality or religious preferences. In an inclusive workplace, our differences are a sign of strength, not a cause of adversity. Each of us is recruited and promoted purely on merit, ie our ability to do the job. Our recruiters, managers and leaders know how to reduce the potential for prejudice and bias in their decision making; they are well trained, and they are encouraged to constantly review and evaluate their commitment to an inclusive workplace.

In an inclusive workplace, every employee is afforded opportunities to listen to and to learn from their colleagues. An inclusive workplace is one where each voice is heard and each contribution is valued. An inclusive workplace requires hard work and action; it demands respect, civility, dignity, dialogue, psychological safety and collaboration.

We understand that an inclusive workplace is not about inane platitudes and superficial pleasantries. It can involve some tough talking, with differing beliefs, values and points of view being expressed, sometimes strongly. That is healthy and perfectly normal.

We recognize that this is the bedrock of an inclusive, innovative and creative organization; it is, after all, an enabler of a transformational culture. We understand that these conversations make us, and our organization, even more successful.

When we disagree, as surely we will, we can be confident that systems have been put in place to protect us from harm, but which enable us to resolve the concerns in a conciliatory, supportive and meaningful way. If we are unable to do so, we do not get penalized or blamed and the issues do not get swept under the carpet. Our managers are there to support us; they know that managing an inclusive team will mean they have to resolve the odd disagreement and the occasional quarrel. They are trained and they are confident to do so. If for any reason they cannot resolve the situation, we don't get dragged into complex policies and divisive processes. Yes, formal procedures do exist, and they are there if all else fails; however, we have access to trained mediators, facilitators, coaches and mentors who can assist us to reach resolution, as required.

In an inclusive workplace, each employee can flourish and achieve their full potential. Our inner brilliance is recognized for what it is; it is nurtured by our managers and leaders because they too can see that inner brilliance. They will work with me to grow it and to bring it to the fore. When we do, they will cherish and nurture it. They will not be threatened by it, they won't try to undermine it and they won't try to claim it as their own.

CASE STUDY
Hounslow Council puts wellbeing, engagement and inclusion at the core of its culture

THIS CASE STUDY HAS BEEN PREPARED FOR TRANSFORMATIONAL CULTURE BY ALISON FORD, STRATEGIC OD AND LEARNING BUSINESS PARTNER, AND STEVE WHITEHEAD, DIRECTOR OF HUMAN RESOURCES AND ORGANIZATIONAL DEVELOPMENT, THE LONDON BOROUGH OF HOUNSLOW

We are proud that Hounslow is a real community of communities and one of the most culturally diverse areas in the UK. Over 250,000 people live in the borough. It's an attractive place to live and work, with miles of river, canals, nature reserves and open spaces.

The council has approximately 2,500 employees, the majority of whom are permanent. One of our key drivers is to work with our partners and our communities to co-create the services, facilities and infrastructure which make Hounslow a great place to live and work. Central to this is our Corporate Plan, recently refreshed, our recovery programme post pandemic, and the One Hounslow programme, which is about the ways in which we need to work (spirit and culture) to achieve our ambition.

Turning the spotlight on people and culture

We have been on a continuous journey of change for the last few years, but the arrival of our new CEO, with a renewed vision and a focus on people, has put our culture under the spotlight. Only with the right culture will we achieve our ambitions, refocusing and revitalizing our public service ethos, to ensure that we are a resilient workforce which puts residents front and centre. We already knew that we need to focus more on joining up internal services and work more collaboratively with our partners to deliver effective services. Empowering our staff to become more creative and entrepreneurial has been essential. A focus on effective leadership at all levels in the organization was also key for us to achieve this transformational change and we wanted our culture change programme to model these ambitions from the start.

The evidence from previous surveys, both internal and with our communities, indicated that there was a need to invest in and empower our people, collaborate much more effectively and ensure that people had equal access to opportunities for development. Interestingly, the pandemic has brought this into much clearer focus, especially how we work with and serve our community.

A dynamic, diverse and inclusive place to work

Our ambition is to become an outstanding council and an exemplar in place leadership. We are determined to remain a dynamic, diverse and inclusive place to live and work, and the council embarked upon a single co-ordinated and outcome-focused transformation programme in mid-2019. The #1Hounslow Programme is reshaping the council's resident offer in a way that will ensure resilience into the future and will deliver the priorities and pledges in the Corporate Plan. (This was written some time ago, before Covid-19, which is developing this original ambition into a dynamic programme of change.)

Over 60 members of staff from across the organization, from all levels and locations, were nominated or volunteered as Culture Change Champions. They took responsibility for engaging with designated areas of the organization (not their own services) to ensure that all staff had the opportunity to take part in the conversation in a way that best suited them – workshops (using world café methodology), conversation hubs, team meetings, informal conversations, postcards, 'empty belly' posters and an online survey. Culture Change Champions were mentored by senior managers and benefited from several other learning interventions.

Values which drive behaviours

Our values are unusual. They were tested and refined with our people before being finalized. There is an ongoing process of embedding them into the way we work which has included storytelling, team discussions, a communications plan, a new approach to managing performance through ongoing conversations, increased involvement and engagement with our people and a new approach to HR policies – a framework based on our values rather than a set of different, directive policies.
Our values are:

- Lead with heart. We're here for the people of Hounslow. We work together with them and for them with care and compassion, with patience and in partnership. We put ourselves in others' shoes, remembering that every person is different and every interaction is a real moment in their lives. We always feel first.

- Do new. We need to do things differently if we're going to help Hounslow people thrive in the future. Hard work is important but it's not enough on its own. We need to challenge ourselves to break new ground, invent new approaches, try new ideas, keep moving forward and keep improving. That means being ready to stop doing things we've done before. It means taking on risk and backing each other when we take a leap.

- Pass on the power. The world keeps on changing and we need to change with it. We won't be able to adapt fast enough to the future needs of our residents if we stick to old-fashioned command and control. We need to hand over responsibility and give people more power to make decisions and take action themselves. It's about being transparent and straightforward. It's about providing tools and support. But most of all, it's about being ready to trust each other to do the right thing.

- Harness the mix. We work together, across disciplines and roles. We talk lots, share our insights, our skills and experience. We're not interested in siloes or defensiveness. We're always open to different approaches, we're flexible and ready to adapt. We break down the barriers between our parts and people to unlock the problem-solving power of our amazing mix of minds.

- Be a rock. There is lots to do and people need us. It is up to us to take the initiative. To take responsibility. To stand up and be counted. Every day. It is about being super focused, effective and efficient. It is about allocating our resources smartly and with good rationale – using data to help guide our decisions. But most of all, it is about having the strength and determination to keep on going through thick and thin.

We want people who work for us to bring their best selves to work and they can only do that for our community if they work for an organization that values and respects people, treats them with kindness and compassion, empowers and values them.

Our World of Work

We know from our response to the pandemic – through the stories about how our values have translated into action and behaviours – that there has been an impact on our culture. Our ways of working – remotely and flexibly – and how we share resources and assets with our community will never be the same. Our World of Work project sets out our ambition to work differently in the future.

We have learned a lot along the way:

1 Having a whole organization conversation about our culture and values was key to embedding our values – we're still on the journey.

2 Continuing to engage people at every level so everyone has a voice and is listened to – a model we continue to use.

3 Compassionate and transformational leadership from the most senior levels is critical.'

Conclusion and calls to action

We see it in the news, in our social media feeds and on our TV screens every day. Exclusion feeds division, which in turn feeds intolerance, which in turn feeds hate. In an increasingly divided society, where diversity is a source of adversity, quarrels turn so toxic so quickly, blame, shame and punishment seem to be the primary source of justice, polarization and dogma are trending, and accountability comes from 120 characters or less, the need to double our efforts to promote wellbeing, engagement and inclusion has never been greater or more urgent.

The areas of wellbeing, engagement and inclusion have perplexed organizations for a great many years. To meet the rising demands for social justice and the call for greater fairness, diversity, equity and inclusion in our workplaces, it is imperative that we reframe this debate and take a fresh look at these issues. Rolling out another ED&I strategy, a wellbeing statement and a programme of unconscious bias training for a group of managers is not going to be sufficient to address these pressing and complex challenges.

When presented with this level of complexity, the answer is sometimes to create more and more complex solutions. What I have advocated in this chapter is the reverse of that. I have suggested that the answer to these complex questions is to go back to some fundamental principles of human need and human relations – respect, civility, authenticity, transparency, dialogue and trust. In this chapter I propose that the areas of wellbeing, engagement and inclusion are aligned as a single discipline and that they become a core strategic priority within the people and culture plan.

The EX equation offers a solid starting point for any organization which is wondering where to begin. The EX equation is designed to generate a dialogue and a big conversation in our workplaces. It is not a magic formula for the perfect workplace, but it is a catalyst for a new way of looking at these issues and a fresh way of exploring how those various factors combine and interrelate. The aim then, of course, is to draw all that data and information into a coherent plan of action. This action plan will sit with the Transformational Culture Hub and will be a key feature of the people and culture function. This will ensure that the process of integrating WEI is a) evidence based, b) inclusive and c) sustainable.

References

Achor, S (2010) *The Happiness Advantage. The seven principles that fuel success and performance at work*, Virgin Books, London

CIPD (2019) *Building Inclusive Workplaces: Assessing the evidence*. CIPD, London

Fitzgerald, M (2019) The CEOs of nearly 200 companies just said shareholder value is no longer their main objective, www.cnbc.com/2019/08/19/the-ceos-of-nearly-two-hundred-companies-say-shareholder-value-is-no-longer-their-main-objective.html (archived at https://perma.cc/AKS7-UUDV)

Liddle, D (2017) *Managing Conflict: A practical guide to resolution in the workplace*, Kogan Page, London

Nadin, G (2021) *Engage for Success Special Wellbeing Report: Covid-19 recovery & employee mental health*, Engage for Success, London

PART TWO

The Transformational Culture Playbook

Introduction

The Transformational Culture Playbook includes practical toolkits and checklists to support you as you develop and integrate a transformational culture. The toolkits are designed for anyone who has an interest in developing a fair, just, inclusive, sustainable, and high-performing organization.

The playbook also suggests reflective practice, and each section of the playbook includes space for transformational thinking. More details and an additional checklist are available from www.transformationalculture.com. This site also includes details of workshops for transformational culture practitioners.

I want to start this section with a powerful example of an organization which has developed a long-term strategy to put its people and values first. *The Financial Times* (FT) is one of the world's leading news organizations, recognized internationally for its authority, integrity and accuracy. While writing this book I had the pleasure of interviewing the chief commercial officer (CCO) at the *FT*, Jon Slade (https://aboutus.ft.com/).

David Liddle: How would you describe the culture of the *FT*?

Jon Slade: The culture at the *FT* is based on our values of integrity, curiosity, trust, ambition, subscriber focus and inclusion. Running through all those values is a culture that values collaboration and honesty, a deep sense of tradition coupled with innovation, and respect for one another.

We know that we make better decisions, and to serve a diverse customer base, we have to create equal opportunities for all and encourage diversity of thinking in our decision making. Our business and industry is changing faster than ever – to succeed we must have a motivated workforce that feel comfortable sharing their opinions.

It is also integral to our culture that our employees feel represented in how the business is run, and a critical dimension of that are the employee-led networks that push us to ask where else we can improve on questions of ethnicity, gender, mental health and sexual orientation.

We have also created a global diversity and inclusion taskforce to drive us ever closer to our goals. We have also created a US taskforce to help address the unique challenges and opportunities in the region.

We have an employee-led sustainability taskforce that conducted an extensive global audit in 2020 to measure the carbon emissions generated from our business operations and within our value chain. The results are being used to define our sustainability goals over the next decade, and we will use an environmental management system to monitor progress year on year.

And the Next Generation Board – a group of talented younger staff who are mapped to, and reverse-mentor, the *FT*'s management board – has been fundamental in connecting senior management to all levels of staff.

DL: How do you measure the impact of your organizational culture?

JS: While we're proud to have won awards for our workplace culture and dedication to inclusion, we measure our success in terms of culture by asking staff themselves on a quarterly basis how they feel using the Peakon engagement survey.

This is a bottom-up collaborative approach where we seek and listen to feedback regularly, and ask specific questions relating to employee engagement and specific matters we know will be of concern and interest. How did staff feel the company's leadership was helping them throughout the pandemic? How is the *FT* doing in terms of offering career progression?

The results are shared with the management teams and managers are expected to engage with staff on a regular basis over the results. We know employee expectations have changed, and they expect to have their voices heard.

DL: This has been an extremely tough year. What steps are you taking to build back better following the global coronavirus pandemic?

JS: We know that staff have valued flexibility in their working arrangements during the Covid-19 crisis but have also missed the 'cultural recharging point' that is the office. Our bank of social capital has been drawn down on heavily in the last year. So we are clear that a hybrid approach to returning to the office is going to be important.

We're going to lean on lessons from our digital culture – iteration, test-and-learn – and we won't pretend to get everything right from the start. We know there will be a lot of testing and adjusting in the next 12–24 months. And we'll be ensuring the voice of the employees is heard in our thinking and planning.

DL: What are your three key lessons for other senior leaders who are considering developing a transformational culture?

JS:

1 Listen to staff, and act on what they are telling you. If you only do the first part, you are failing.

2 Talk to staff and share as widely and frequently as possible what is going on around the business. Transparency has been critical to us during the Covid-19 crisis.

3 And finally, experience the parts of the business you do not know well enough. I have tried to challenge myself by learning more about other areas of the business and stepping into mini secondments. A

couple of summers ago, I had the privilege of spending a week with our product and tech team and learned a lot about a business area that is outside of my own expertise. Other leaders have since followed the example. I would highly recommend others try this too.

TRANSFORMATIONAL THINKING

What could you learn from the *FT*'s commitment to people and values?

What three actions could you take within your organization to start your own transformational culture journey?

What are the key drivers for you to adopt this approach?

What internal and external resources might you need to support you?

11

Transformational Toolkit 1

Building the business case for a transformational culture

This section provides guidance to support you as you develop your business case for developing a transformational culture. The business case is a critical document which sets out the rationale for the development of a transformational culture.

Developing a business case delivers several additional benefits:

- It ensures that your culture is built on strong evidence. This evidence can be used to evaluate your current situation and provides a set of baseline indicators for evaluating the impact of the transformational culture over the short, medium and longer terms.

- It ensures that the appropriate resources have been identified prior to engaging on the cultural transformation journey.

- The process of developing the business case presents an opportunity to undertake a cultural audit and to map your existing organizational structures to assess trends and patterns.

- During the development of the business case, the process of engaging key stakeholders gives them a voice and builds a sense of collaboration and connection.

Your business case should align to the Transformational Culture Model as described in Chapter 3 (see Figure 11.1).

FIGURE 11.1   The Transformational Culture Model

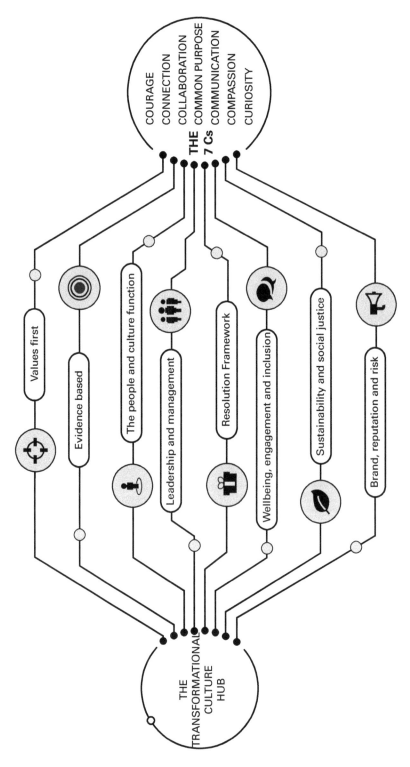

THE 7 Cs

COURAGE
CONNECTION
COLLABORATION
COMMON PURPOSE
COMMUNICATION
COMPASSION
CURIOSITY

Values first

Evidence based

The people and culture function

Leadership and management

Resolution Framework

Wellbeing, engagement and inclusion

Sustainability and social justice

Brand, reputation and risk

THE TRANSFORMATIONAL CULTURE HUB

© The TCM Group

Transformational culture business case template

1. Vision and objectives

This section of your business case allows you to set your vision and objectives for the development of a transformational culture.

- What is the purpose and the values of your organization?
- How does a transformational culture align to your purpose and values?
- What are the key benefits of adopting a transformational culture, ie a culture which is fair, just, inclusive, sustainable and high performing?
- What are the key drivers for adopting a transformational culture?
- How does a transformational culture align with your wider corporate strategy and objectives?

2. Situational analysis (current context)

This section of your business case allows you to explain your current organizational culture.

- What emphasis do you currently place on the eight enablers of a transformational culture (see Figure 11.1)?
- What are the strengths, weaknesses, opportunities and threats (SWOT) relating to your organizational culture?
- Who is currently responsible for shaping and managing the culture of your organization?
- What policies and procedures do you have in place now? Do they draw from the retributive justice models as described in this book?
- How would you describe the climate (micro-cultures) in departments and teams within your organization?

3. Evidence of the case for change

This section of your business case allows you to set out the evidence which supports the need for change. This evidence can also be used to develop baseline measures with which you can evaluate the impact of the cultural transformation.

The following data can be gathered using a variety of means. Some examples of the tools for gathering the data are set out in Transformational Toolkit 2.

- Do you currently measure the culture of your organization?
- What data do you have relating to the following areas of your organization?

  a. Conflicts, grievances, disciplinary cases, performance management cases, bullying, harassment and discrimination, whistleblowing cases, etc. (I have developed a cost of conflict calculator which was explained in my first book, *Managing Conflict*. The calculator can be used to gather forensic-level data relating to the costs of these issues.)

  b. Absence and attrition.

  c. Employee engagement, wellbeing and inclusion.

  d. Sustainability and responses to social justice issues.

  e. Customer experience.

  f. Brand and reputation.

  g. Productivity.

Triangulating your primary data against your secondary data means that relationships can be discovered, and patterns and trends can be identified. The above data can be triangulated against any of the following secondary data sets to provide a more detailed analysis:

- Use of alternative dispute resolution (ADR) or restorative processes.
- Employee engagement initiatives and programmes.
- Wellbeing and inclusion programmes.
- Sustainability and social justice activities.
- Leadership and management development programmes.
- Organizational change programmes.

4. Benchmarking

This section of your business case allows you to consider what other organizations are doing in relation to culture change and to examine best practices from relevant professional bodies and associations such as the CIPD or SHRM.

5. Stakeholder analysis and impact assessment

This section of your business case allows you to consider who the key stakeholders are within your organization and what role they will play in developing, deploying, integrating and evaluating the transformational culture (see Table 11.1).

- Who are the stakeholders?
- What role will they play in the development of the transformational culture?
- What impact will the transformational culture have on the stakeholder group?

6. Developing the Transformational Culture Hub

This section of your business case explores the potential role, objectives, benefits and scope of the Transformational Culture Hub (Culture Hub).

- What are the benefits of adopting a cross-functional Culture Hub?
- What are the proposed terms of reference for the Culture Hub?
- How will the Culture Hub integrate into your organization and what resources will be required?
- Who will chair the Culture Hub, what decision-making authority do they have and what governance processes will need to be developed to ensure accountability?
- Who will be involved in the development of the Culture Hub?
- Which workstreams will be developed and what processes will be put into place for the reporting and accountability of the workstreams?

TABLE 11.1   The key stakeholders and their role in the transformational culture

Stakeholder group	Role in the development of a transformational culture	Potential impact of a transformational culture
Board/C-suite		
HR/ER etc		
Learning and development		
Organizational development		
Unions/works councils/ employee reps		
Senior and line management		
Diversity and equality groups		
Occupational health		
Lawyers/counsel		
Change agents		
Employee engagement/internal communications		
Shareholders/investors		
Local community groups and organizations		

More details can be found in Chapter 3 and in Transformational Toolkit 3.

7. Project plan, timetable and key milestones

This section of your business case allows you to begin shaping the project plan. It includes the proposed roadmap and timescales for the delivery and deployment of the transformational culture:

- What does success look like, what are the critical success measures?
- When will the cultural change programme start, what are the key milestones and deliverables?

- What are the key workstreams and who are the project teams to support these?
- Where do you want to be in 12, 24, and 36 months?
- What are your key milestones for the next 12, 24 and 36 months?
- What is the approach to the assessment and management of risk?

8. Resource requirements

This section of your business case allows you to set out the costs and the resources required to support the implementation of a transformational culture. It is advisable to link the costs and the resource requirements to the eight enablers of the transformational culture model.

9. Anticipated benefits and return on investment

This is a key part of the business case and as such it should be evidence based and persuasive. This is the part of the business case which will 'sell' the concept of a transformational culture to senior leaders and to other stakeholders. The following is just a selection of questions that will need to be answered in this section:

- What are the potential benefits of adopting a fair, just, inclusive, sustainable and high-performance workplace?
- How can the organization harness the potential of the 7Cs of a transformational culture, as set out in Chapter 4?
- What are the potential benefits and ROI from reframing HR to people and culture?
- What are the potential benefits and ROI from developing a cross-functional Transformational Culture Hub?
- What are the potential benefits and ROI from adopting wellbeing, engagement and inclusion as a unified and integrated discipline?
- What are the potential benefits and ROI from developing a Resolution Framework?
- What are the potential benefits and ROI from developing a values and behaviours framework?

- What are the potential benefits and ROI from investing in our managers and leaders?
- What are the potential benefits and ROI from developing a commitment to sustainability and social justice?
- What are the aggregated benefits and potential ROI from adopting a transformational culture?

10. Programme resilience

This section of your business case allows you to assess the potential blocks and barriers to integrating a transformational culture and explains how they should be managed and overcome. It is advisable to cross reference to the threats identified in the SWOT analysis in section 2.

11. Internal communications

This section of your business case allows you to consider how you will let your stakeholders know what you are doing and how you will maintain the momentum. The development of a detailed communications strategy will be a priority for the new Culture Hub.

12. Additional information

Please use this space to add any areas that you believe will need to be included within your transformational culture business case.

_____

_____

_____

_____

_____

_____

_____

_____

_____

_____

_____

_____

_____

_____

_____

_____

_____

_____

_____

_____

_____

_____

_____

12

Transformational Toolkit 2

Measuring and evaluating your culture

'A great company culture can make each member of the company better. And it can make the company ascendant.' (Schmidt and Rosenberg, 2014, p. 65)

In *How Google Works*, the authors Eric Schmidt and Jonathan Rosenberg share their learning following Google's acquisition of Motorola in 2012. 'There are a couple of important steps to take. First, recognize the problem. What is the culture that defines your company today (not the one described by the mission or value statements, the real one that people live in every day)? What problems has this culture caused with the business? It is important not to simply criticize the existing culture which will just insult people but rather to draw a connection between business failures and how the culture may have played a hand in those situations.'

Schmidt and Rosenberg provide five practical steps to support the process of driving and sustaining cultural change. They are summarized below.

1 Articulate the new culture you envision and take specific high-profile steps to start moving that way.

2 Promote transparency and sharing of ideas across divisions.

3 Open up everyone's calendar so that employees can see what other employees are doing.

4 Hold more company-wide meetings.

5 Encourage honest questions without reprisal and when you get these tough questions, answer them honestly and authentically.

This toolkit will help your organization develop a robust system for capturing and evaluating data which supports the development of the business case outlined in Transformational Culture Toolkit 1.

It must be stressed that most of the data that your organization requires to measure its culture already exists in one form or another. The methodology that I recommend for gathering quantitative and qualitative data is based on a research model called Participatory Action Research (PAR). The analysis is a participatory and an active means for gathering quantitative and qualitative data which seeks to understand the world by reflecting and trying to change it collaboratively.

> Quantitative data is information about quantities; that is, information that can be measured and written down with numbers. As part of a conflict analysis, quantitative data will include measures such as: how many grievances were received in the last year; how much time was spent handling conflict; how many cases ended up in a formal process; how much money was spent on legal advice, etc.
>
> Qualitative data is descriptive and draws on people's personal experiences, feelings, interactions and concerns. It is, by nature, subjective; however, the stories that are gathered can be profoundly powerful and can provide valuable insights into the reality of managing conflict in a way that statistics, numbers and percentages fail to do.

When combined as part of your cultural analysis, quantitative and qualitative data provide a valuable overview of the current culture and climate within your organization.

The transformational culture index that I recommend includes four distinct data-gathering methods:

1 Desktop review.

2 Culture, engagement, climate and pulse surveys.

3 In-depth interviews.

4 Focus groups.

1. Desktop review

This is an opportunity to draw together historical data gathered from existing data sources and gathering processes within your organization. The data may be collected from the past 12, 24 or 36 months. For purposes of expediency, I don't generally recommend going back further than three years. However, my experience has led me to believe that the further back in time you can go, the more detailed and valuable the subsequent trend analysis will be.

TRANSFORMATIONAL THINKING

Data that is typically collected as part of the desktop review may include any of the following:

- Grievance levels including action taken and outcomes.
- Bullying and harassment allegations including action taken and outcomes.
- Data relating to productivity and performance.
- Data from stress audits or other audits into workplace wellbeing.
- Allegations and findings of discrimination including action taken and outcomes.
- Employment tribunal levels and outcomes.
- Volume and value of settlement agreements.
- Absence data, particularly any that relates to stress absence or suspensions due to workplace conflicts or allegations of bullying.
- Data gathered from exit interviews.
- Data gathered from analysis of whistleblowing cases.
- Data gathered from appraisals.
- Customer complaints or serious incidents.
- Levels of public awareness relating to the culture of your organization such as through press clippings, comments on social media or in the news media.

2. Surveys

A survey can be a useful way of gathering data from a selection of your employees. There are no hard and fast ways that the survey should be set up. However, it needs to generate data which will stand up to scrutiny and from that point of view it is generally better that the respondents can supply their answers anonymously.

The following surveys can be useful for diagnosing and evaluating an organizational culture and understanding the cultural profile of your organization:

- Employee engagement surveys.
- Culture surveys.
- Climate surveys.
- Pulse checks.

3. In-depth interviews

Interviews can be a powerful way of gathering qualitative data and to ascertain people's felt experiences of the culture and the climate (micro-cultures) of your organization. In the past, I have interviewed the following representatives of a particular function as part of undertaking a culture change programme. It is generally helpful to interview a senior leader from many of the functions as well as those in a frontline role.

4. Focus groups

Focus groups bring people together to discuss a particular topic or issue. Used as part of a cultural analysis, focus groups are a highly effective way of getting people talking about their experiences of the climate and the culture of their workplace and generating valuable qualitative data. Invite a wide cross-section of stakeholders to attend the focus groups. Such cross-functional focus groups are an effective way of generating debate and therefore yielding more valuable data for use as part of the conflict analysis.

By conducting a focus group with a broad cross-section of your stakeholders, you are also sending a powerful message to your stakeholders about your commitment to listening to them and valuing their views and experiences as part of the development of a transformational culture.

Reference

Schmidt, E and Rosenberg, J (2014) *How Google Works*, John Murray, London

Resources

Cameron, K and Quinn, R (2011) *Diagnosing and Changing Organizational Culture*, Jossey Bass, San Francisco

Financial Times (2021) About the *FT*, https://aboutus.ft.com/ (archived at https://perma.cc/SVT5-E26H)

Grote, D (2006) *Discipline Without Punishment*, 2nd edn, AMACOM, New York

Liddle, D (2017) *Managing Conflict: A practical guide to resolution in the workplace*, Kogan Page, London

An up-to-date copy of the Resolution Framework™, plus additional guidance documents for implementing the Framework, are available from www.ResolutionFramework.com (archived at https://perma.cc/9Z9M-HQM3)

Additional guidance and checklists to help you develop and integrate a transformational culture are available from www.TransformationalCulture.com (archived at https://perma.cc/LDT8-8C3H)

For best practice guidance relating to workplace mediation, investigations and associated training programmes, please visit www.thetcmgroup.com (archived at https://perma.cc/W9U4-ATKJ)

13

Transformational Toolkit 3

Establishing the Transformational Culture Hub

The Transformational Culture Hub (the Culture Hub) is a cross-functional group of stakeholders who work together to develop, deploy and evaluate a fair, just, inclusive, sustainable and high-performing culture – a transformational culture. The Culture Hub meets two to four times a year, although in some organizations it will meet more frequently than this. It also includes a number of workstreams which support the Culture Hub to deliver its strategic objectives.

This toolkit expands on the detail provided in Chapter 3. It explains the role and the purpose of the Culture Hub and it sets out several suggested workstreams/subgroups to support the Hub.

The role of the Culture Hub

The Culture Hub supports the people and culture function (HR) to develop and deploy its people and culture strategy. It provides consultation, accountability and governance to support the people and culture function as it delivers its strategy and it can provide feedback in real time regarding its impact and effectiveness.

The Culture Hub supports the development and deployment of the organization's Resolution Framework. This is the framework which replaces the traditional performance, discipline and grievance procedures. See Chapter 5 for more details of the Resolution Framework.

One of the subgroups of the Culture Hub is the Resolution Unit, thus ensuring that this important activity is fully integrated into the people and culture activities of the organization.

The Culture Hub offers a safe space for stakeholders to generate and test ideas about all matters pertaining to the areas of purpose, values, behaviours, people and culture. One example of this is the development of a values and behaviours framework which I explore in more detail in Chapter 5.

It provides a forum for collective disputes to be resolved proactively and constructively. The Resolution Unit has access to a range of intermediaries and adjudicators who can support collective dispute resolution, as and when required.

The Culture Hub engenders organizational learning and organizational memory. To do so, it gathers data and it undertakes reviews into critical incidents and serious events which impact on the culture of the organization. Applying a transformational methodology (fair, just, restorative and inclusive), the Culture Hub ensures that insights are gathered, lessons are learned and the learning and insights are embedded into the organization. The learning and insights are disseminated companywide via training, mentoring and coaching, all of which is resourced and administered through the people and culture function (HR).

The Culture Hub delivers an evidence-based approach to cultural change and cultural management. The Hub generates, collates and commissions research and data to analyse and evaluate the impact of the culture and to inform the future direction of the organizational culture. To do so, the Hub can utilize the Transformational Culture Index™ (TCI). The TCI offers a cultural management balanced scorecard which is explained in more detail in Transformational Toolkit 1.

Examples of the data and evidence that the Culture Hub may gather and analyse include:

- data gathered from cultural audits;
- data arising from the management of complaints, concerns and conflict at work;
- employee engagement surveys and engagement pulse checks;

- customer experience and employee experience metrics;
- health and wellbeing data;
- data from exit interviews;
- analysing users' experience data from people processes such as the Resolution Framework;
- sustainability and social justice measures;
- brand, reputation and risk data.

Typically, the Culture Hub includes representatives from the board/ senior leadership team, the people and culture function, trade unions, employee reps, line management, customer experience, CSR, communications and health and wellbeing among others. There are no limits to the size of the Transformational Culture Hub, although it is important that it remains manageable.

The Culture Hub workstreams (or subgroups)

The day-to-day work is carried out via the Culture Hub workstreams, all of which report into the Culture Hub. Workstreams are constituted on a 'task and finish' basis and the meeting frequency, and the terms of reference for workstreams will be decided on a case-by-case basis.

Suggested workstreams of the Transformational Culture Hub

It must be stressed the formation of the Culture Hub workstreams is underpinned by a commitment to collaboration, consultation, common purpose and interconnectedness. The workstreams should model and demonstrate the transformational principles described throughout this book.

Typically, the workstreams of the Culture Hub include:

- Purpose, values and behaviours workstream. This group is responsible for developing, reviewing and aligning the purpose, values and behaviours of the organization and developing the organization's behavioural framework.

- Leadership and management workstream. This subgroup is responsible for reviewing the management and leadership competencies and ensuring that they are aligned to the organization's purpose, values and agreed behaviours. This subgroup supports the strategic and the operational deployment of the transformational culture.

- Research and data workstream. This group is responsible for ensuring an evidence-based approach is utilized including gathering and evaluating data for the design, deployment and evaluation of the transformational culture.

- Communications workstream. This group is concerned with the ongoing communication throughout and after the process of cultural change. They will be responsible for designing and delivering the communitarians' strategy and working relentlessly to engage people and to celebrate and share success stories.

- The Resolution Unit/Hub. The Resolution Unit administers the Resolution Framework. It is a unit concerned with integrating transformational justice and developing person-centred and values-based approaches for managing concerns, conduct, complaints and conflict at work.

- Wellbeing, engagement and inclusion workstream. This group is concerned with ensuring that the organization's commitment to these three strategic priorities is achieved. It also acts as a powerhouse of creativity and ideation.

- Sustainability and social justice workstream. This subgroup supports the delivery of the organization's commitment to sustainability and social justice.

- Brand, reputation and risk workstream. This subgroup considers all matters relating to the organization's transformational culture and its impact on the brand and reputation of the organization. It also considers any risks that could arise during and following the cultural change.

- Learning and development. This subgroup is concerned with ensuring that adequate levels of training, coaching and mentoring are in place to support the delivery of the transformational culture.

14

Transformational Toolkit 4

Integrating a Resolution Framework

The following section provides an explanation of the Resolution Framework followed by guidance for integrating it within your organization.

The Framework comprises six phases which are summarized in Figure 14.1:

1 Attempts made to achieve a local resolution.

2 Request for resolution submitted to the Resolution Hub.

3 Resolution Hub undertake a resolution assessment.

4 Route to resolution: early resolution or formal resolution.

5 Outcome agreed, with the option to appeal the outcome from a formal resolution meeting.

6 Ongoing follow-up, evaluation and support as required.

An example of a forward-thinking organization who have adopted the Resolution Framework as part of their culture journey is Nationwide Building Society. Kirsty Knight, Senior Manager in the People and Culture team at Nationwide BS has been leading the changes and explains:

> 'The aim of our Resolution Framework is to help accelerate and support the culture journey we are on. It promotes accountable freedom, aids even more constructive conversations and moves our People and

Culture team to be more of an enabler and strategic partner to the rest of Nationwide Building Society. Our new Resolution Framework, which has been developed in partnership with TCM, focuses on promoting and actively encouraging positive and constructive behaviours in the workplace. This is being done using mediation and early resolution techniques, which aligns to our values-based and person-centred approach which exists within our present culture.'

FIGURE 14.1   The Resolution Framework

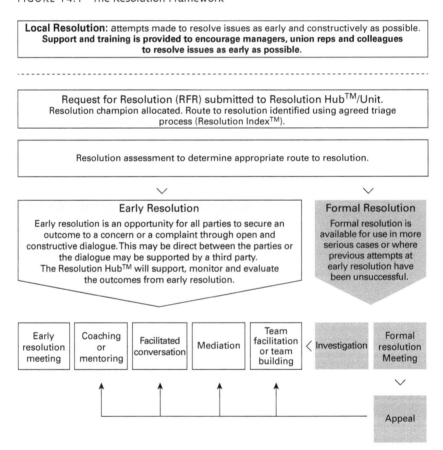

The Resolution Unit (also known as the Resolution Hub™)

The Resolution Unit is a multidisciplinary team which is representative of the organization. If the organization has developed a Transformational Culture Hub (see page 233), the Resolution Unit is a subgroup of that body. If the organization has not created a

Transformational Culture Hub, the Resolution Unit operates as a semi-autonomous unit, aligned to the people and culture function.

The Resolution Unit is led by the head of people and culture or a delegated person who reports to them on a regular basis. The Resolution Unit manages the day-to-day administration of the Resolution Framework and the associated resolution processes. The Resolution Unit comprises HR and ER specialists, trade union representatives and senior managers. Other members may include lawyers, employee groups (LGBTQ+, BAME, disability, etc), and employee and customer experience colleagues. Members of the Resolution Unit are fully trained, and they are experts in the resolution process.

The role of the Resolution Unit is set out below:

- Developing the communications strategy and ensuring that adequate levels of communication are in place to promote the Resolution Framework across the organization.

- Responding to enquiries about the Resolution Framework from employees, managers, union reps and others.

- Coaching and mentoring line managers and supervisors during local resolution, as required.

- Undertaking the resolution triage assessment following the submission of a request for resolution (RfR).

- Chairing facilitated conversations (round table meetings) as required.

- Setting up and managing mediations as required (or working closely with the organization's mediation scheme co-ordinator to do so).

- Setting up and managing investigations as required.

- Setting up and managing formal resolution meetings and ensuring that the chairs of formal resolution meetings are suitably trained and supported.

- Arranging appeals as required.

- Ensuring that Resolution Framework users' feedback is gathered and undertaken and is reviewed as part of a cycle of continuous improvement.

Governance and accountability

To ensure that the Resolution Framework is being applied fairly, consistently and appropriately, it is important to ensure that a system of accountability and governance is in place. This will ensure that trust is built in the Framework, and that your employees can be confident in the knowledge that the resolution systems are fair, just, inclusive, equitable, legally compliant and they are aligned to the core values and the purpose of your organization.

To assist with the overall governance and accountability, data should be captured and evaluated relating to the overall effectiveness of the Resolution Framework. The data should include:

- volume of cases going through each stage of the Resolution Framework. Broken down by type of issues, department, etc;
- number of requests for resolution received. Broken down by category of issues, demographic data, departmental data, etc;
- use of the assisted dialogue stages such as facilitated conversations, mediation, etc;
- outcomes from the above stages;
- resilience analysis (measuring the long-term sustainability of outcomes that are achieved through the Resolution Framework);
- user feedback and satisfaction metrics;
- numbers of second and third reminders issued, broken down by type, etc;
- use of formal resolution processes including investigations;
- time and costs associated with each resolution stage;
- legal fees, tribunal fees, awards and compensation costs.

In addition, the above data can be triangulated with the following data to generate a valuable and holistic assessment of the impact of the Resolution Framework.

- Absence and/or other measures of employee health and wellbeing.
- Talent retention/employee attrition.

- Employee engagement/employee experience.
- Performance/productivity.
- Legal costs/costs of litigation.
- Reputation and brand.

By using data in this way, it is possible to identify patterns and to undertake detailed trends analysis. These can be useful for predicting future issues, and for taking a proactive approach to allocate resources to hotspots or areas that may require support. The data also allow organizations to examine the impact of the Resolution Framework over the longer term and in relation to its impact on some of the key people and culture strategic drivers. See the case study in Chapter 4 for a transformational culture.

Resolution champions

Resolution champions play a critical role in the deployment and sustainability of the Resolution Framework. The resolution champions are a diverse team of people from within your organization. They are specially trained to support the parties before, during and after the resolution process. They are accountable to the Resolution Unit and they receive training, support and professional development from the Resolution Unit.

The resolution champions' role is to provide impartial support and guidance to all parties involved in the resolution process. They also support the parties for a full year after the resolution process concludes. I think of the resolution champions as the 'long nose' and the 'long tail' of resolution.

We know that engaging in resolution and restorative processes can be stressful – it requires courage from all parties. We also know that the process can be laden with jargon and may be confusing, especially when emotions are heightened and suspicions have been raised. Perhaps most notably, we know that after a resolution process concludes, the issues might resurface and the agreements made during resolution can begin to unravel and break down. The fear of the agreement unravelling is one of the factors that can create distrust and scepticism in the resolution process. Although evidence suggests that agreement reached through mediation is generally sustained, parties tell me they are concerned that the agreement will not be sustained, and things will go back to how they were. This is particularly prevalent when we are resolving complex and serious cases such as bullying, harassment or discrimination. These are genuine and legitimate concerns, and they are addressed through the resolution champions' role.

The role of the resolution champions can be summarized as:

- offering impartial and jargon-free guidance for the parties in advance of resolution commencing;
- providing coaching and mentoring support for the parties once the resolution process has concluded to help them sustain the agreement;
- maintaining contact with all parties for a year after the resolution process has concluded to ensure that the agreement is sustained and that any future issues are identified and resolved quickly.

The resolution champions offer a modern and highly effective way for an organization to demonstrate its commitment to securing and sustaining a fair, just, inclusive and sustainable outcome to complex workplace issues. The parties benefit by knowing that the resolution process is not a one-hit wonder. They can have confidence that any future issues will be picked up early and that their emotions, their needs, their goals and the issue of psychological safety remains of paramount importance – even after the mediators and the facilitators have left the building. This knowledge helps the parties to build trust in the Resolution Framework and the various routes to resolution available to them.

The organization benefits in the knowledge that future issues will be identified and resolved before they escalate. In the best traditions of restorative justice, this is a win/win situation.

Local resolution

In any workplace it is inevitable that conflicts will occur, concerns about performance will arise, questions of employees' behaviour or conduct will surface and team members will have complaints about one another or their managers. In most cases, if caught early enough, the first and most important step for resolving a concern, a complaint or a conflict is to have a prompt, informal conversation with the person who is causing the concern or has a complaint; to try to find an outcome that is acceptable to all parties.

At this stage, it is incumbent on local managers and supervisors, supported by a coaching and facilitative people and culture function, to encourage constructive and conciliatory efforts by all parties. In practice, this means that managers and supervisors should possess the skills and the capability to spot issues early, and to create the conditions for dialogue.

As a minimum, line managers and supervisors should be able to:

- understand and demonstrate the three restorative principles:
  - Do no harm
  - Follow our values
  - Listen to learn
- understand how to create a psychologically safe space by developing boundaries and ground rules;
- understand the importance of empathy and self-awareness (emotional intelligence) and display these qualities during a discussion;
- listen actively and understand the importance of questioning, clarifying and summarizing as part of the listening process;
- remain impartial and objective, even when faced with people trying to get them to take sides;
- understand how to role-model the right behaviours. For instance, how to invite feedback and how to respond non-defensively to criticism;

- understand how to craft an agreement or a Resolution Action Plan which is collaborative, supportive, focused and has clear objectives;
- understand the power of feeding forward, as well as feeding back;
- articulate the consequences of not achieving an objective in a way which is clear and assertive, and which avoids sounding threatening or confrontational;
- demonstrate humility, for instance they can say sorry and can forgive errors and mistakes, as required;
- recognize that local resolution is an opportunity for gaining insight, learning and growth for everyone involved.

The Resolution Unit provides mentoring and coaching support to assist local resolution by managers, employees and people partners (HR).

The outcomes from local resolution may include:

- a verbal agreement between the parties;
- a Resolution Action Plan which is agreed between the parties. The RAP sets out the nature of the agreement and the agreed timescales;
- a first or a second reminder issued by the line manager. The aim of the reminder is to explain clearly what the expected behaviours are and to agree objectives to drive behavioural changes and/or improvements of conduct. See below for more details.
- Any of the above may also trigger a request for coaching or mentoring.

Reminders not warnings

Within the Resolution Framework, reminders are the new name for disciplinary warnings. There are three reminders:

The first reminder is between the line manager and the employee. The terms of the reminder may be in writing and will form the basis of a Resolution Action Plan. In other cases, they will be given verbally (in all cases, the manager should make a file note that a first reminder has been issued in case of future escalation). The aim of the first reminder is to restate expectations and to remind the employee of the values and behaviours framework. It also sets out specific steps that the employee is required to make and clarifies the consequences of failing to do so. There are no limits to the number of first reminders that can be issued. However, care should be given to ensure that the reminders are delivering the desired outcomes. If not, then a second reminder may be required.

The second reminder is used in more serious cases, or where the first reminder has failed to bring about the necessary improvements within the agreed timeframe. The second reminder is always made in writing and this reminder is notified to the Resolution Hub. This enables the Resolution Hub to support the manager and the employee with the necessary improvements. It also allows the Resolution Hub to review progress made. The reminder does not go into the employee's personnel file and will be deleted at an agreed point in time, and in any event no longer than 12 months after it was issued. In some cases, the line manager will arrange an investigation prior to a second reminder being given. To reduce the risk of harm and allegations of bias, managers should not arrange an investigation without first notifying the Resolution Hub. The Resolution Hub should always consider whether a restorative justice process, such as a facilitated conversation, mediation or a team conference could be beneficial.

The second reminder fulfils the same requirements as the first reminder; however, it is made in writing and therefore it is more formal. If the employee is unhappy about the way the second reminder has been managed, they can submit a request for resolution to the Resolution Unit.

The third reminder can only be issued following a formal resolution meeting, which is chaired by a trained and independent chair (typically a senior manager). The formal resolution meeting is administered by the Resolution Hub. The chair of the formal resolution meeting may request an investigation before the hearing can be held. In more serious cases, they may also request for the employee to be suspended. In either event, advice should be sought from the Resolution Hub to ensure that the investigation and suspension processes are undertaken correctly, and they are done so in a way which is proportionate, compassionate and supportive.

The formal resolution meeting is run using the restorative principles and the process is inclusive, safe and supportive. The employee has the right to be accompanied to the resolution meeting. Where a third reminder is issued, this is always put in writing. It is placed into the employee's personnel file for an agreed period and in any event no longer than 12 months. While this constitutes a final reminder, the emphasis remains on addressing the behaviours, conduct or performance in a supportive and constructive way. The chair of the resolution meeting should always consider mediation or restorative justice as an option for resolving any underlying issues between the parties. Restorative justice can also be used as an opportunity for apologies to be given and for an employee to build deeper insight into the impact of their behaviour.

Dismissal

In some cases, such as the three below, the organization and the employee may need to part company:

- if the behaviour falls so far below what is expected, or:
- the performance has not improved in line with the agreed expectations, or:
- the misconduct has been continuing for a prolonged period.

In these cases the employee should be advised in advance that dismissal is a potential remedy. The case should always be subject to a full and thorough investigation. Failure to investigate properly, even if the allegations amount to gross misconduct, could result in the employee being unfairly dismissed. The chair of the formal resolution meeting should ensure that they have access to the full range of evidence including interviewing witnesses as required.

As part of the governance and accountability frameworks which I described earlier, a third final reminder, or a dismissal, generates an automatic case review by the Resolution Unit. This is an opportunity to review the case and to draw out and integrate any lessons learned.

The shift from warning to reminder was inspired by the work of Dick Grote (2006).

Submitting a request for resolution

If local resolution is not successful, a request for resolution should be submitted to the Resolution Unit which will triage the case. The Resolution Unit will then recommend an appropriate course of action – the route to resolution. In each of the routes to resolution, dialogue has primacy, and the focus is on applying the restorative principles to assist the parties to secure a constructive and lasting outcome.

Depending on the circumstances, this might include an early resolution meeting between the two parties or a restorative justice process such as a facilitated conversation, mediation, coaching or team facilitation.

The Resolution Triage and the Resolution Index™

Once a request for resolution is received, a member of the Resolution Hub will triage the case and identify the most appropriate route to resolution. The following factors, which make up the Resolution Index, will be considered.

1 The seriousness, frequency and complexity of the issues being raised.

2 The impact of the situation.

3 The needs and expectations of the parties.

4 Previous attempts to resolve the situation.

5 Any perceived risks to the employee and/or the organization.

For each of the above a score is given from 1 to 5. An aggregate score is then created, and the aggregate score will suggest the most appropriate route to resolution in that case. Typically, scores over 20/25 will move to a formal resolution. Below 20/25 and consideration will be given to one of the early resolution processes.

Where there is insufficient information available on the request for resolution, the person(s) undertaking the resolution triage may speak to either or both parties to gather additional information to allow them to complete the triage process.

Defining the routes to resolution

In *Managing Conflict* (Liddle, 2017), I set out the Resolution Spectrum. This comprises several processes which can be applied to help the parties achieve a resolution. The Resolution Spectrum has become the routes to resolution, which are explained below. They fall under two headings of informal or formal resolution.

Informal resolution

EARLY RESOLUTION MEETING

Many workplace issues can be resolved at an early resolution meeting. Within many organizations which are using the framework, they are finding that over 60 per cent of cases that are referred for an early resolution meeting following the submission of a request for resolution are being resolved to the satisfaction of all parties. The impact of this is considerable in terms of cost savings but also in terms of the reduced stress and anxiety for all parties.

The early resolution meeting is a simple process which involves a conversation between the parties involved. It is a restorative conversation, and it provides an opportunity for colleagues, managers and employees to discuss the issues or concerns in a supportive and constructive forum.

The guiding principles of the early resolution meeting follow the same three restorative principles that have run through this book:

1 Do no harm.

2 Follow our values.

3 Listen to learn.

On pages 243–44 I provide guidance for managers and leaders on how to set up and run a successful early resolution meeting.

FACILITATED CONVERSATION

The facilitated conversation is a confidential discussion between all parties which draws on the same restorative principles as outlined above and throughout the book. The meeting is chaired by a member of the Resolution Unit or a trained senior manager. The facilitated conversation is shorter and less structured than mediation. It is therefore used in less serious cases than mediation. A facilitated conversation would never be used in cases that included allegations of harassment or discrimination which would, if deemed suitable, be managed via mediation or a restorative team conference.

The facilitator provides a safe, confidential environment for the parties to discuss their concerns in a supportive, constructive way.

The facilitator creates the opportunity for dialogue between the parties and assists them to reach a mutually acceptable outcome – a Resolution Action Plan. One of the key characteristics of the process is that the facilitator creates a psychologically safe space for all parties. This is generated through the development of ground rules and boundaries.

The facilitation conversation generally includes:

- a separate private meeting with each of the parties so that the facilitators can understand the issues and can answer any questions;
- a facilitated face-to-face meeting;
- reaching agreement and closing the meeting.

Most facilitated conversations are completed in half a day. The facilitation process is confidential, and the facilitators are trained to a high standard. They will remain neutral and non-judgemental throughout the process.

MEDIATION

Mediation is a powerful restorative justice process which is proven to be highly effective at resolving complex workplace disputes, disagreements, complaints or concerns.

As well as being used to resolve a wide variety of workplace issues, mediation can also be used in complex and serious cases including allegations of harassment and discrimination. This includes allegations of sexual harassment and racial discrimination, ie in a situation where the issue is not a conflict between two parties, but an issue of harm caused by one party's behaviour against the other. The suitability of mediation in serious and complex cases is carefully assessed at the resolution triage assessment by the Resolution Unit. If all parties agree to take part in mediation, the issue will be referred to either an internal or an external mediator. If the case involves allegations of harassment or discrimination, the mediators should hold an advanced qualification such as TCM's Restorative Mediator Certificate (RMC).

HOW MEDIATION WORKS

The mediator, who is impartial and non-judgemental, will contact both parties by phone and explain the principles and processes of mediation. To assist practitioners and organizations wishing to integrate restorative and just principles within their organizations, I developed a restorative process: the FAIR Model™ (see Figure 14.2). This model draws on best practice from several mediation and restorative disciplines – transformative narrative, evaluative and facilitative.

The FAIR Model™, when applied to mediation and restorative processes, generally includes:

- the parties signing an Agreement to Mediate form;
- a phone call with the mediator(s);
- two separate private meetings with the mediators(s);
- a facilitated face-to-face meeting;
- reaching agreement and closing the meeting.

FIGURE 14.2 The FAIR Model™

© The TCM Group

Most mediations are completed in one full day, but it may take longer if more than two people are involved. Mediation is a voluntary and confidential process.

The mediator will help the parties have an open and honest dialogue with the aim of identifying a mutually acceptable outcome. If this is the case, the mediator will encourage parties to draw up an agreement.

After mediation has finished you may agree that, if appropriate, others can receive a copy of this final written agreement. However, the employer will not receive any other feedback from the mediator about issues raised and discussed or any other factors raised during the mediation process.

In *Managing Conflict*, I dedicated an entire chapter to the role and benefits of workplace and employment mediation. I also wrote a chapter to support organizations which wish to embed a mediation programme into their own organization, with various case studies – the text aimed to bring mediation to life and to promote mediation as a powerful remedy to workplace and employment disputes.

TEAM FACILITATION

Team facilitation is also known as team mediation or a restorative conference. This powerful process is designed to repair the harm from a dispute or a breakdown in team relations. It is useful for supporting a team as it turns from toxic to transformational.

The team conference should be facilitated by skilled and expert facilitators. By applying the restorative principles, team facilitation provides an opportunity for a team to:

- gain insight and understanding of the root cause of the problems and the various issues affecting the team. These may include behavioural, cultural, systemic, structural, environmental or political factors;
- analyse and discuss their concerns in a safe space;
- renew and build connections within the team – connections which may have broken down because of a conflict or a change;

- develop agreed behaviours and boundaries for the team. These should be aligned to the organization's values, purpose and agreed behavioural framework;

- understand the impact of the problems on individuals within the team and the whole team;

- identify and agree a set of common needs which can then foster a sense of common purpose within the team;

- agree a way forward which is sustainable, and which builds individual and team resilience. Ultimately the focus is on building high performance by stimulating creativity, innovation and a renewed sense of purpose.

Formal resolution

A formal process is available where it has not been possible to resolve matters informally or it is not suitable to do so. This may be due to the complexity or serious nature of the issues, or when previous attempts to resolve issues through informal resolution have failed to generate the desired outcome.

The Resolution Unit will appoint a chair for the formal stage of the Resolution Framework. The chair will be at an appropriate management level to the parties involved in the issue and from outside the team or department concerned. In conjunction with the Resolution Unit, they will advise on the appropriate steps of formal resolution which may involve one, or more, of the following:

- An early neutral evaluation. This process is used to scope out the issues when a situation is complex in order that the chair of the formal resolution process has all the information at hand before the meeting.

- A formal investigation into the facts and circumstances relating to an allegation, or a series of allegations. This is particularly important where the allegations could result in a third reminder or dismissal.

- A formal resolution meeting with the parties to hear the case and to determine the most effective remedy.

- Referral to an alternative policy/procedure.

The chair of the formal resolution stage will oversee the formal resolution process and decide the outcome of that process in terms of a formal recommendation for resolution.

Handling suspensions

In more serious cases, the line manager, or the chair of the formal resolution process, may consider suspending the employee before undertaking a full investigation. In these cases, guidance should always be sought from the Resolution Hub. Suspension is not a neutral act; employers must be satisfied that it has reasonable and proper cause to do so. The decision to suspend must be proportionate and it must not be a knee jerk reaction. As the Imperial College Hospital Healthcare NHST case study on page 141 demonstrated vividly, care and consideration should be given to the pastoral needs of the suspended employee.

What can employees expect during the formal resolution stage?

The following provisions apply to all formal meetings at the investigation, formal resolution meeting or appeal stage:

- The employee(s) will be invited in writing to the investigation and/ or formal resolution meeting.
- The chair will make provision to meet the employee and the other party, either separately and/or together, without unreasonable delay. The parties will be able to talk about their concerns and explain how they would like them to be resolved.
- Each party has the right to be accompanied to the meeting if they wish.
- A note-taker may attend the meeting. Notes will be sent following the meeting and without unreasonable delay.
- Where possible, meeting times will be agreed with all parties. All parties must make every effort to attend; however, provision will be made for some flexibility if it is required.

- The outcome of a formal resolution meeting will be confirmed in writing after the meeting and without unreasonable delay.

Investigation/fact finding

If the issue is particularly sensitive or complex, an investigation may be appropriate prior to the formal resolution meeting. The purpose of the investigation is to discover all the relevant facts and information in a fair, reasonable and objective manner. Investigators will be trained, unbiased and neutral without personal or close professional links with the main parties or any other perceived conflict of interest with the case.

The investigator will develop terms of reference for the investigation from the start, eg the incident(s), who was involved, the format of the final report and who they are reporting back to. The investigation will then be undertaken using the terms of reference.

Once the investigation is concluded, all the evidence will be analysed objectively and with impartiality by the investigator and presented in an investigation report for use by the Resolution Unit and/or chair of the formal resolution meeting.

Right of appeal

Parties have the right of appeal against the outcome of the formal resolution meeting within five working days from the date of notification. Grounds for an appeal might include:

- procedural errors where there is evidence that the process was incorrectly followed;
- new evidence has come to light that may change the outcome of the original decision;
- fairness and reasonableness of the outcome.

Appeals should be heard without unreasonable delay, where possible, by a manager who is senior to the chair who made the original decision and from a different part of the organization. At the appeal meeting, the appeal manager will clarify their understanding of the basis for the appeal and ask relevant questions. Through discussion, they will explore solutions and attempt to achieve resolution. The decision of the appeal manager will be conveyed in writing and will be the final stage of the process.

The appeal chair will always bear in mind the restorative principles and the primacy of dialogue. In cases which do not result in a dismissal, it is common for appeals processes to refer the parties to mediation or one of the other available routes to resolution.

Collective disputes

In circumstances where a complaint applies to more than one person, the details of the complaint must be set out in the request for resolution. Normally one person will be nominated to represent the group. Details of a collective complaint will only be considered at one resolution meeting and (if applicable) one appeal hearing. Where employee complaints are not identical or where there is not a full voluntary agreement among the complainants, the issues will be dealt with on an individual basis in line with the Resolution Framework.

The following case study provides a useful insight into the way that a complex community health service integrated a Resolution Framework. Kent Community Health NHS Foundation Trust provides NHS services in the community across the whole of Kent, some parts of East Sussex and London. Their services are practitioner led and therapy focused. They treat the whole person, not just the condition.

CASE STUDY

Integrating a Resolution Framework within Kent Community Health NHS Foundation Trust

CASE STUDY PREPARED FOR TRANSFORMATIONAL CULTURE BY NICOLA RUTTER AND CAROLINE HANLON, KCH

Why did you introduce a Resolution Framework?

We recognized that the antiquated grievance and bullying and harassment procedures were not working and were leaving individuals at best unsatisfied and at worst damaged and unable to contemplate repairing broken relationships or re-engaging in the workplace. We were also motivated to try to reverse the spiralling cost and significant time commitment that increasing numbers of tribunals were having for the organization.

How did you do it?

We initiated a task and finish group in which we sought membership from staff-side colleagues, our staff networks and operational colleagues and ensured we had an executive sponsor to ensure executive buy-in. We have developed our framework collaboratively with these stakeholders and are at a point where we are ready to launch it now. We have trained eight mediators, so we have an internal service ready to support colleagues who mediation has been identified as being suitable for. We also have several resolution champions to support the roll-out. We used David Liddle's book *Managing Conflict* as a blueprint for our framework and it was key to establishing the principles and philosophy that underpins it.

What evidence did you use to inform your decision-making process?

We analysed historic grievance and bullying and harassment cases alongside numbers and cost of tribunals. Feedback from the task and finish group was also considered when developing the framework and how it should be implemented.

How did you engage your stakeholders in the development of your Resolution Framework?

The implementation of the framework has been a joint HR/OD project. The executive sponsor is the Director of HR, OD and Comms and project leads are the Head of ER and the People and Business partner for one of our operational services. Recently the ER team and OD colleagues have attended a three-day training workshop about the framework and to equip them with the skills required to deliver conflict resolution coaching as a precursor to local resolution, facilitation or mediation.

We did experience resistance from our wider staff-side colleagues and regional representatives. We engaged the support of TCM to help us dispel some of the misunderstandings they had and have engaged staff-side colleagues in regular dialogue seeking to understand what misgivings remain so we can identify compromises to overcome these.

We are already applying the transformational principles (just and learning) when assessing the need for investigation processes that may lead to disciplinary action. The intention is that we move towards a restorative justice model in the coming months.

References

Grote, D (2006) *Discipline Without Punishment: The proven strategy that turns problem employees into superior performers*, AMACOM, New York
Liddle, D (2017) *Managing Conflict: A practical guide to resolution in the workplace*, Kogan Page, London

15

Transformational Toolkit 5

Restorative justice in action

This toolkit uses two examples to bring the restorative principles, described throughout this book, to life. They include an example of a restorative conversation between a manager and a member of their team, and a case study from Mersey Care which has integrated the just and restorative principles across its organization.

Scenario 1: The restorative manager

The example below shows how a manager might use the restorative principles in a conversation with a member of their team.

Manager: Jenny, I wondered if you could help me out with something?

Jenny: Sure, how can I help?

Manager: [invites Jenny to sit] Thanks for taking the time to have this chat when I know how busy you are. I am trying to make sure that we get the management reports out on time. I know that you are responsible for producing them for the weekly management meeting; how are things going with them?

Jenny: Um, I thought you may bring this up. I have been really struggling to get the information I need to produce the reports and that has meant the last two have been late. I am sorry about that. I should have let you know but I could see you were busy.

Manager: [listens carefully] OK. Look, thanks for apologizing. I am never too busy for you to discuss these with me Jenny; the sooner I know we have a problem, the better placed I am to help you to resolve it. I know you understand that it is important that we get the reports out on time.

Jenny: Yes, I do, and that is why this is so frustrating.

Manager: [summarizes what they have heard] I hear that it is frustrating for you, it is for me too. However, it is good to be talking about it with you. I'd like to understand what is happening. You mentioned that there is a delay getting information to you; can you give me your view on what is happening and what you would like to see happen to resolve it?

Jenny: Thanks, it is good to know that you are supporting me on this. The problem is that the report templates on the database have not been updated. It is taking me twice as long to manually pull the data off the report. I know IT are working on it, but they said it could be another four weeks before the report templates are updated.

Manager: [responds empathetically] Thanks for explaining the problem to me and yes, I can understand that must be frustrating for you. It seems that we are both feeling a bit frustrated by this and we both need to get it resolved. Now that I understand the root cause of the problem, let's work together to get this problem fixed. What can I do to help?

TRANSFORMATIONAL THINKING

In the above scenario please reflect on the following questions:

- How did the manager behave?
- How did those behaviours align to the restorative principles?
- What skills and strategies did the manager use during the conversation?
- How did the situation feel from Jenny's perspective?
- What outcomes were achieved through this conversation?

CASE STUDY

Developing a restorative just and learning workplace

The following is a case study which highlights how Mersey Care NHS Foundation Trust has developed and integrated a restorative just and learning culture.

Setting the scene: our Mersey Care strategy

Since 2012, Mersey Care NHS Foundation Trust has been recognized for delivering a strategy for perfect care within a restorative just and learning culture. Initially a mental health Trust with high, medium and low secure services, community and inpatient mental health, learning disability and addictions services, the Trust has doubled in size with the acquisition of Liverpool Health Care and now includes all community physical health services in Merseyside, with a workforce that has increased from 3,500 to 8,000 staff in the last three years.

Through this period of significant change, the Trust has continued to improve its quality indicators, staff indicators and maintain financial balance (despite acquiring Trusts in difficulty), which is a rarity in the NHS.

At the heart of all that is done in Mersey Care is the commitment to 'perfect care' – care that is safe, effective, positively experienced, timely, equitable and efficient, with our own stretching targets for improvements in care. This is underpinned by the Trust aspiration for a restorative just and learning culture, with compassion, fairness and civility ingrained into day-to-day life and an emphasis on learning from mistakes and asking what is the problem instead of who is to blame. Crucial ambitions are framed into 'big hairy audacious goals', and staff demanded a staff BHAG around a culture change. They wanted to work in a safe place, be treated fairly and compassionately and so the Just and Learning Culture was born.

Our restorative just and learning culture

Psychological safety is present when colleagues trust and respect each other and feel able, even obligated, to be honest. It is the ability to show and employ yourself without fear of negative consequences. Mersey Care leaders are purposefully building psychological safety by setting the scene for their team: framing the work and emphasizing purpose, followed by inviting participation from team members through demonstrating situational humility, practising inquiry and setting up structures and processes. Proactively responding is also crucial to ensure psychological safety by expressing appreciation, destigmatizing when things do not go to plan and avoiding language such as sanctions and violations – to Mersey Care such language does not embody restorative just culture principles.

In this culture of clarity, co-operation, structure and processes, just and learning come in to create an environment where staff feel supported and empowered to learn when things do not go as expected, rather than feeling blamed.

'A Just culture accepts nobody's account as "true" or "right" and others wrong … Instead, it accepts the value of multiple perspectives, and uses them to encourage both accountability and learning.' (Dekker, 2017)

In a culture of retribution, the questions that are asked include: Which rule is broken? Who did it? How bad is the breach? What should the consequences be? This approach, however, is counterproductive to learning and the team and their method of review, and also in terms of enduring trust, humanity, compassion, forgiveness, understanding and healing.

In a culture of restoration, the questions are quite different: Who is hurt? What are their needs? Whose obligation is it to meet those needs? How do we involve the community? The goals and outcomes to approaching situations that do not proceed as planned in this way include moral engagement, emotional healing, the reintegration of practitioner into their work, learning for the organization and prevention to avoid the adverse event being repeated in the future.

A culture that instinctively asks in the case of an adverse event 'What was responsible?', not 'Who is responsible?', is not finger pointing and not blame seeking. However, it is not the same as an uncritically tolerant culture where 'anything goes', as that would be as inexcusable as a blame culture.

A restorative justice culture compassionately asks those involved to give an account of how the event happened and what it meant to those involved. Together, it is determined how to meet the needs that have arisen. By reviewing an event in this way, the differences between 'work done' and 'work imagined' can become clearer, and when and what changes would make a difference can be identified.

Mersey Care worked with Professor Sidney Dekker in our journey to develop the Trust's restorative just and learning culture. For Mersey Care, Sidney's was the literature we most connected to, as in our view he focused on understanding, sense making within the context of which an event occurred, bringing the language of restorative practice into fruition. Sidney is a widely respected academic, Safety II pioneer and has also been a first officer on Boeing 737s in Europe. In Sweden, he was a professor of human factors and system safety and in Australia Sidney founded the Safety Science Innovation Lab. His book, *Just Culture* (Dekker, 2017), has become a standard text for organizations across the world which are redefining what accountability means, offering a way for workplaces to respond to mistakes and restore relationships and trust. Sidney's studies of patient safety and understanding human behaviours are a celebration of the expertise that makes things go well and offers compassion when they don't.

For Mersey Care, delivering the ambition for perfect care depends on the development of a non-punitive culture; with personal responsibility and professional accountability driving the organizational learning, and a prospective outlook rather than a retrospective bias ensuring the focus on the future and the next event. Recognizing all systems are not perfect, the emphasis is always on asking what and how, not who, because a bad system will always beat a good person.

Our restorative just and learning programme

Mersey Care has found that the introduction of a restorative just and learning culture with restorative justice has coincided with many qualitative improvements for staff, such as a reduction in suspensions and dismissals, an increase in the reporting of adverse events as staff feel safe to do so, an increase in the number of staff that feel encouraged to seek support and an improvement in staff retention. The Trust has seen an 85 per cent reduction in disciplinary investigations over the last five years, while its workforce has increased during the same period by over 135 per cent.

The economic benefits of restorative practice appear significant. Our research study in 2016 conservatively estimated the total economic benefit of restorative justice in the case of Mersey Care NHS Foundation Trust to be about £2.5 million or approximately 1 per cent of the total costs and 2 per cent of the labour costs.

Many staff have been able to share their experiences of how a just and learning culture ensures they are able and supported to share their views and experiences – restorative justice is applied to adverse events and as a result learning and the implementation of productive changes has increased and the outcome has been an improvement in staff engagement, innovation and patient safety, with data being reviewed to support this result.

In June 2019 Mersey Care NHS Foundation Trust and Northumbria University developed an accredited four-day training and development programme in restorative just culture and practices. Our founding belief is that restorative just and learning culture cannot be bought off the shelf but must organically grow within an organization. This programme equips participants with the skills needed to apply the principles in practice and shares the years of application and learning from Mersey Care NHS Foundation Trust, which has had the benefit of working alongside world leaders such as Professor Sidney Dekker and colleagues.

TRANSFORMATIONAL THINKING

Drawing on the above case study from Mersey Care, please reflect on the following questions:

- What have you learned because of this case study?
- What are the benefits of a restorative just and learning workplace?
- How can you adopt these principles into your own organization?

Reference

Dekker, S (2017) *Just Culture: Restoring trust and accountability in your organization*, 3rd edn, CRC Press, London

16

Transformational Toolkit 6

Vitamin R – the resolution vitamin

I often hear all manner of weird and wonderful ideas about what mediation is and what it is not. I have sometimes heard mediation confused with meditation and medication. Of course, it is neither of these things. However, I began to ask myself what would happen if I amalgamated mediation, meditation and medication? The more I thought about it the more I was drawn to the idea of a virtual pill which could resolve dysfunctional conflict, increase empathy, encourage collaboration, promote a high-growth mindset and facilitate adult-to-adult dialogue. Okay, it is not a real pill and it has not been subjected to any clinical trials. However, I am delighted to announce that I have discovered a new vitamin which can support the development of a transformational culture. I call it Vitamin R. The Resolution vitamin.

So here is it. This is the Resolution vitamin that anyone can use to help them resolve a workplace conflict, have a courageous conversation with a colleague or a manager, use during a performance conversation or simply as part of the day-to-day conversations that happen in our organizations.

Viewpoint. Impact. Thoughts. Actions. Meaning. Insights. Needs. Resolution.

Viewpoint

This is a chance to consider what you observed happening in a calm and neutral way. Ask yourself, what did you observe happening? Be realistic and avoid blame and making it a personal attack. Try to be neutral and objective. Engage in some deep breathing and deep reflection. Give yourself the time and the permission to reject the self-blame and paranoia that the situation may have caused you. Now look back and describe what you see.

Impact

This is a chance to reflect on how the situation has made you and the other person feel. Ask yourself, how did the situation make you feel? Try to put yourself in the other person's shoes and imagine how it made them feel. How did the situation impact the relationship between you and the one within which you are working?

Understanding the impact that a situation is having on me and the other person helps to build self-awareness and empathy – two core elements of emotional intelligence. As we describe the impact of a situation to each other, we often come to realize that the impact (hurt, stress, anxiety, confusion, isolation, fear, underactivity, etc) is common between us and that we are often living a shared experience.

Thoughts

This is a chance to reflect on what you were thinking. Ask yourself, what did you think at the time? Were your thoughts rational or irrational? What do you think now? Did the situation affect your thought processes? Did you find it hard to think and/or do you find yourself thinking about it all the time?

A good question to ask is what you think needs to happen to change the situation. Thinking ahead and thinking about a positive solution can break the cycle of negative thoughts.

Actions

This is a chance to reflect on how you acted, interacted and reacted to the situation. In other words, how you behaved. Ask yourself, how did you and the other person act, interact and react? This is the AIR that we create. Did you overreact or did you respond calmly? What would it take to promote better actions, interactions and reactions in the future? How can you ensure you respond calmly in the future?

Meaning

This is a chance to consider what interpretations you drew from the situation. Ask yourself, what did you interpret and understand from the situation? Were you biased in any way? Did your biases affect your interpretation? Did you have an open or a closed view of the situation? Are you open to hearing the other person's interpretation and meaning? What would it take to open your mind to hearing them and encouraging them to hear you?

Insights

This is where we see a transformation in the situation as we turn from the past to the future. Ask yourself, what have you learned from the situation that could make you stronger and which could enrich your relationship with the other person? What insights have you gained about yourself, about the situation and about the other person? How can you convert those insights into practical actions?

Needs

This is a chance to reflect on what you both need from the situation. Ask yourself, what do you need to make this situation better? What does the other person need? Do the needs converge or complement each other's? If so, how can you achieve an outcome which might meet both your needs and their needs? How can you secure a win–win outcome?

Resolution

This is a chance to focus on a new future – a resolution. Ask yourself, what would a fair outcome look like? What actions will you take to help you achieve the outcome? How will you get there? What support do you need? The resolution might be written as a resolution action plan (RAP) or it can be a verbal resolution.

17

Transformational Toolkit 7

Best practice for tackling workplace incivility

While I was conducting my research for *Transformational Culture*, I had the good fortune to interview Dr Chris Turner. Chris is a consultant in emergency medicine at University Hospitals of Coventry and Warwickshire, a major trauma centre in the West Midlands, and one of the co-founders of Civility Saves Lives. Civility Saves Lives is a grassroots organization dedicated to raising awareness of the impact of behaviour in healthcare.

I wanted to understand the impact of incivility, and to learn about the practical steps an organization can take to create a psychologically safe organization. At the end of this interview is an opportunity for reflection.

Can you say a few words about incivility in the workplace, and what you believe is at the heart of this issue?

In healthcare, how we treat each other has traditionally played a distant second fiddle to how we treat patients, with statements like 'it's all about the patients' and 'he may be unpleasant, but he's a really good doctor' regularly heard. For many, the idea that treating staff badly may result in poorer outcomes for patients is frankly novel.

There are times, of course, when treating co-workers in an assertive fashion may be necessary, for example in a time critical moment during an operation or a resuscitation – when the right decision needs to be taken and immediately acted upon. Unfortunately, we appear to have taken this this brusque command-and-control leadership style and translated this into a template for how people might be managed on a day-to-day basis.

It seems obvious to state but cultures where incivility and disrespect can flourish are not cultures where people are able to make their fullest contribution. When we treat each other with respect we open up the working memory of our colleagues which allows them to generate more and better creative solutions to the complex problems that we face day to day.

Is there any evidence that can demonstrate the impact of incivility?

Over the last 15–20 years there has been an ever-increasing number of scientific papers showing that behaviour matters in healthcare contexts, and that negative behaviours result in poorer outcomes for both patients and staff. The studies come from the business world, the academic world and from healthcare. What these studies show, and they do this with remarkable consistency, is that when we treat people poorly it has a direct impact on their ability to think and perform.

Alongside this academic work, we have the results of various inquiries into poor care and poor outcomes in the NHS, such as Mid Staffs, that consistently show that in failing organizations staff tend to be treated poorly and treat each other poorly. Organizations have developed safety cultures that look for error and are then seduced by blame, with the result that staff do not feel safe to speak up and when they admit mistakes the result is frequently that they are punished. These psychologically unsafe environments are a genuine risk to creating safe environments because staff learn to keep quiet about the things that go wrong and the opportunities for learning are lost.

What is the impact of incivility/a toxic culture?

Incivility has a direct impact on our ability to think and it does this by reducing our working memory. This happens because when we feel threatened, and incivility causes us to feel threatened, then our working memory competes with our fight or flight response and the consequence is that the capacity of our working memories are reduced. This is true not just of the direct recipient but of those around the incident.

Perceived incivility has been shown to reduce the cognitive ability of the recipient by 61 per cent. This is the reason why, when somebody is offensive to us, we frequently fail to think of the smart reply when that happens with it only coming to mind many hours later. When somebody is rude to us in the moment, we aren't able to think as quickly or clearly as we would like to; instead, we are busy trying to make sense of what happened and preparing ourselves for what other onslaught, verbal or otherwise, is about to occur.

What impact does incivility have on bystanders, ie people who observe it happening?

Incivility does not just have an impact on the recipient, it also has an impact on bystanders, with studies showing that the average cognitive decline for people who are around uncivil acts is 20 per cent. For these bystanders their working memory is being stolen because they are preparing themselves for whatever is about to come next and they know that how the person was treated before them may well how they will be treated next. It is easy to see why this can have significant impact when many people work near each other, for example in an operating theatre or an office. This immediate impact on the recipient has a lingering tail – studies have shown that should someone witness incivility and then leave a room, when they turn the corner and somebody asks for help, those who have been exposed to incivility are 50 per cent less likely to help.

Recent research has shown that we are not all impacted equally by witnessing incivility. Those of us who are more empathetic are significantly cognitively worse off after witnessing incivility. This has relevance for workplaces that explicitly wish to have more empathetic people working within them. If we select people for their empathetic natures and then put them into hostile toxic workplace cultures where incivility is accepted, if not the norm, then what we will achieve is a workforce who cannot fulfil their potential. This seems like a crazy situation.

What is the impact of incivility within teams?

Incivility amongst teams has been shown to reduce individual and team performance. When teams work in an environment where respect is not shown, the result is that they share less information, probably because team members fear the consequences of sharing. It is known that in complicated and complex situations, the chances of getting the best outcome are mediated by information sharing.

When teams are toxic, they spend more time managing their own image and less time sharing information to the overall pool. The result is that the team leader has less information on which to base their decisions, thus decisions made in these circumstances are usually less effective. We turn off the taps of information, reduce the information pool and have worse outcomes.

What experience do you have of leadership and incivility?

At a leadership level, incivility is both more frequent and more damaging than at other levels. It is easy to see how, as a leader, if being the most important person in the room matters to us, then we can create situations where that is the case by simply treating those around us in a rude and disrespectful fashion. When we permit and even tacitly encourage uncivil behaviours, we create situations where those around us are quite literally worth less cognitively. The result of this is that the leader becomes the smartest person in the room but only at the cost of reducing the cognitive ability of those around them.

What is also interesting is that, in the longer term, many successful leaders learn that their own emotions are not more important than the emotions of people around them. They know that how we speak to each other, and how we treat each other is fundamental to what the climate of a team is and ultimately, of course, what our cultures are.

There are many routes through which staff may feel heard. One way we have recently achieved this is within the emergency department where I work. We asked staff what areas they feel are risky, and where risk lies. This may seem like an obvious thing to do – however, this highlights the day-to-day difficulties of delivering healthcare, where staff often see risk that is not visible to senior and managerial positions.

What are the benefits of a more civil workplace?

Workplaces that are more civil result in multiple benefits from multiple perspectives. At an individual level, more civil workplaces result in improved performance with both quality and creativity increasing. Civil workplaces are known to increase the wellbeing of staff and with this comes increased discretionary effort.

From a team perspective, more civil environments have been shown to increase the amount of information that is shared and, as above, the quality of information and ideas rises as well. For teams, working in civil environments increases psychological safety, which in turn leads to improved outcomes and enhanced productivity.

In the 2017 Gallup opinion poll about 'does your voice count?' only three out of 10 workers felt that this was the case. If we were to move to six in 10 workers feeling that their voice counted and that they were heard, then we would potentially see a:

- 27 per cent decrease in turnover of staff;
- 40 per cent decrease in safety incidents;
- 12 per cent increase in productivity.

What practical steps can organizations take to promote a civil, safe, and healthy workplace?

1 Recognise the impact of incivility – knowing that how we treat each other, and feel is fundamental to our experience of work. Understand that when we feel undervalued by our workplaces and

by our colleagues, the consequences extend beyond just us in the moment and into our ongoing efforts in the workplace and the efforts of those around us.

2 Rather than negotiating to win , start by taking a position where we listen to understand each other so that we might appreciate others' perspectives and the world in which they live.

3 Introduce evidence-based systems that genuinely let organizations know what it feels like to work there. This can make for uncomfortable reading and the information should be packaged in such a way that it does not induce an instantaneous deny-and-defend stance from those receiving it.

4 Work on creating a culture where people understand that there will be misunderstandings. We all work in complex areas and at times under immense stress. In these circumstances nobody can be their best self all the time. If we can get to a position where we believe that people come to work to do a good job and that their purpose is not to harm those around them, then we might get to a position where when we are hurt by somebody's actions, we allow ourselves the thought that this may not have been intentional. This is not an easy position to take.

5 Introduce the idea that it is a professional responsibility to find mechanisms through which we can let other people know if they have left co-workers distressed after an interaction. Further to this, it is our responsibility to ensure that we use those mechanisms in a way that leaves the person on the receiving end feeling heard and causes the least distress to the supposed perpetrator.

TRANSFORMATIONAL LEARNING

- What have you learned from this interview with Dr Chris Turner?
- What actions will you take to tackle incivility in your workplace?

18

Transformational Toolkit 8

Getting investigations right first time

Organizations need to ensure that from the moment informal resolution has not been effective or has not been taken forward, complaints are investigated thoroughly, fairly and objectively, following their internal policies and procedures.

The failure to follow these basic principles at the earliest stage of any investigation has potentially disastrous consequences for organizations. Even the initial scoping of the terms of reference for an investigation can be scrutinized and result in the tribunal finding flaws in the way that these have been orchestrated to influence the direction of an investigation outcome (www.gov.uk/employment-tribunal-decisions/mr-j-truscott-v-norfolk-and-norwich-university-hospitals-nhs-foundation-trust-3332455-2018).

A simple, easy-to-understand and use process should reflect that of a TRIAGE framework, which provides the key stages for any investigation.

The TRIAGE approach (see Figure 18.1) ensures that the key areas of an investigation are followed and that investigators, and those managing investigations, are clear on each phase of the process. It provides consistency and objectivity, to prevent organizations from becoming criticized over a flawed investigation and, ultimately, an unfair dismissal.

FIGURE 18.1   The TRIAGE Investigation Model

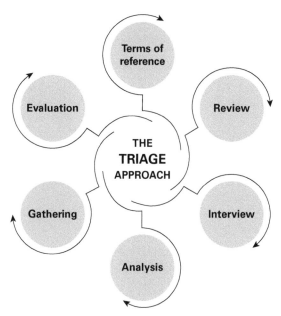

© The TCM Group

TABLE 18.1   The steps of investigation

Stage	Conducting investigations	Managing investigations
Terms of reference The most important aspect of an investigation is to understand what is to be investigated. This is why the terms of reference for the investigation are paramount. This outlines what is to be investigated so that the investigator has a clear remit to adhere to while conducting their enquiries, without straying into areas that may misdirect their focus.	Read the complaint carefully and identify what is being alleged. Agree with the commissioning manager what is to be investigated and is within the scope of your remit. For complex complaints, identify common themes to provide succinct areas for investigation.	Do the terms of reference align with the complaint being made? Are they agreed with all relevant parties? Do they need to be reviewed during the investigation? Are there any other complaints to be included?

(Continued)

TABLE 18.1 (Continued)

Stage	Conducting investigations	Managing investigations
Review An investigator has to review all the necessary documentation. This includes the initial complaint or allegation, and organizational policies and/or procedures. They must then identify any additional evidence or witnesses that may need to be included in the investigative process.	Make a list of all the individuals who are to be interviewed as part of the investigation process. Ensure you outline realistic, achievable timescales in light of the complexity of the investigation. Ensure you have available, and have read, any and all policy documentation which is relevant to the case.	Have all witnesses been identified? Are there any not included and if so, is it clear why they have not been included? Is the documentation relevant to the complaint being made? Is anything missing?
Interview A good proportion of evidence that the investigator will analyse will be drawn from witness interviews, so excellent interviewing techniques are essential. Creating an open and safe environment for witnesses to feel comfortable to share as much information as possible is key. The investigator must also be skilled to draw pertinent, reliable information from the witness.	Interview the complainant(s) first, followed by the respondent(s) and subsequently all identified witnesses. Remember, if you need to obtain further information or ask a wider range of questions, you may interview a party more than once. Begin with open questions to allow each party to give an open account of what has happened, before using closed questions to address key details.	Have interviews been conducted objectively – no leading questions or questions not asked, not relevant? Have notes been accurately taken and been shared with the witness?
Analysis Analysing the documentary evidence at hand prior to undertaking any further interviews, or evidence gathering, enables the investigator to establish any potential flaws in the early stages of the investigation. A lack of policies or directives covering the allegations or complaint to be investigated, for example, allows an investigator to explore other potential areas to be included or reviewed.	Draft a list of additional evidence that you require from all the information gathered. This helps ensure you do not miss any key information. Prioritize your evidence. Digital evidence may be available for a specific period only, so time is of the essence. Explore alternative solutions. Is it evident that, for example, mediation may be a more suitable resolution approach?	Has all relevant evidence been identified? Is the evidence available? If not, why not? Has the investigator explored other solutions, such as mediation? If so, has this been explored? If not, why not?

(continued)

TABLE 18.1 (Continued)

Stage	Conducting investigations	Managing investigations
Gathering Gathering evidence in a timely manner is important, particularly if such evidence is time-critical. Some organizations store CCTV images, for example, for a set time period only and so it is important to identify and gather evidence swiftly. Other evidence, such as policies, will be available for longer and so prioritizing evidence gathering is a skill for the professional investigator.	Use your interviews to identify any additional evidence that may be important to the process. Request additional pieces of evidence as soon as possible, to prevent costly delays. Collate all your evidence, interviews and other documentary evidence and review 'as one'. Don't miss out any important pieces of the jigsaw.	Has all relevant evidence been obtained? If not, why not? Is there evidence not referenced? If so, has it been clearly explained why?
Evaluation Once the investigator has compiled and collated all the necessary evidence and interview notes, they must begin to draw their conclusions by evaluation of all the details available to them at the time of the investigation. In workplace investigations, the investigator will collate all the information and evaluate their findings based upon the 'balance of probabilities'. The commentary of their rationale and findings needs to be clearly constructed within the investigation report in a way that a lay person could read. The reader needs to understand what took place, how, and why the investigator came to their conclusions.	Include an initial 'Executive Summary' at the beginning of the report which outlines the key findings in a clear and concise manner. Ask a relevant colleague to proofread the investigation report prior to its final submission. Be sure that you thoroughly understand the content of the report as you may later be questioned on its contents.	Has the investigation covered the terms of reference? Is the report clear and easily understood? Are the outcomes clearly justified, based upon a genuine belief and the balance of probabilities? Is the evidence referenced in the report? Is it clear what evidence has and has not been included?

Following these simple steps, as outlined in Table 18.1, will provide reassurance that your investigation will withstand both internal and external scrutiny, resulting in a fair, objective and thorough investigation.

With thanks to The TCM Group's Gary Rogers for his support developing this toolkit.

CONCLUSION AND CALLS TO ACTION

This book represents the accumulation of a lifetime spent working with organizations to embed fair, just, inclusive and sustainable approaches for managing complex people and organizational issues. The text can be summed up in very simple terms: if we want to develop a modern and progressive organization, we need to put our people and our values first.

This, of course, is easier said than done. As the book, supported by numerous case studies and contributions, has demonstrated, the prevailing systems, structures, processes and cultures of our organizations are often designed around orthodoxies of blame, retribution, power, autocracy, paternalism and control. If an organization wishes to develop a transformational culture, these systems, structures, processes and orthodoxies will need to be challenged robustly. The vested interests of those who benefit from blame and retribution will surely be threatened, and the response from a great many may be to reject or oppose the development of a truly transformational organization.

However, if these vested interests can be overcome – if the needs of your diverse stakeholders can be voiced and heard, if you are ready to reject division and dogma in favour of co-operation and dialogue, if you are willing to put your people and your values first – your organization will become one of the great organizations of the future.

A transformational culture is flexible and adaptable. It can be applied in any organization, from a start-up to a global blue chip, from a community charity to a complex public body. However, this book has demonstrated that some guiding principles must be put in place if an organization is going to implement a fair, just, inclusive, sustainable and high-performing culture:

- Dialogue must have primacy.
- Evidence and data should be gathered to help build the business case and to support the design and the deployment of a transformational culture.

- HR should evolve into an independent people and culture function.
- A cross-functional Transformational Culture Hub should be established, with board-level authority to drive the necessary changes.
- A new social contract should be adopted with unions, management and employees.
- Transformational justice should replace the current retributive justice models, so clearly demonstrated through the traditional discipline, performance and grievance procedures.
- The purpose and the values of the organization should be expressed through a clearly defined values and behaviours framework. This framework sets out the desirable and the undesirable behaviours and it equips managers and others to have better-quality conversations using approaches such as radical listening, nudge theory, positive psychology and principled negotiation to resolve issues at work.
- A Resolution Framework should be developed and integrated which provides a modern and legally compliant vehicle for the management and resolution of concerns, conduct, complaints and conflicts at work.
- Leaders and managers should adopt the transformational principles. These principles should be integrated into recruitment processes, job designs, competency frameworks, training programmes, reward and bonus systems, etc.
- Employee experience and customer experience should be fully integrated.
- Sustainability and social justice should become embedded into the strategic narrative of our organizations.
- Wellbeing engagement and inclusion should be combined to form a single strategic focus for the board and the people and culture function.

This list represents a short summary of the principles that are required for an organization to adopt a transformational culture. The full details are contained in the pages of this book. It may appear daunting; it may look like a huge mountain to climb. However, it need not be. This is not a sprint, it is a marathon. Taking one's time, building a coalition, gathering the evidence, and applying sound project and change management disciplines will assist as you begin your journey and navigate the course. The rewards will be great and the effort will be more than worth it – you will be a transformational trailblazer. The other option is to do nothing. In the current context, and with the challenges that the future holds, doing nothing is most definitely not an option.

Good luck.

OVERVIEW OF THE MODELS THAT UNDERPIN A TRANSFORMATIONAL CULTURE

I drew on the following theories, models and frameworks as I developed the Transformational Culture Model.

Appreciative inquiry (AI): AI is a process of driving change in which greater focus is placed on what is working well and on an employee's strengths rather than what is not working and their weaknesses. One example of the use of AI within a transformational culture is during performance meetings. Using AI, the manager and employee are encouraged to focus on the strengths and the positive achievements and to look ahead (feed-forward) rather than focus on what has not worked and look backwards (feedback). Errors, mistakes and achievements present an opportunity for learning and insight which is used to develop and agree short- and medium-term goals. These are subject to regular review, with continuous dialogue between an employee and a manager. In this way, managers put their people first and they use coaching skills to create a high-performance climate rather than relying on historic records, formal processes or punitive sanctions.

Emotional intelligence (EQ): this term was made famous by Daniel Goleman in the 1990s. EQ focuses on the ability to be aware of our own emotions (self-aware) and to develop empathy with others. If organizations valued EQ in the same way that they value cognitive intelligence (IQ), I would not have needed to write this book.

Flow: popularized by Mihaly Csikszentmihalyi in the 1970s, being in a state of flow (in the zone) makes us happier and is thought to release the DOSE hormones: dopamine, oxytocin, serotonin and endorphin. Flow can work at a human level and as seen in this text, it can work at a relational and a systemic level in our organizations: a flow of ideas, of insight, of dialogue, of empathy etc. A transformational culture aims to generate flow between culture and climate. The cultural flow model is explained on page 139.

Non-violent communication (NVC): NVC was developed by Marshall Rosenberg and is based on the principles of ahimsa – the natural state of compassion where there is no violence presence in the heart. NVC has been one of the most important models in my work as a mediator, a restorative justice practitioner and a leader. It comprises four distinct elements:

○ Observations: express what you see without blame or criticism.

○ Feelings: describe how you feel and the impact it has had.

○ Needs: explain what you need to change.

○ Request: make a request not a demand.

Nudge theory: credited to American academics Richard H Thaler and Cass R Sunstein, nudge theory is a system of changing behaviour and reshaping choices through positive means rather than through the threat of retribution or enforcement. For instance, in a transformational culture, the values and behaviours framework codifies the desirable and non-desirable behaviours into an overarching structure. Leaders and managers use coaching techniques to reinforce and reward the desirable behaviours and to address and transform undesirable behaviours. In this way, the need for rigid rules and HR processes is reduced. As a result, employees can be nudged into collaborative interactions by using a resolution-oriented lexicon where reminders replace warnings, resolution meetings replace hearings, action plans replace performance improvement plans and a request for resolution replaces the grievance form.

Positive psychology: this branch of psychology was popularized by Martin Seligman in the late 1990s. It is future focused and aims to reinforce our positive experiences, traits and relationships rather than trying to treat the negative elements. It also aims to create flow (see above).

Principled negotiation: this process of negotiation was made famous by Roger Fisher and William Ury in their seminal text *Getting to Yes* (Fisher and Ury, 2011). The objective of principled negotiation is to help the parties achieve a mutual gain or a win/win outcome by focusing on their underlying interests and needs rather than trying to negotiate their relative positions (which is known as positional bargaining).

Psychological contract: this is the unwritten contract between an employee and their manager. It is used to foster a trusting, mutually respectful relationship. The psychological contract is a combination of the expectations that an employee has of their manager, many of which are made during the first few weeks of their employment, and subsequently through their various interactions with their manager. It includes promises made, expectations raised, values and beliefs defined, and behaviours agreed. It is tacit and unwritten, and it can flex and adapt as the relationship develops. When it breaks, it can be a trigger for a significant breakdown in trust and confidence, giving rise to conflict. Understanding the psychological contract and how to maintain it should be obligatory training for every single manager. Organizations should also have robust systems in place for repairing and restoring the psychological contract, one example being the Resolution Framework.

Social contract: this can be defined as the amalgamation of the purpose, the values, the rules, the culture, the strategy, the climate and the acceptable behaviours of our organizations. In other words, the social contract is the way that we think about justice; it seeks to balance the rights and the responsibilities of employers and employees. Transformational culture, and the principles of transformationalism, seek to redefine the nature of the social contract at a macro level by redefining the culture and the systems of the organization, and at a micro level by modifying the way that managers and employees act, interact and react.

Systems theory: organizations can be viewed as a set of interconnected systems which make up a whole. The Transformational Culture Model is an example of a whole-systems approach for driving change within an organization. It draws heavily on systems theory, which is an amalgamation of several fields of academic study. In this book I have taken systems theory to mean the interrelation between autonomous but connected functions within an organization, and the ability to discern patterns and insights from these interconnections and the changes that occur within the system. Systems theory proposes that changing one part of the system has an impact elsewhere on the organization. For instance, enhancing employee wellbeing may increase customer experience due to employees feeling less stressed at work. In this regard, a transformational culture requires ongoing monitoring and evaluation to develop a deep understanding of the relationship between the eight enablers of the model.

Transactional analysis (TA): in this system for understanding human interactions (transactions) developed by Dr Eric Berne in the 1960s, Berne identified three ego states, Parent, Adult and Child, which define the roles that people will adopt during conflict. The common transaction that exists at times of conflict is an unhealthy parent–child relationship. The aim of mediation, facilitation and other ADR approaches is to enable the parties in a conflict to engage in healthy adult-to-adult dialogue.

Reference

Fisher, R and Ury, W (2011) *Getting to Yes: Negotiating agreement without giving in*, 3rd edn, Baker & Taylor, New York

Resources

Boniwell, I (2012) *Positive Psychology in a Nutshell: The science of happiness*, Open University Press, Berkshire

Cooperrider, D *et al* (2008) *The Appreciative Inquiry Handbook: For leaders of change*, Crown Custom Publishing, Ohio

Csikentmihalyi, M (2002) *Flow: The classic work on how to achieve happiness*, Rider, London

Goleman, D (2020) *Emotional Intelligence: Why it can matter more than IQ*, 25th anniversary ed, Bloomsbury, London

Lapworth, P and Sills, C (2011) *An Introduction to Transactional Analysis: Helping people change*, Sage, London

Lockey, A and Wallace-Stephens, F (2020) *A Blueprint for Good Work: Eight ideas for a new social contract*, RSA, London

Rosenberg, M (2015) *Nonviolent Communication: A language of life*, PuddleDancer, California

Stroh, P (2015) *Systems Thinking for Social Change: A practical guide to solving complex problems, avoiding unintended consequences, and achieving lasting results*, Chelsea Green, Vermont

Thaler, R and Sunstein, C (2009) *Nudge: Improving Decisions about health, wealth and happiness*, The final edition, Yale University Press, New Haven, CT

INDEX